FRONTIER MILITARY SERIES
XXI

Scalp Shirt of Crazy Horse, purchased by Lt. John G . Bourke
from Little Big Man at Pine Ridge in the 1880s.

Reproduced from the *Ninth Annual Report*, Bureau of Ethnology.

The Surrender and Death of
CRAZY HORSE

a source book
about a tragic episode
in Lakota history

compiled and edited by
Richard G. Hardorff

THE ARTHUR H. CLARK COMPANY
Spokane, Washington
1998

Other publications by Richard G. Hardorff:

The Oglala Lakota Crazy Horse: A Preliminary Genealogical Study and an Anotated Listing of Primary Sources (Mattituck, NY, 1985)

Markers, Artifacts and Indian Testimony: Preliminary Findings on the Custer Battle (Short Hills, NJ, 1985)

The Custer Battle Casualties: Burials, Exhumations and Reinterments (El Segundo, CA, 1989)

Lakota Recollections of the Custer Fight: New Sources of Indian-Military History (Spokane, WA, 1991)

Hokahey! A Good Day to Die! The Indian Casualties of the Custer Fight (Spokane, WA, 1993)

Cheyenne Memories of the Custer Fight: A Source Book (Spokane, WA. 1995)

Camp, Custer, and the Little Bighorn: A Collection of Walter Mason Camp's Research Papers on General George A. Custer's Last Fight (El Segundo, CA, 1997)

LIBRARY OF CONGRESS CARD CATALOG NUMBER 98-19984
ISBN 0-87062-283-8

The surrender and death of Crazy Horse : a source book about a tragic episode in Lakota history / compiled and edited by Richard G. Hardorff.
    p. 288   cm. —(Frontier military series; 21)
Includes bibliographical references and index.
ISBN 0-87062-283-8 (alk. paper)
    1. Crazy Horse, ca. 1842–1877.   2. Oglala Indians—Kings and rulers—Biography.   3. Oglala Indians—History—Sources.   4. Oglala Indians—Interviews.   5. Soldiers—United States—Interviews.
6. Indians of North America—Wars—1866–1995—Personal narratives.
I. Hardorff, Richard G.   II. Series.
E99.O3.C72944 1998
978.004'9752'0092—dc21   98-19984
[B]   CIP

To Bo, Koko, and Paco
and Baby and Princess

Contents

Illustrations

Preface

Although the tragic death of Crazy Horse on September 5, 1877, continues to captivate the general interest, the published works on his life have been sporadic and few. Of the biographical treatments, only two works stand out among the others. First and foremost is the biography by Mari Sandoz, *Crazy Horse: the Strange Man of the Oglalas* (1942). Although some scholars have classified her work as an historical novel containing contrived dialogue, the fact remains that the biography was based on her fieldwork among the Lakotas in the 1930s. Motivated by a driving compassion for her subject, Sandoz told a stirring story which touched the emotions of all her readers.

The second biography which should receive mention is *Crazy Horse and Custer* by Stephen Ambrose (1975). The uniqueness of this volume lies in the fact that it explores the parallel lives of two warriors, each representing a different and opposing culture, whose fates were sealed forever at the battle of the Little Bighorn.

Because the writing of history must rest by necessity on primary evidence, the publication of such data is crucial in the accurate understanding of our history. In addition to the newspaper accounts and the official documents relative to Crazy Horse, we also have at our disposal journals, magazine articles, and book editions. Among the first of such sources to appear were the accounts by Major Jesse M. Lee and Capt. Henry R. Lemley in *The Journal of the Military Service Institute of the United States* (1914). Lee was the military Indian agent assigned to Camp Sheridan, while Lemley had charge of the escort which was to transfer the imprisoned Crazy Horse to Omaha.

A major primary work to appear was *Crazy Horse, the Invincible Ogalala Sioux Chief* by Earl A. Brininstool (1949). The entire corpus of this publication consists of eyewitness information obtained from five individuals relative to the death of Crazy Horse: Accounts by Major Jesse M. Lee and Capt. Henry R. Lemley (albeit reprints of the 1914 *Journal* article); an extract of Lee's diary; a narrative letter by Lee's wife, Lucy; a deposition by Pvt. George W. McAnnulty, Ninth Infantry; and the composite correspondence between Dr. Valentine McGullycuddy and Brininstool.

Additional primary evidence may be found in *McGillycuddy: Agent* (1941) which contains his posthumous recollections published by his wife Julia (1941). Before being appointed as an Indian agent at Pine Ridge, Dr. McGillycuddy served as a contract surgeon at Camp Robinson where he witnessed the stabbing of Crazy Horse and attended to his mortal wounds.

The works cited heretofore represent, more or less, the military view of this tragic episode. In addition, we have at our disposal the statements made by Indian and mixed-blood eyewitnesses whose recollections stand, more often than not, in sharp contrast with the military views. One of the first publications to represent the Indian view on Crazy Horse was *My People, the Sioux* by Luther Standing Bear (1928). Standing Bear was an educated Brulé Lakota whose stepmother was related to Crazy Horse.

Another work produced by a Native American was *Indian Heroes and Great Chieftains* by Charles Eastman (1929). Eastman was a full-blooded Santee Dakota who was employed as an agency physician at Pine Ridge. This work contains a chapter on Crazy Horse which provides details on his childhood and youth. Eastman obtained his information from the elders of the Oglala tribe.

Mention should also be made of *Black Elk Speaks: Being the Life Story of a Holy Man of the Oglala Sioux* by John G. Neihardt (1932). This volume contains Black Elk's recollections of Crazy Horse who was related to him, both having the same grandfather.

In *Custer's Conqueror* (1951), William J. Bordeaux gives the recollections of his father, Louis Bordeaux, an interpreter employed at Camp Sheridan. Of French/Brule blood, Bordeaux' account is rich in detail and represents the Indian view. In addition, this work contains an interview with Tom Laravie which provides background information on the Laravie family, among which was "Nellie" Laravie, the third wife of Crazy Horse.

The Nebraska State Historical Society made a major contribution with the publication of "Oglala Sources on the Life of Crazy Horse" (Spring 1976). It contains the field interviews conducted by Eleanor H. Hinman and her assistant Mari Sandoz at Pine Ridge and Rosebud, South Dakota, in 1930. This research resulted in ten interviews with six Lakotas whose recollections are rich in detail, although somewhat guarded in extent. The Hinman interviews are the cornerstone of our primary sources on Crazy Horse.

Another noted contribution to the existing body of source material was made by Robert A. Clark who edited *The Killing of Chief Crazy Horse* (1976). This work includes an account by the Oglala He Dog told to his son; a deposition by William Garnett; and the latter's correspondence with Dr. McGillycuddy. Unlike some of the other sources, this work has the benefit of a scholarly preface which allows the reader to view the source material in their proper historical context.

Current Native American attitudes are represented in *To Kill an Eagle: Indian Views on The Last Days of Crazy Horse* (1981) by Edward and Mabel Kadlacek. These recollections are the hearsay statements of elderly Lakotas as told to them by their fathers and grandfathers. This publication includes original field research on the camp locations of Crazy Horse's band after the surrender, and Crazy Horse's burial sites.

The works cited heretofore are not intended to represent a complete listing of references. There are numerous other sources which in one way or another have contributed to our store of knowledge. In spite of all these contributions, our information on Crazy Horse is fragmentary and incomplete, and much of his life, therefore, will remain shrouded in obscurity. Being the subject of continued speculation, Crazy Horse has become an enigma in modern literature, a Lakota culture hero whose name has become a symbol of resistance against white oppression.

This volume deals primarily with the period May through September 1877, approximately the last four months in Crazy Horse's life. The bulk of the interviews treat the surrender and death of Crazy Horse, events which are viewed through the eyes of a number of Indian and mixed-blood contemporaries. These interviews are supplemented by military orders, telegrams, and reports which reflect the view of the Military on this matter. The eyewitness accounts are rounded out with dispatches from numerous newspaper correspondents, which sources reflect the civilian view of these tragic events.

I have annotated the text of the interviews with extensive footnotes. Although this proved to be a time-consuming exercise in discipline, I feel that the benefit derived from these annotations far outweighs any drawbacks. The contextual information adds dimension to the individuals and events spoken of in the narrative accounts, enriches the reader's understanding and appreciation of the recorded oral evidence, and enhances the overall historiographic value of the resulting work.

This volume was completed with the assistance of numerous individuals over a period which spanned more than a decade. They have my enduring gratitude and I gladly share with them any and all credits which may come from this endeavor. The following have been especially helpful. Andrea I. Paul, Assistant State Archivist, Nebraska State Historical Society; Joseph G. Svoboda, Archivist, and Robert Boyce, Librarian, both of the University of Nebraska; Phyllis E. McLaughlin, Librarian, Iowa State Historical Department at Des Moines; Father Joseph D. Sheehan, S.J., Holy Rosary Mission, Pine Ridge, South Dakota; Dennis Rowley, Curator, Brigham Young University Library at Provo; Virginia Lowell Mauck, Assistant Curator, Indiana University Library, Bloomington; Gene M. Gressley, Director, and David Crosson, Research Historian, University of Wyoming Heritage Center at Laramie; Archibald Hanna, Librarian, Yale University Library; Tim Wehrcamp, Manuscript Curator, South Dakota Historical Research Center, Pierre; Jack Haley, Assistant Curator, University of Oklahoma Library; James R. Glenn, National Anthropological Archives, Smithsonian Institution; Bonnie Gardner, Photo

Curator, South Dakota Historical Society; James J. Heslin, Director, New York Historical Society; Beatrice A. Hight, Librarian, University of New Mexico Library; Hilda Neihardt Petri; and my wife Renee.

RICHARD G. HARDORFF
Genoa, Illinois
March 28, 1997

Introduction

The westward expansion of this nation has led to armed resistance by many American Indian tribes. None of these conflicts, however, lasted as long as the confrontation with the Sioux Indians. Spanning nearly half a century, the resistance to white encroachment reached its culmination in the embarrassing defeat of George Custer's Seventh Cavalry in 1876. Ironically, this Indian victory proved to be a hollow one because increased military pressure, famine, and division in the ranks of Indian allies forced the surrender of most of the hostiles in 1877.

Late in 1875 U.S. Army intelligence had become aware of the leadership abilities of a charismatic Oglala Sioux named Crazy Horse, and with the defeat of the armies in 1876, his name had become the epitome of Indian resistance. However, on May 7, 1877, Crazy Horse surrendered at Camp Robinson, Nebraska Territory, an historical event which received national media coverage.

Born in 1840 in a small Oglala camp near Bear Butte, Dakota Territory, Crazy Horse proved to possess a remarkable ability to distinguish himself through military valor. As a mere waterboy to a small Oglala war party in 1856, he experienced the glory of combat by slaying several of his Crow adversaries. During the succeeding years of tribal warfare, he compiled a long record of valor through his numerous deeds of bravery. It was this remarkable combat record, achieved against red and white opponents alike, which in 1868 earned him the rank of Shirt Wearer—the highest military rank among the warlike Sioux.

From composite statements by Indian contemporaries, Crazy Horse emerges as a man of medium stature, and light in frame and weight. His hair was of a sandy color, fine in texture and reaching well below the waist. Of light complexion, with a narrow face and sharp, straight nose, Crazy Horse lacked the prominence of cheekbones so typical of his race. His left check was disfigured by a bullet scar, giving his mouth a somewhat fierce expression. It was said of him that his eyes were restless, with a wandering gaze which rarely focused straight at another person.

Crazy Horse never wore a war bonnet or any of the gaudy trappings so cherished by the Indian peoples of the plains. In combat he generally dressed in a cotton shirt and a breechclout, discarding his fringed leggings. His spirit powers were evoked from the Winged Beings—a spotted eagle—who instructed him to wear a single feather on the back of the head, the tip pointing down. His medicine pouch contained the heart of the same spotted eagle, while one of the wing bones was used as a whistle which he wore around his neck. He also carried a sacred stone which was invested with a protective spirit helper.

Crazy Horse was one of the very few Indian leaders capable of exercising authority over his tribesmen. This authority was neither absolute, nor was it inherited through rank; rather, it was the result of influence gained through unprecedented bravery. Social esteem among the Lakotas was based on military achievements. As a rule, therefore, warfare was waged for the greater glorification of its combatants. Loosely adhering to a common objective, each warrior applied his martial skills as he saw best to further his own interests. Other than planning and coordination, most Indian leaders had very little control over the conduct of each warrior.

In the case of Crazy Horse, however, his authority was based on the profound respect and honor accorded him by his fellow Sioux. It was said that he always led the charge, well in advance of his line of warriors, not allowing anyone to get ahead of him. He was known for his mounted charges in front of the enemy to test the fire power of his opponents. Such exhibitions of valor made the hearts of his men strong. Some of his most daring deeds were performed by him in hand-to-hand combat to cover the retreat. To gain greater firing accuracy, he nearly always dismounted, a practice considered rather unusual among the equestrian Sioux. This unorthodox habit may have led to his nickname Horse Stands in Sight.

If Crazy Horse excelled in military abilities, his social conduct was subject to extreme introversion. Yet, this stark contrast only served to reinforce his unusual military stature among the Lakotas. He never participated in any of the social dances so thoroughly enjoyed by the Sioux. He was a quiet man who moved through the village without noticing people, or saying much. He rarely spoke in councils, always using a spokesman to express his thoughts. He was an introverted man without any political ambitions, who was considered an eccentric among his own people. Yet, he was a person of authority and the possessor of one of the most powerful medicine bundles. In fact, he was a man of contrasting Sioux ideals who was feared somewhat by his own Oglalas. Nonetheless, he was always spoken of in a reverent way.

When Crazy Horse appeared on the battlefield, so the Lakotas said, everybody became brave.

The Lakota way of life changed drastically in May of 1877 when Crazy Horse and his hostile Oglalas surrendered at Camp Robinson. Located in Nebraska near present Crawford, Camp Robinson was established in 1873 to protect nearby Red Cloud Agency. Some forty miles to the northeast lay Camp Sheridan and Spotted Tail Agency where the Minneconjous and other Sioux bands surrendered.

The Oglala agency was named after Red Cloud, a wily politician who controlled the more progressive element of the Oglalas since the peace treaty of 1868. The same held true for Spotted Tail in regards to his Brulé Sioux. A favorite with the military, Spotted Tail proved to be a visionary equipped with political skills and the gift of oration. Although Red Cloud was not as skilled a politician, he compensated for the shortcoming with a cunning ability to manipulate both the military and his own kindred. To maintain his prominence, Red Cloud would remove any obstacle which posed a threat to his political aspirations.

The significance of Crazy Horse's surrender did not escape the military. With a view to appease him and better control the recent hostiles, the military intended to make him the civil leader of all Sioux, subject to the condition that he and a delegation visit the President in Washington. Unfortunately, the military overestimated the political ambitions of Crazy Horse.

Upon the persuasion of the military Indian Agent, Lieutenant William P. Clark, Crazy Horse and fifteen members agreed to enlist as U.S. Indian Scouts. Accordingly, he was sworn in as a noncommissioned officer with the rank of sergeant on May 15, 1877. However, he postponed his decision to go to Washington and, instead, expressed his desire to establish his Oglala agency near the Black Hills. His anxiety about this promised agency comes to expression once again when he reiterated this request on May 25 during a meeting with General George Crook.

Crazy Horse's anxiety about his agency was the result of the U.S. Government's removal politics which intended to relocate the Sioux along the Missouri River. Crazy Horse had objected against this relocation and feared that the military would proceed with the removal during his visit to Washington. Whether through rumors or otherwise, Crazy Horse had became extremely suspicious of the intentions of the military and other Indian leaders. He knew about the pressure being exhorted by the whites to sell Indian lands, especially the Black Hills. He was suspicious, therefore, of any documents presented to him to affix his mark, and for that reason, he refused to place his mark even on ration receipts. In June, therefore, Crazy Horse informed the military that he would not depart for Washington until his agency was established near the Black Hills.

On July 27, 1877, a council was called by Lieutenant Clark who read to the Indian assembly a message from General Crook, permitting the Sioux to go on a buffalo hunt. As was customary, this council was to conclude with a feast, proposed to be held at the camp of Crazy Horse. This suggestion resulted immediately in the jealous departure of Red Cloud and his delegation from the council room.

That same evening, Indian Agents Benjamin K. Shopp and James Irwin received an Indian envoy who proceeded to relate Red Cloud's displeasure with the proposed feast at Crazy Horse's camp. They explained further that the location of the feast would boost the political status of Crazy Horse, while undermining the prestige and authority of Red Cloud. Shopp and Irwin were warned not to trust Crazy

Horse who was a hostile, "tricky and unfaithful to others, and very selfish as to the personal interest of his own tribe." However, the envoy stressed that the Indian agents could count on Red Cloud in case of any confrontation with Crazy Horse.

In August of 1877 the military had learned of the flight of the Nez Perces from their reservation with intent to cross into Canada. Consequently, General Crook decided to enlist a large contingent of Oglalas to fight the Nez Perces. This proposal, however, was met with the objections of both Crazy Horse and Touch the Cloud, the latter a leader of the Minneconjous. Through misinterpretation the military was given the understanding that the Sioux would leave the agencies and go north, but would not fight the Nez Perces. This mistaken impression was fueled by rumors from Red Cloud's camp that the coming buffalo hunt was merely a pretext by Crazy Horse to leave the reservation and resume hostilities with the whites.

On August 4 the sale of ammunition to the Indians was halted, while the buffalo hunt was postponed to August 5. This news resulted in some remonstrations by Crazy Horse who now was convinced not to rely on any promises by the military. Crazy Horse's defiant conduct was magnified by fabricated intelligence reports submitted to Lieutenant Clark by Indians friendly to Red Cloud. Rumors also began to circulate in Crazy Horse's camp that either he or his family would be killed during the proposed visit to Washington. As a result, Crazy Horse informed Clark on August 18 that he himself would not go to Washington, but that he had selected several prominent men of his band who would go instead. At the same time, Crazy Horse reiterated his position on the Nez Perces, stating that the Oglalas were not to partake in the pending campaign.

As a result of the heightening crisis and the influence exhorted by Red Cloud, most of Crazy Horse's former allies began to move their bands away from the vicinity of his camp. The climax came on August 31 when Crazy Horse bluntly told Lieutenant Clark that he intended to leave the reservation. His patience taxed to the utmost, Clark telegraphed Crook regarding the explosive situation, and on September 1 Crook issued orders to disarm Crazy Horse's band. However, for tactical reasons these orders were rescinded the same day.

On September 2 General Crook arrived at Camp Robinson with intent to have a final council with Crazy Horse. On the way to the former's camp, Crook was informed of a plot by Crazy Horse to assassinate him. Significantly, the bearer of this news was a nephew of Red Cloud. Consequently, General Crook issued orders to surround and disarm Crazy Horse's band, while Crazy Horse himself was to be arrested and brought under guard to Omaha. These orders were executed on September 4 by a battalion of the Third U.S. Cavalry and a large contingent of Indians friendly to the military. Upon arrival at the camp site, however, it was learned that Crazy Horse had left for Spotted Tail Agency.

The following day, September 5, Crazy Horse agreed to return to Red Cloud Agency for a reconciliatory council with the commanding officer of Camp Robinson. Expecting to meet the commandant, Crazy Horse was taken to the guardhouse instead. Upon entry, he realized the true intentions of the military, and while resisting arrest he was bayonetted in the back by a military guard. Mortally wounded, Crazy Horse passed away just before midnight, September 5, 1877, his final moments gone unnoticed by those who attended him.

WILLIAM GARNETT
Date and origin of this youthful portrait are unknown.
Courtesy Little Bighorn Battlefield National Monument

William Garnett Interview

INTRODUCTION

Born on April 25, 1855, near the confluence of Saline Creek and the Laramie River, William Garnett was the son of Brigadier General Richard B. Garnett and the Oglala Lakota named Looks at Him. Better known as Billy Garnett, William later married one of the mixed-blood daughters of Nick Janis, a rancher and stage station operator on the North Platte near the present Wyoming-Nebraska state line. In 1873, Billy Garnett gained employment as interpreter for Agent James J. Saville at Red Cloud Agency, a position he held until 1876 when he was employed by the Army at Camp Robinson as a guide, interpreter and chief of Indian scouts. After 1878, he was employed once again by various officials of the Indian Office which he served in positions of trust during unsettled and troublesome times on the frontier. Garnett died at his home in the Medicine Root District on Pine Ridge in 1929. The following extracted interview is contained in the Eli S. Ricker Collection, Nebraska State Historical Society, reel 1, tablet 2, pp. 79-100, which is reproduced hereafter by special permission. The Ricker interviews were recorded in penciled longhand, and with the passage of time, some fading and "bleeding" of the text has occurred, reducing its legibility. This interview contains several passages which were corrected by Ricker, and also a number of notes which were recorded out of sequence. Where necessary, I have corrected punctuation and have inserted the notes in the proper sequential order. For another account by Garnett, see his 1920 deposition in Robert A. Clark, *The Killing of Chief Crazy Horse* (Lincoln, 1988), pp. 75-100. Said to have been Garnett's personal copy, this published document is incomplete in that several essential passages were found to be missing. The original deposition is housed in the Hugh L. Scott Collection, Smithsonian Institution, while a copy was filed with the South Dakota Historical Society. To the latter is appended a statement of biographical information and a copy of Garnett's pension application. A brief statement on the slaying of Crazy Horse given by Garnett to the Military in 1878 is reproduced hereafter.

THE WILLIAM GARNETT INTERVIEW
Cane Creek, S.D., 1907

The death of Crazy Horse was as spectacular as it was unexpected and momentous. It has been regarded by writers acquainted with outside facts only–and with only some of these–as a plain, unromantic affair. But it will be the provence of this chapter to uncover some of the hidden influences which hastened the end of this man's life and cast over it an investiture of the tenderest and saddest pathos.

After his return from the north, Crazy Horse fell into a domestic trap which insensibly led him by gradual steps to his destruction. A half blood woman,[1] not of the best frontier variety, not lightly measuring her intentions and power by casting glances, but fixing her captivating gaze upon this man who had never known fear or a single conqueror before,

[1]Reference is made to Helen "Nellie" Laravie. Born along the South Platte about 1860, she was one of four daughters of Joseph Laravie, a French trader, and a Southern Cheyenne woman. Among her mother's people, Helen Laravie was known as Chi-Chi. In 1878 she settled among the *Wajaje* band of Lip near Eagle Nest Butte on Pine Ridge and was known among the Lakotas as *Ista Gli Win* 'Brown Eyes Woman'. See the statement by Tom Laravie in William J. Bordeaux, *Custer's Conqueror* (No place, no date), no pagination; and also the Walter Camp Manuscripts, transcripts, Indiana University Library, p. 288.

in defiance of the warnings which a trustworthy adviser to whom he turned for counsel in the matter had given him, surrendered to her as her husband. There cannot be the slightest question, for the evidence of circumstances points unmistakably that way that Crazy Horse had come to the Agency with nothing but honorable intentions to accept the strains of the government and the inevitable situation of affairs. His mind was induced by no more presentation; the influences and precautions addressed to his mind were not induced by this government or borne by any of his direct agents; the arguments and entreaties to which he listened fell not from any white man's lips, but were uttered by tribesmen of his own blood; and he had brought his people in at a season when they all might have stayed out. This alliance was a misfortune which overcame this chief with ease, whereas, had it been a case of bullets, his ability to extricate himself would have been unequaled. This woman at once set out to imbue his mind with poisons.

In the course of the representations by the scouts who first went to Crazy Horse, and of the later ones made by Red Cloud[2] on his trip north to see him, he was told of the contemplated mission to Washington by the Sioux chiefs to lay before the authorities the claim of the Oglalas to be allowed to remain in their country and to have an agency there, notwithstanding the treaty of 1876. So on his arrival at Red

---

[2]Promised greater political influence over the Oglalas, Red Cloud accepted a mission from the U.S. Military to persuade Crazy Horse and his band to surrender. Accomplishing his objective through his nephew, Owns Sword, the hostiles were escorted to Camp Robinson by Red Cloud personally, the surrender taking place on May 6, 1877; see Harry H. Anderson, "Indian Peace-Talkers and the Conclusion of the Sioux War of 1876," *Nebraska History* (December, 1963): 233-54.

Born east of the Black Hills in 1821, Red Cloud was the dominant leader of the Bad Face Band of the Oglalas. He is perhaps best known for his determined resistance against the establishment of forts on the Bozeman Trail along the eastern slope of the Big Horn Mountains. Best known as the Red Cloud War, the hostilities culminated in the Fetterman Battle of December 21, 1866, and led to the abandonment of these military posts two years later. For biographical information on Red Cloud, see George Hyde, *Red Cloud's Folk* (Norman, 1937), and also James C. Olson, *Red Cloud and the Sioux Problem* (Lincoln, 1965).

Cloud [Agency],[3] Crazy Horse was not surprised with any new propositions; nor was the journey to Washington to be arranged for him and his fellow chiefs anything he had not heard before. An instance will be introduced in this connection which shows that Crazy Horse was arranging in his mind for the Washington mission, and that his frame of mind was tranquil and pacific. Three or four days after he got back, Garnett, who is well acquainted with him and on account of his position as interpreter was destined to have much intercourse with him, invited him and Little Big Man[4] and two or three others to dinner. It was on this occasion that he [Crazy Horse] remarked he would begin to learn the use of the fork at the table. He said he had got to do it. And then he began to ask Garnett questions about traveling to Washington, how the Indians were provided for, all of which were answered to his satisfaction by the interpreter who had been there as Agency interpreter for Dr. Saville[5] in 1875.

From the moment that this insidious and evil woman came into Crazy Horse's confidence and exerted her insidious art, disaffection began to assert itself over him. She told him that the trip to Washington was a trick to get him out of his country and keep him; that if he went away he would not be allowed to return. These representations might not have been insurmountable but for another conspiring circumstance which went a long way with Crazy Horse to confirm

---

[3]Named after the renowned Oglala leader, Red Cloud Agency was established in August 1873 as a distribution center for annuity goods. The site was situated along the White River, about a mile southwest of the present town of Crawford, Nebraska.

[4]Also known as Charging Bear, Little Big Man was a member of Big Road's (Wide Trail) Oglala band of Bad Faces which surrendered at Camp Robinson in 1877. Having enlisted as a U.S. Indian Scout, Little Big Man was transferred to the Pine Ridge Indian Police in 1879 in recognition of his valuable service to the Military. He was a close ally of Crazy Horse and was said to have been his cousin. A son of Little Big Man, named Bad Whirlwind, and a daughter were living at Standing Rock Agency as late as the 1920s. See Hyde, *Red Cloud's Folk*, p. 243; Frank Salaway Interview, 1906, Ricker Tablets.

[5]A physician nominated by the Episcopal Church, James J. Saville served as Indian agent to the Oglalas from July 1873 through December 1975, when he resigned under the stigma of suspected fraud. See Olson, *Red Cloud's Folk*, pp. 158, 216.

what his new (his second or double) wife had said. Black Elk,[6] who had fought in the Fetterman massacre and had a leg crushed which made him a partial cripple for life, and had always been an inveterate hater of the encroaching whites, possessed the same kind of spirit as Crazy Horse to whom he would most naturally become endeared through association and sympathy, added his own vicious suggestions to those of this woman. He repeated substantially the same silly falsehoods. John Provost,[7] the son-in-law of Black Elk, one of the Indian scouts, likewise had the Chief's ear into which he, too, poured the same misleading strain. These latter tried to convince Crazy Horse that when once he was conveyed east he would be imprisoned; perhaps placed upon some island in the sea and indefinitely confined, or otherwise disposed of so that he would never return. The talk of the day in relation to the motive of fear and the punishment meted out by the government was fresh on the popular tongue and did not fail of furnishing a convincing example to excite the imagination of this warrior, though he possessed as little imagination as the

---

[6]A member of Big Road's band, Black Elk participated in the Fetterman Battle on December 21, 1866, during which his right leg was crushed, the injury making him a cripple for life. Black Elk's father, named Black Elk also, was a brother of Makes the Song who was the paternal grandfather of Crazy Horse. Black Elk was married to White Cow Sees, and upon his death at Pine Ridge in 1889 she married Good Thunder, a brother of the deceased. Of the children born out of the first marriage, the one best known to the whites was Nicholas Black Elk who was immortalized by John G. Neihardt in *Black Elk Speaks: Being the Life Story of a Holy Man of the Oglala Sioux* (Lincoln, 1961), and by Joseph Epes Brown in *The Sacre Pipe: Black Elk's Account of the Seven Rites of the Oglala Sioux* (Norman, 1963). However, Lakota traditionalists do not rank Nicholas Black Elk very high among the Shamanic heroes. See William K. Powers, *Sacred Language: The Nature of Supernatural Discourse in Lakota* (Norman, 1987), p. 226. For Nicholas Black Elk's brief account of the surrender and death of Crazy Horse, see Raymond J. DeMallie, *The Sixth Grandfather: Black Elk's Teachings Given to John G. Neihardt* (Lincoln, 1984), pp. 202-04.

[7]Born along the Cache La Poudre in Colorado, John Provost was the son of "Old Man Provost" and a Lakota woman. In 1879, John Provost was employed as interpreter at Red Cloud Agency when his brother, Charley Provost, committed suicide after a dispute with Agent Valentine McGillycuddy. Unable to control his mixed-blood emotions, John Provost avenged his brother's death by wantonly slaying Bernard Clementi, for which he served five years in the Detroit House of Corrections. See Julia B. McGillycuddy, *McGillycuddy: Agent* (Stanford, 1941), pp. 114-18.

ordinary man possibly could. The foundations of his latter dispositions were broken up. Not very long afterwards, Lieutenant Clark[8] had him and some twenty of his warriors up to his quarters to see what could be done in his camp in getting scouts for serving in the campaign against the Nez Perces.

Garnett was set to work among the Red Cloud Agency Indians, letting them know there were chances for more scouts to be enlisted, and he was met with favorable responses. When returning from the Agency to the fort, he met [Frank] Grouard[9] who accosted him, saying, "Billy, go back to Lieut. Clark's office, it is too hot for me!" "What's the

---

[8]A graduate of West Point, Second Lieutenant William Philo Clark was assigned to the Second Cavalry on June 15, 1868. He was promoted to first Lieutenant on July 10, 1869, and served as regimental adjutant until July 1876. On January 25, 1881, he was promoted to captain, which rank he held until his death on September 22, 1884. This data, and all data on military personnel which follows hereafter, was extracted from Francis B. Heitman, *Historical Register and Dictionary of the United States Army* (Washington, 1903). Upon the transfer of reservation management from the Indian Bureau to the War Department in 1876, Lieutenant Clark was assigned to Camp Robinson as the military agent and placed in charge of the U.S. Indian Scouts. He was a confidant to General George Crook, commander of the Department of the Platte, with whom he was in constant communication regarding the volatile state of affairs at Red Cloud Agency. After the ill-fated removal of the Lakotas to the Missouri River late in 1877, Clark was relieved from his assignment and returned to Company K, Second Cavalry, for field service. Although the need for a military agent ceased to exist after the removal, Mari Sandoz, nonetheless, speculated that Clark's removal resulted from Crook's displeasure with the escape of several Lakota bands during the removal. She further added that Clark had been romantically involved with Helen Laravie, both before and after Crazy Horse's death, a charge, however, which she was unable to substantiate. See Mari Sandoz to Eleanor Hinman, Thanksgiving, 1947, and December 10, 1947, Eleanor H. Hinman Collection, Nebraska State Historical Society. Known to the Indians as White Hat, Clark was an expert in sign communication. As a result, he was directed in 1881 by General William T. Sherman to compile a manual for use by army officers. Clark had barely finished his research in 1884 when he suddenly died. His work was published the following year under the title, *The Indian Sign Language.*

[9]Born on September 20, 1853, Frank Grouard was captured by Lakotas in 1869 and stayed among them for six years. However, after a domestic quarrel with his Oglalas in-laws, Grouard left the Lakota camps and drifted into Red Cloud Agency in 1875, destitute and dressed in a loincloth only. He was hired by General George Crook's staff as a scout and rendered valuable services throughout the Indian wars of 1876 and 1877. Upon Crook's recommendation, Grouard obtained permanent employment as a scout and interpreter with the government at $150 per month.

According to William Garnett, Grouard had been married to two or three women, but he did not have children with any of them. Mari Sandoz claimed that his second wife was Sally Garnett, the sister of William Garnett. Sally eventually left Grouard and went to Pine

matter?" He says: "Crazy Horse is up there with his people!" Garnett reached Clark's office and found some twenty Northern Indians in the room when he went in. Clark directed him to ask Crazy Horse if he would not go out with the scouts and some of his men; that the Nez Perces were out and up in the country where he used to roam.[10] Crazy Horse said, "No." Garnett did not know what had taken place with

---

Ridge where she married Charles Twist, the mixed-blood son of a former Indian agent. It should be noted further that Sally Garnett was actually known as Sally Bouyer and that she was a half sister of William, she having been born from the second marriage of Garnett's mother. Apparently, Sally's marriage to Twist did not last either, because William Garnett stated that she had married Philip White. Grouard's third wife was Eulalie Garnier, the sister of Baptiste Garnier who was known on the frontier as Little Bat. Nicknamed LaLie, she had been married to John Hunton, a roadhouse operator on the Chugwater in Wyoming. She had left him about 1886 and had married Grouard; but this marriage failed, too, and she eventually settled on Pine Ridge with someone else. See Sandoz to Hinman, December 10, 1947; letter to the editor, *Nebraska History* (April-June, 1940): 113; and L. G. Flannery, ed., *John Hunton's Diary*, Vol. III (Lingle, 1960), pp. 47-8.

In later years Grouard left his government job at Fort McKinney, Wyoming, and went to Pine Ridge to live with the Oglalas. However, he did not stay long. Frank Goings, a native judge on the Court of Indian Offenses, recalled that the last time Frank Grouard visited the reservation was in 1902. Grouard wanted his name entered on the agency rolls to be eligible for a land allotment, a scheme he tried to accomplish through the help of Standing Soldier, an elderly Oglala. However, during the bribing process, Standing Soldier became dangerously intoxicated, and Grouard, fearing arrest, fled the reservation and was never seen again. He went to Missouri, and on August 20, 1905, he suddenly died in the town of St. Joseph where he lies buried in a forgotten grave in Ashland Cemetery.

History has not been kind to Frank Grouard. Scholars are still debating whether he was a mixed-blood Lakota or a Mulatto who lied about his ancestry. Grouard himself consistently repeated he was born in Tahiti, on the Isle of Taiarapu. Newly discovered evidence corroborates his claim. See Richard G. Hardorff, "The Frank Grouard Genealogy," *Custer and His Times. Book Two* (Fort Worth, 1984), pp. 123-33. For a biography, see Joe DeBarthe, *Life and Adventures of Frank Grouard* (Norman, 1958).

[10]As a result of state pressure to occupy ceded Indian lands, the Nez Perce Indians were ordered by the U.S. Army to leave the Wallowa Valley in Oregon and settle on a reservation by April 1, 1877. This removal policy resulted in an armed confrontation on June 17, 1877, during which the U.S. troops were decisively defeated. Fearing indiscriminate reprisals by the whites, Chief Joseph's Nez Perce decided to seek sanctuary in Canada and began an epic trek of some 1,300 miles which carried them across the Bitterroot mountains, through Yellowstone Park and into present Montana. During this remarkable retreat, the Indians fought six battles in four months and inflicted heavy casualties on their white adversaries. However, the end was inevitable, and as a result of the extreme suffering of the young and the elderly, Chief Joseph finally surrendered on October 5, 1877, in the Bear Paw Mountains of Montana, only a short distance from the Canadian border. For a scholarly treatment of this remarkable retreat, see Helen Anderson Howard and Dan L. McGrath, *War Chief Joseph* (Caldwell, 1941).

Grouard, but he could see that Crazy Horse was not right. Crazy Horse continued: "I told him (Lt. Clark) what I wanted to do. We are going to move; we are going out there to hunt. You are too soft; you can't fight," speaking to Clark. Clark answered: "You can't go out there. The trouble is on; I don't want anybody to go out there. That's the reason I am trying to get scouts to go out there to head them off from that country." Crazy Horse said: "If you want to fight Nez Perces, go out and fight them; we don't want to fight; we are going out to hunt." "You cannot go out there, I tell you," said Clark. That was all. Crazy Horse turned and remarked to his Indians, saying, "These people can't fight; what do they want to go out there for; let's go home; this is enough of this," and they all obeyed him and went right out.

This passage with Crazy Horse was a revelation. Though nothing was spoken out on the subject, something was wrong, and this evident fact was soon to receive what seemed to be corroboration. Gen. Crook[11] shortly arrived, and it was arranged to hold a council the next day out on White Clay Creek, along which the Oglalas were collected, and two miles southeast of Red Cloud. Crazy Horse had his camp at the mouth of this stream, some six miles below the Agency (west). A few Cheyennes were around the Agency. All the chiefs had been notified. Garnett and Pourier,[12] who were to

---

[11]A graduate of West point, Brevet Second Lieutenant Crook was assigned to the Fourth Infantry on July 1, 1852, and obtained a regular commission on July 7, 1853. He was promoted to first lieutenant on March 11, 1856, and to captain on May 14, 1861. On September 13, 1861, he became the colonel of the Thirty-Sixth Ohio Infantry, after which he was promoted to brigadier general of volunteers on September 7, 1862, and to major general of volunteers on October 24, 1864. He was honorably mustered out of volunteer service on January 15, 1866. On July 18, 1866, he was awarded a commission of major in the Third Infantry, and was transferred to the Twenty-Third Infantry on July 28, 1866 to become its lieutenant colonel. Crook was promoted to brigadier general on October 29, 1873, and to major general on April 6, 1888. Crook died on March 21, 1890. For a biography of this gallant soldier, see Martin F. Schmitt, *General George Crook: His Autobiography* (Norman, 1946).

[12]For biographical information on Baptiste Pourier, see the Ricker interview hereafter.

be present, had been told next morning to meet Crook and Clark in front of Frank Yates'[13] store at the Agency. In the meantime, these two had gone to Garnett's house northeast of the Agency buildings. Woman's Dress[14] happened to join them, and hearing their business as they were going back to meet the two officers, he unraveled a tale which brought the most important affair of the day to a sudden pause. He recounted how Crazy Horse had planned to meet General Crook in an apparent friendly manner and intention to shake hands, and then treacherously take his life, while his adherents would kill his attendants. At the store where all the parties met, this information was imparted to the General who received it with some incredulity, yet weighed it with that consideration which a prudent man would, and had it not been for the assurances of Pourier that Woman's Dress was veracious and the plea of his subordinate against his going further, he would probably have proceeded to the council.

---

[13]Known to the Indians as Cut Foot, Frank D. Yates was a partner in the Yates Trading Company located at Red Cloud Agency. He was a brother of Captain George F. Yates, Seventh Cavalry, who was slain with Custer's battalion at the Little Bighorn, June 25, 1876. See Roger T. Grange, "Fort Robinson, Outpost on the Plains," *Nebraska History* (September, 1958): 196. Frank Yates and his father-in-law, Captain W. H. Brown, also operated the first passenger, mail, and express stagecoach from Cheyenne north to Custer city in January, 1876.

[14]Born in 1846, Woman's Dress was the son of the Oglala, Bad Face, and was a paternal grandson of Chief Smoke in whose camp both Crazy Horse and Red Cloud grew up. Woman's dress was a brother of Keeps the Battle, both being related to the renowned Northern Oglala, Iron Hawk. Apparently, they had come from one family, but being orphaned at an early age they were raised by different relatives. Woman's Dress was also related to Louis Shangreau and Baptiste Pourier through marriage. In 1877, Woman's Dress enlisted in the U.S. Indian Scouts and was later transferred to the Pine Ridge Indian Police. His service record includes some twenty reenlistments, each for a period of six months, for which service he received rations and $40 per month. Some traditional Oglalas described Woman's Dress' character as that of "a two-edged sword against his own people." Later in life he became a lonely, embittered man who complained that he had been "thrown away"–discarded not only by his own people, but also by the whites who never gave him the recognition which he so rightfully deserved. Woman's Dress died on Wounded Knee Creek, Pine Ridge, January 9, 1921. See Clark, *The Killing of Chief Crazy Horse,* pp. 97, 77-78; Eleanor H. Hinman, "Oglala Sources on the Life of Crazy Horse" (Spring, 1976): 7; Interview with He Dog, June 30, 1931, Mari Sandoz Collection, University of Nebraska Library; James H. Cook, *Fifty Years on the Old Frontier* (New Haven, 1923), p. 192.

An omission from the story of Woman's Dress was made. Crazy Horse was killed by lies and liars. Woman's Dress was a scout. He pretended that he had been keeping a brief on Crazy Horse after his return from the north. He said that Little Wolf,[15] who stayed in that camp, was learning from Crazy Horse the intentions of that chief. This Little Wolf is not the Cheyenne chief by that name, but a Sioux Indian who had been in the Custer battle. He was a brother to Lone Bear.[16] Woman's Dress claim was that Little Wolf was keeping Lone Bear, his brother, advised of what he found out, and then Lone Bear told it all to Woman's Dress. Woman's Dress was magnifying his own consequence by making it appear that he was doing voluntary detective work for the benefit of the public service. His political antecedents must be taken in account to understand him. He belonged to the Bad Face band[17] over which was Red Cloud. Lone Bear was also a Bad Face on his mother's side, and it is barely possible that he was being actuated by precisely the same motives that Woman's Dress was, though this can be mentioned only as supposition. The Bad Faces had a reputation all over the Oglala tribe

---

[15]Upon his surrender in 1877, Little Wolf enlisted as a U.S. Indian Scout along with his brother Lone Bear. They had kinship ties with the Oglala Bad Face Band, and may have been cousins of Woman's Dress, although the Oglala, He Dog, told Hinman that they were brothers. However, other sources contradict He Dog's statement, the contradiction perhaps resulting from a mistranslation of Lakota kinship terminology, which identifies the male children of one's paternal uncle as brothers also. See Hinman, "Oglala Sources," p. 31.

[16]Lone Bear was a Northern Oglala who as born about 1847. Upon his surrender in 1877, he enlisted as a U.S. Indian Scout and was later transferred to the Pine Ridge Indian Police. In this capacity he served the white authorities for more than twenty years. It was said of him that he had fought in the Custer Battle of 1876, and that he had cut off the tongue of one of Reno's wounded troopers, keeping the grizzly momento the remainder of his life. See Richard G. Hardorff, *Lakota Recollections of the Custer Fight: New Sources of Indian-Military History* (Spokane, 1991), p. 153.

[17]The Bad Face Band was one of seven bands which made up the Oglala tribe. They were known among the Lakotas as the *Itesica*, which is derived from *ite*, which means "face," and *sica*, which means "bad." According to Hyde, *Red Cloud's Folk*, p. 305, the name Bad Face was applied to Smoke's nephew, Spotted Bear, and later to the whole camp, as a result of domestic quarreling between the latter and his wife. However, Powers, *Oglala Religion*, p. 31, states that the name was derived from their manner of painting their faces for war.

WOMAN'S DRESS IN THE
UNIFORM OF THE PINE
RIDGE INDIAN POLICE.
Date and origin of
photo unknown.
Courtesy Little Bighorn
Battlefield National
Monument

of seeking to be chiefs. They were much occupied with Indian politics, and were reported to be tricky, an inseparable art from the actual manipulations of partisan politics without reference to the color of the actors. This slur or twit or sneer was always being thrown up in the Indian councils at or about these Bad Faces when some of them were cropping and tasseling out with schemes or ambitions in this line.

This story of a plan to kill General Crook and his attendants, as in the case of General Canby and Reverend Thomas,[18] was a fabrication. The reason for it must be sought in the secret corners and crevices of the human mind. These are alike to the understanding–identical in all men to

[18]On April 11, 1873, General Edward R. Canby and Reverend Eleazar Thomas were shot to death by Modoc Indians during a truce council in the Lava Beds near the California-Oregon border. The killers were apprehended and hanged in October, 1873. For a scholarly treatment, see Keith A. Murray, *The Modocs and Their War* (Norman, 1959).

the students of human nature. I have stated Woman's Dress'
political antecedents as a fact to aid in accounting for his
falsehood.

About ten years after these occurrences, Little Wolf and
Garnett were sitting in the guardhouse at Pine Ridge talking
over the times, when Little Wolf asked reflectively: "What do
you suppose caused Crazy Horse to be killed?" Quick as lightning Garnett replied, "You killed Crazy Horse!" This he said
remembering the tale that Woman's dress had told in 1877 of
Little Wolf's part in eavesdropping and reporting to Lone
Bear. Garnett believed that if Little Wolf had not done this,
Crazy Horse would not have been the subject of so much gos-
sip and the victim of misrepresentation and an innocent con-
spiracy of army officers to confine him, and that his life,
instead of being a forfeit, would have been saved. "You killed
Crazy Horse!" Little Wolf stared as he paused to collect his
senses. Had a thunderbolt shivered the roof of the building
the Indian could not have been more astounded. "I killed
Crazy Horse?" he inquired in a reasoning way, like one recov-
ering from a reeling blow. "I—how can that be? I fought with
him all through the north—have always been with him—was
his friend—how did I kill Crazy Horse?" Garnett coolly told
him the story with which Woman's Dress had regaled Garnett, Pourier, and General Crook and Lieut. Clark in 1877.
Little Wolf denounced his part of it as a base falsehood, and
declared that he would see Lone Bear on the subject to find
out if he had ever told Woman's Dress such a story.

Afterwards—not long afterwards—Garnett was at Pine
Ridge and so was Woman's Dress. The latter began a conversation, betraying easily enough that Little Wolf had been
calling him to account for his misrepresentations. He was
abusive to Garnett, calling him a liar for what he had said,
denying that he had ever stated that Little Wolf and Lone
Bear had acted such parts, and affirming now that it was he
himself who overheard the secret utterances of Crazy

Horse–that he had sat behind him, enveloped in his blanket when the chief was unbosoming himself, supposedly in secret.[19] The mischievous prevaricator had, in the course of justice, which ever runs in a circuit, been overtaken and entrapped; and he had recourse to the device of cutting Little Wolf and Lone Bear off the piece of his weaving and putting himself in; this would make him the sole master of the whole story. It was now nothing more than a game to save his reputation. But he was too late. There was one factor he could not eliminate. Baptiste Pourier had joint knowledge with Garnett of all the facts. Both men were known to speak the truth–truth–truth.

While Woman's Dress was arraigning Garnett with severity, Pourier unexpectedly appeared, his presence in the neighborhood not being known. Garnett appealed to him and recited what Woman's Dress had said. Pourier asked Woman's Dress if that was what he said, "Yes," was the answer. "Woman's Dress, you are a liar!" exclaimed Pourier, whose eyes flashed with indignation. The last story was not like the first, with which Pourier was as familiar as Garnett. Woman's Dress had caused to be spread among the officers of the post a falsehood against Crazy Horse, imputing him to the basest criminal purpose. It precipitated the immediate marshalling of force against him–his flight; his pursuit; his voluntary return; the deception to get him into the guardhouse and close the doors on him before he should suspect he was a prisoner–his discovery of betrayal at the last instant; his revolt; the fierce struggle; his mortal wound; his death. Pourier was a relative of Woman's dress, cousins by marriage;

---

[19]Although Ricker dismisses this whole matter as a fabrication, Woman's Dress' statement merits some serious consideration because of corroborating sources. According to Lieutenant Clark, one of his enlisted Indian Scouts commenced a liaison with an Oglala girl who lived in the lodge next to Crazy Horse so as to be able to monitor the chief's intentions. Clark did not disclose the name of this scout, but He Dog reveals that both Lone Bear and Woman's Dress spied at Crazy Horse's lodge. See W. P. Clark, *The Indian Sign Language* (Philadelphia: 1885), p. 130; Hinman, "Oglala Sources," p. 23.

he it was who piled on the last straw to add force to Lieut. Clark's argument to prevail on Gen. Crook to abandon the council which he had called with the Indians, and which made that argument effective by declaring that Woman's Dress was one of the most credible Indians.

In 1891, when Gen. Crook was negotiating the treaty which is known by his name,[20] this matter was discussed with him at Pine Ridge by Garnett and Pourier together, and he was informed of the deception of Woman's Dress and how his falsehood had been detected and exposed. When the subject was laid before him in 1877 and the council was given over, he remarked that he did not like to start and do a thing and not finish it. In 1889, he remarked thoughtfully that he always thought he should have gone to that council.

After giving directions to Garnett to repair to the place of meeting, [Crook told him to] select from the chiefs such as were known to be of loyal brand, excluding all of the northern chiefs who had lately come in, and quietly notify them to come to headquarters at the fort. In two or three hours they were all gathered at the post in the presence of Gen. Crook and Lieut. Clark. The meeting was held in the reception room of Col. Bradley's[21] residence. There were present Red Cloud (?), Red Dog,[22] Young Man Afraid of his Horse,[23] Little Wound,[24]

---

[20]On March 2, 1889, President Grover Cleveland signed a Sioux Bill which provided for division of the Sioux reservation, allotments in severalty, and cession of surplus lands. The terms were that purchasers were to pay $1.25 per acre for three years, 75 cents for the next two years, and 50 cents thereafter; the Government was to provide for surveys and pay for them; benefits with respect to education and farming were not to be charged to land sales; a $3,000.00 trust fund was to be established; and Indians from the Red Cloud and Red Leaf bands were to be paid $40 a head for horses taken away from them in 1876.

During June of 1889, a special commission consisting of former Governor Charles Foster of Ohio, Senator William Warner of Missouri, and Major General George Crook was able to persuade the Lakotas to accept the land agreement and thus obtained the required signatures necessary for its approval. As a result of the land sale, South Dakota became a state on November 2, 1889, and on February 10, 1890, Congress passed a Homesteading Bill for the region between the White River and Cheyenne River, the land rush commencing on February 12. See Don C. Clowser, *Dakota Indian Treaties* (Deadwood, 1974), pp. 244-47.

[21]Luther Prentice Bradley was appointed lieutenant colonel of the Fifty-First Illinois Infantry on November 6, 1861. He was promoted to colonel on October 15, 1862, and to brigadier general of volunteers on July 30, 1865. He resigned on June 30, 1865. On July 28, 1866, he accepted a commission of lieutenant colonel in the Twenty-Seventh Infantry, from which he was transferred to the Ninth Infantry on March 15, 1869. On March 20, 1879, he was promoted to colonel of the Third Infantry, and was transferred on June 14, 1879 to the Thirteenth Infantry, from which he retired on December 8, 1886. In March of 1867, Bradley received brevets of colonel and brigadier general for gallant and meritorious services in the battles of Chickamauga and Resaca, both in Georgia. In 1877, Bradley commanded the District of the Black Hills, a subdivision of the Department of the Platte.

[22]Red Dog was the leader of the *Ohyuhpe* Band, which Lakota verb means "to throw down," translated by George Hyde as "where they lay down or throw down their packs." This was one of the oldest and strongest groups among the Northern Oglalas. Red Dog was married to a sister of Red Cloud and maintained close association with the Bad Face Band. Contemporary sources describe Red Dog as an orator, rather heavy set and with an intelligent face. His family was the keeper of the band's Winter Count, which record was later maintained by Cloud Shield, Red Dog's son. See Hyde, *Red Cloud's Folk*, pp. 96, 180.

[23]Born about 1835, Young Man Afraid of His Horses was the son of Old Man Afraid of His Horses (1802–1887) who was known among the Oglalas as "Our Brave Man," and who really was not afraid of anything. Old Man was the leader of the *Hunkpatilla* Band, which later took the name *Payabya* Band, meaning that they camped near the head of the circle; that is, near the eastern entrance. In 1868, Young Man succeeded his father in leadership and was elected as Shirt Wearer, one of six so chosen to lead the Oglala tribe. Young Man married the daughter of Henry Chatillion, and later married an Oglala full blood. In 1877, Young Man enlisted as a U.S. Indian Scout with the rank of sergeant. Termed a progressive Oglala, he died of heart failure near Newcastle, Wyoming, in 1899, while en route to the Crow Agency in Montana. See Hyde, *Red Cloud's Folk*, pp. 60, 312, 313; Powers, *Oglala Religion*, p. 30; William Garnett to Valentine T. McGillycuddy, no date, Agnes W. Spring Collection, University of Wyoming Library; and Clark, *The Killing of Chief Crazy Horse*, p. 109.

[24]Little Wound was born about 1828 near the headwaters of the South Fork of the Cheyenne River, in present Wyoming. He was the son of Bull Bear and grew up in a very powerful family of the *Kiyuksa* Band, which means "breakers of the rule," so named from the custom of relatives intermarrying. This band was led by Stone Knife, paternal grandfather of Little Wound who remembered him as the shamanic leader of all the Oglalas. Upon Stone Knife's death, Bull Bear became head of the *Kiyuksa* Band, which formerly had been known as the Ground Squirrel Eaters. Dominant in nature and labeled by historians a tyrant, Bull Bear received a gunshot wound in the abdomen during a drunken brawl with the Smoke family of the Bad Face Band on Chugwater Creek, Wyoming, in 1841. He died a month later in agony from blood poisoning, the killer said to have been a young Bad Face Oglala who became known as Red Cloud. As a result of the slaying, the Bear People and the Smoke People separated, and the rift then caused by traders' whiskey never healed.

In 1846 Francis Parkman visited the Bear People along the Platte and commented that Bull Bear's surviving family numbered some thirty males. Among the older relatives was One Eye, Bull Bear's brother, who was known as *Le Borgne* to the early French. One of these Frenchmen was Henry Chatillion who had married Bear Robe, the daughter of Bull Bear. The family was now led by Little Wound's brother, Young Bull Bear, who was born about 1825. Little is known about the latter who, perhaps, at an early age had become

[footnote 24 continued on next page]

Slow Bull, American Horse,[25] Yellow Bear,[26] Chief Day, Blue Horse,[27] Three Bears,[28] Frank Grouard, William Garnett, Baptiste Pourier (?), and possibly some others.

The Woman's Dress story was repeated to the assemblage, and the chiefs learned for the first time why the council had failed. The business transacted all related to the disarming of Crazy Horse and the scouts in his camp. This was simply an undoing under the most trying and dangerous surroundings of Lieut. Clark in trusting these newly-returned northern Indians in the matter of enlisting scouts on an equality with those who had been in service and tested by utmost experience. Crook put the question to these chiefs how the movement against Crazy Horse should be planned and managed. It was their opinion which was finally adopted that each chief present should pick two of his best men who should have

---

a casualty of the tribal wars with the Crows and the Shoshones. Upon his brother's death, Little Wound, also known as Swelled Face, became the leader of the *Kiyuksa* Band, whose prominence among the other Oglala bands was further enhanced by the emergence of Sitting Bull, newly-elected head soldier and a nephew of Little Wound.

The *Kiyuksa* settled on the reservation in the 1870s, where Little Wound became a leading agency chief. He shared this power with Red Cloud, his father's assassin, who he bitterly opposed throughout the remainder of his life. Little Wound died of natural causes on Little Wound Creek, Pine Ridge, during the winter of 1899. He was survived by two sons, James and George, and a daughter who had married the Oglala, Turning Hawk. See James R. Walker, *Lakota Society* (Lincoln, 1982), pp. 21, 88; James R. Walker, *Lakota Belief and Ritual* (Lincoln, 1980), pp. 195, 284; William Garnett to Valentine T. McGillycuddy, December 14, 1927, Agnes W. Spring Collection, University of Wyoming Library; Francis Parkman, *The Oregon Trail* (Boston, 1891), pp. 106-09; Hyde, *Red Cloud's Folk*, pp. 85, 209, 222; Walter Camp Manuscripts, transcript, p. 276, 291, IU.

[25]For biographical information on American Horse see the Ricker interview hereafter.

[26]Married to Sans Arc Woman, Yellow Bear was one of the principal Oglala chiefs of the *Oyuhpe* Band. In 1877 he enlisted in the U.S. Indian Scouts with the rank of corporal and in the same year visited Washington, D.C., as a member of the Oglala delegation to see the President. See Hyde, *Red Cloud's Folk*, p. 174.

[27]Born about 1821, Blue Horse was known to the whites as a progressive Oglala. He was a member of the U.S. Indian Scouts and resided in the Wakpamni District on Pine Ridge. See Walker, *Lakota Belief and Ritual*, p. 283.

[28]Three Bears was an Oglala band chief. In 1877 he enlisted in the U.S. Indian Scouts with the rank of sergeant and in the same year visited Washington, D.C., as a member of the Oglala delegation. See Olson, *Red Cloud and the Sioux Problem*, p. 248.

support of other warriors, all to go in the night to Crazy Horse's camp and surround it, and call out the chief and his scouts who had been armed for service to the government, and to require them to give up the guns and revolvers, and if he refused, they were to be taken even at the cost of Crazy Horse's life. Crook told Clark to issue ammunition for this service, and the chiefs were directed to return to their camps and make due preparations for the work that night. Then the General immediately took his departure for Sidney.[29] He had been gone but a few hours, when Col. Bradley, who was in command of the Post, sent for the interpreter to learn what maneuver was about to take place. The agent was there from Red Cloud with his interpreter (Dr. Irwin[30] and Leon Pallady)[31] and He Dog,[32] one of the northern chiefs under Crazy Horse. The startling undertaking had leaked out through the Indians. Bradley was desirous to find out from the interpreter what had transpired at the recent conference, but he was reluctant to make any communication in the presence of others; as the room was cleared, and when the Colonel and the interpreter had entered a more secluded apartment, the officer was told to repeat what he had heard. When he had done this, Garnett confirmed what had reached his ear. Bradley said, "It was too bad to go after a man of the standing of Crazy Horse in this manner in the nighttime without his

[29]Reference is made to Sidney Barracks. Situated along the Union Pacific Railroad near present Sidney, Nebraska, this post was manned in 1877 by a unit of the Fifth Cavalry under command of Major G.A. Garden.

[30]James Irwin served as the Oglala Indian agent from July 1877 through December 1878. He resigned for philosophical differences with the commissioner of Indian affairs and with the Indian Bureau, stemming from the mismanagement of the department. See Olson, *Red Cloud and the Sioux Problem*, pp. 240, 264.

[31]Employed by James Irwin as his personal interpreter, Leon Pallardy was born of French parents in St. Louis about 1830. His experience with the Lakotas dates back to 1845 when he was employed by the American Fur Company at Fort John, the forerunner of Fort Laramie. See Agnes Wright Spring, *Caspar Collins: The Life and Exploits of an Indian Fighter of the Sixties* (Lincoln, 1969), p. 109.

[32]For biographical information on He Dog see the Eagle Hawk Interview hereafter.

knowing anything about it. They ought to do this in broad daylight. There are plenty more soldiers after we are gone. The life of Crazy Horse is just as dear to him as my life is to me. It was a mistake in the first place to give him a pistol and gun," said Bradley.

Lieut. Clark immediately sent for Garnett and dispatched him to countermand, under directions from Bradley, the preparations which were then in progress to move that night with an armed force to Crazy Horse's camp; and to leave orders with each chief to appear at an early hour the next morning with all his warriors. These having arrived, between seven and eight o'clock, the command consisted of the chiefs before mentioned, several companies of cavalry under Lt. Col. Mason,[33] and some cannon and gatling guns, which marched down the south side of White River; and Lieut. Clark with Little Wound's Cutoff band of Oglalas, the Arapahoes and a small number of Cheyennes moving down the north side of the river. Specifying more fully the forces on the south side, they were in this way: Garnett went over to the Oglala camp and led the Indians along from their camp until Col. Mason was moving in their rear. When the forces were on the march, couriers were passing at high speed between the camp and the advancing column on the south, keeping the camp advised of what was taking place. Garnett and a few of the best informed Indian scouts were extremely solicitous and suspicious regarding the main body of the Indians that were marching toward the camp, for among these were many Crazy Horse Indians, and besides these a large majority of the

---

[33]Julius Wilmot Mason obtained a commission as second lieutenant in the Second Cavalry on April 26, 1861, and was promoted to first lieutenant on June 1, 1861. Having been transferred to the Fifth Cavalry on August 3, 1861, he was promoted to captain on December 6, 1862, and was transferred on July 1, 1876 to become a major in the Third Cavalry. In 1863 Mason received brevets of major and lieutenant colonel for gallant and meritorious services in the battles of Beverly Ford and Brandy Station, both in Virginia. He died on December 19, 1882. On September 2, 1877, Mason and Companies D, E and G, Third Cavalry, arrived at Camp Robinson from Fort Laramie to strengthen the garrison.

others were considered ticklish and unsafe in the extreme; these men who had this knowledge and concern, passed word around among the trusty ones, to gather in a body by themselves and march apart from the rest, so that in the event of a battle those who were in the procession in the guise of friends yet would be certain to assist the other side, should not have quite everything their own way by taking these wholly at disadvantage.

When within half a mile of the camp, Little Big Man, who had been going and coming continually, now met the Indians again, bringing word this time that Crazy Horse had fled, taking with him his full-blood wife,[34] Kicking Bear,[35] and Shell Boy. The command was halted. Something like seventy of Crazy Horse's braves had collected on a knoll on the east side of the creek, about 600 yards above the river. A boy, about fifteen years of age, dashed down from this hill and passed through the halted Indians, [the] men standing apart to let him through. This was pretty strong evidence that his friends had insinuated themselves among the supposedly friendly

[34]The name of this full-blood wife was Black Shawl Woman. Born in an Oglala camp about 1843, she was the daughter of Old Red Feather whose family maintained close kinship ties with Big Road's band of *Itesica*. In 1871 Black Shawl Woman became the second wife of Crazy Horse. This marriage resulted in the birth of their only child, a daughter named They are Afraid of Her, who passed away in 1873 as a result of frail health. Black Shawl died in 1927, at age eighty-four, apparently a victim of the influenza which swept the reservations in the 1920s. See Hinman, "Oglala Sources," pp. 13, 29, 32; and DeBarthe, *Life and Adventures of Frank Grouard*, pp. 181-82. For an account of Crazy Horse's death witnessed by Black Shawl's brother, see the Red Feather Interview in Hinman, "Oglala Sources," pp. 24-30.

[35]Born in 1848, Kicking Bear was the son of Old Black Fox, an Oglala chief, and Iron Cedar Woman, a sister of Chief Sitting Bull. Although an Oglala by birth, Kicking Bear became a Minneconjou band chief through his marriage to Woodpecker Woman, a niece of the Minneconjou leader Big Foot. Kicking Bear was a close ally of his cousin Crazy Horse, both having an inveterate hatred for the whites. According to Garnett, Kicking Bear ambushed and killed Frank S. Appleton, chief clerk at Red Cloud Agency, on February 9, 1874, to avenge the death of a Lakota relative who was slain by white men along the Platte. However, his main rise to notoriety came through his leading part in the Ghost Dance troubles of 1890. Kicking Bear died near Manderson, Pine Ridge, in 1904. See M. I. McCreight, *Firewater and Forked Tongues* (Pasadena, 1947), pp. 3-4; Robert M. Utley, *The Last Days of the Sioux Nation* (New Haven, 1963), p. 62; and Camp Manuscripts, p. 266, IU.

Indians. After this came a man, Black Fox,[36] magnificently decked in war costume, who rode down from the hill on a gallop and speaking these words: "I have been looking all my life to die; I see only the clouds and the ground; I am all scarred up." Drawing his knife, he placed it between his teeth. At this instant American Horse, standing with the body of selected Indians, advanced a few steps, and holding in his hand a pipe, extended it toward Black Fox, saying: "Think of the women and the children behind you; come straight for the pipe; the pipe is yours." Black Fox ejaculated, "How." The two met and smoked. Then Black Fox spoke again: "Crazy Horse is gone. He listened to too many bad talks. I told him we came in for peace, but he would listen to them. Now he is gone, and the people belong to me. I come to die, but you saved me."

His warriors were riding in a drill of the most beautiful fashion and keeping near to his person while this talking and smoking had been taking place. He now cried out to them: "All over. Go back." They returned in perfect order to the camp. American Horse told Black Fox now that they were coming to get Crazy Horse's arms, but as he was gone he supposed they would all probably have to move up to the Agency. Black Fox said they would move; and this was done the same day.

[On the subject of] Black Fox. This chief was a surprise to Garnett who had never heard of him. He rose up without a moment's notice like a king. The Indians have the most luadible comments of him as a brave Indian. Some of them speak of him as the last of a race of brave Oglalas. The way he rode down to meet the firing from the front shows that he was a man of the greatest determination and grandest courage. He came to the front that morning unheralded, but

---

[36]Young Black Fox was the half brother of Kicking Bear and Flying Hawk. On September 4, 1877, Young Black Fox commanded Crazy Horse's warriors in his absence. The courage displayed by Black Fox on that occasion earned him the respect of both Indians and whites alike. In the same year Young Black Fox sought sanctuary in Canada, but he was killed on his return to the United States in 1881 by Indians of an enemy tribe. See McCreight, *Firewater and Forked Tongues,* p. 4.

it was seen that the warriors were under most perfect discipline. A word and a wave by the hand and the braves behind him—caparisoned for conflict, boiling with passion, and thursting for blood—calmed down from a tempestrious lake of fire to a quiet company of warriors who went demurely to their tents at his bidding. The Indians with Garnett that day knew that Black Fox was a prominent Indian among them. When he came forward he said when Crazy Horse was not there he was the chief—that the people were his. He was worthy of them. He got away with others from the agency in 1877, and went north and crossed into Canada to Sitting Bull;[37] and when he returned among the last, and on the way in, he was killed in a fight with some other tribe of Indians. He was remarkable cool and self-possessed, never exhibiting the slightest excitement under the most sudden surprise. His relations were all noted for their courage. His relatives were: Black Fox, his father, [who] was a chief signing the Mayanadier Treaty made the year after Fants [sic][38] was killed at the mouth of Horse Creek, and the treaty was effected at Fort Laramie; Kicking Bear, the messiah, [who] died about three years ago; Flying Hawk,[39] who lives on the east

---

[37]Sitting Bull was a ranked member of the Strong Heart Society and the spiritual leader of the Hunkpapa Lakotas. He was born on the Grand River near the present town of Bullhead, South Dakota, in 1831, near which location he was killed while resisting arrest on December 15, 1890. For his biography, see Stanley Vestal, *Sitting Bull, Champion of the Sioux* (Boston, 1932); and also Stanley Vestal, *New Sources of Indian History, 1850–1891* (Norman, 1934).

[38]While escorting several Oglala and Brulé bands to Fort Kearney to be held as prisoners, Captain W. D. Fouts and four enlisted men of the Seventh Iowa Cavalry were slain near the junction of Horse Creek and the North Platte River in June of 1865. According to the Oglala Thunder Bear, Captain Fouts was killed by Charging Shield and Foam. See Hyde, *Spotted Tail's Folk: A History of the Brulé Sioux* (Norman, 1961), pp. 102-05; Walter Camp Manuscripts, transcript, p. 650, Brigham Young University Library.

[39]One of two sons of Black Fox and Iron Cedar Woman, Flying Hawk was born in an Oglala camp near present Rapid City, South Dakota, in 1852. He was a brother of Kicking Bear, and a nephew of the Hunkpapa, Sitting Bull. Flying Hawk was also related to Crazy Horse, who was his cousin. Flying Hawk married two sisters, White Day and Goes Out Looking, of whom the latter bore him a son name Felix. Flying Hawk passed away at Pine Ridge on December 24, 1931, the cause rumored to have been starvation. See McCreight, *Firewater and Forked Tongues*, pp. xxi-xxii, 3. For Flying Hawk's brief account of Crazy Horse's life, see ibid, pp. 31-39.

side of Wounded Knee Creek and ¾ mile south of White River and [who] was in the Custer Battle and can tell of the death of Lt. Harrington,[40] [and who] was a half brother to Black Fox who was in command when Crazy Horse fled; those are all the blood relatives he [Garnett] can remember and all related to the second Black Fox.

Lieut. Clark soon crossed over to where the main command rested. He promptly dispatched thirty Indian scouts under No Flesh[41] in pursuit of Crazy Horse who had just been seen at some distance. Twenty-five more were selected from the main body and placed under charge of No Water[42] and sent forward on the same errand.

All the Indians and troops now went back. All the outlying Indians were brought up close to the Agency, and when they had pitched their lodges in close order, the camp covered more than a section of ground. Garnett thinks there were at least 700 Indians in line when they marched down to the camp. Garnett did not go down [with the scouts] to Fort

---

[40]Second Lieutenant Henry Moore Harrington was a member of C Company, Seventh Cavalry, and participated in the Battle of the Little Bighorn on June 25, 1876. After the engagement, survivors were unable to identify the remains of Harrington, who was declared MIA and presumed killed. His whereabouts on June 25 have been the subject of continued speculation. See Kenneth Hammer, *Men with Custer* (Ft.Collins, 1972), p. 82.

[41]No Flesh was an Oglala band chief who was born about 1845. He enlisted in the U.S. Indian Scouts in 1877 and in the same year visited Washington, D.C., as a member of the Oglala delegation. He lived on No Flesh Creek, near Kyle, Pine Ridge Reservation. See Olson, *Red Cloud and the Sioux Problem*, p. 319.

[42]No Water was the leader of the *Hoka Yuta* (Badger Eaters), a band of the *Itesica* Oglalas. His brothers were Holy White Buffalo and Holy Bald Eagle, the latter being one of the last six Oglala Shirt Wearers. Although Hyde stated that No Water surrendered with his camp on March 19, 1877, No Water's cousin, He Dog, recalled that the former did not join the hostiles in 1876, but that he remained with the Oglala Loafers at Red Cloud Agency. This statement is corroborated by the *Chicago Times,* issue of May 26, 1877, which commented that No Water was an Agency Indian who had successfully negotiated to the surrender of several hostile Oglala bands.

No Water was married to Black Buffalo Woman, a daughter of Red Cloud's brother, and had a family of three children. The oldest child was a son also named No Water, who was still living at Pine Ridge in 1930. Born about 1863, Young No Water is chiefly remembered for his failed assassination attempt on the life of Indian Agent Valentine T. McGillycuddy in 1880. See DeMallie, *Lakota Society*, p. 21; Hinman, "Oglala Sources," pp. 16, 17; Hyde, *Spotted Tail's Folk*, 243; and McGillycuddy, *McGillycuddy, Agent*, p. 219.

Sheridan.[43] He is now stating second hand, and will give the report of the scouts. The scouts did not come within shooting distance of Crazy Horse that day, but were in sight of him. The woman was seen in the lead and the three men behind.

Garnett explains Crazy Horse's own system of retreating, which is always talked about by the Indians. He always ran downhill and across level country, but slowed down to a walk at the foot of a hill, and when he got to the top his horses were fresh and in this way he conserved the strength of his animals. The scouts complained that this was his tactics in this flight. While they kept about as near to him for a long time, they noticed toward the end he was lengthening the distance between them because his way of using his steeds

[43]Located at Spotted Tail Agency, Camp Sheridan was established in March, 1874, under the command of Captain H. H. Lazelle. In September 1877 the garrison housed only two companies with an aggregate total of 113 military personnel, commanded by Captain Daniel W. Burke. See Roger T. Grange, Jr., "Fort Robinson, Outpost on the Plains," *Nebraska History* (September, 1958): 199; Schedules "C" and "G," *Report of the Secretary of War*, House of Representatives Ex. Doc. No. 1, Pt. 2, Vol. 1, 45th Congress, 2nd Session.

saved them, while his pursuers raced uphill and down, were wearing theirs out, when at length, ten miles from Fort Sheridan, they were played out.

This same day that Crazy Horse fled from his camp below Red Cloud, he reached the camp of Touch the Cloud.[44] His arrival threw the camp into the wildest excitement, and the warriors mounted their steeds and came out to meet the scouts. The Touch the Cloud camp was on Beaver Creek where Frank N. Corn[45] now [1907] lives, about three miles below Camp Sheridan. Touch the Cloud was the son of Lone Horn and succeeded his father to the chieftaincy on the Cheyenne Agency. The present Chief (1907), son of Touch the Cloud,[46] succeeded his father when the latter died about three or four years ago; but he bears the name of his noted grandfather, Lone Horn.

Lone Horn[47] was a celebrated chief of the Minneconjous

---

[44]The son of Lone Horn, Touch the Cloud was born in 1837, and became a Minneconjou band leader upon his father's death in 1875. Evidence suggests that Touch the Cloud was related to Rattle Blanket Woman, the mother of Crazy Horse, who may have been his paternal aunt. Upon his surrender in 1877, Touch the Cloud enlisted in the U.S. Indian Scouts with the rank of sergeant. He died on the Cheyenne River Reservation on September 5, 1905. See the Camp Manuscripts, p. 234; and Richard G. Hardorff, *The Oglala Lakota Crazy Horse: A Preliminary Genealogical Study and an Annotated Listing of Primary Sources* (Mattituck, 1985), pp. 27-28.

[45]Although not identified positively, Frank N. Corn was probably the father of the Oglala, Charles Corn. Born in 1853, Charles was a Carlisle graduate who had fought against Custer at the Little Bighorn in 1876. The Walter Camp Collection at the Little Bighorn Battlefield National Monument contains several letters written by Corn.

[46]The name of this son was Charging First. He was a member of the Minneconjou contingent of U.S. Indian Scouts which was commanded by his father, Touch the Cloud. Known to the whites as Amos Charging First, he later took the name of this grandfather, Lone Horn, whose ancestors are frequently mentioned in the Minneconjou Winter Counts. See Camp Manuscripts, p. 234, IU; Thomas R. Nelson to Bill Garnett, March 28, 1924, copy in the Spring Collection, University of Wyoming Library.

[47]The son of Crippled Warbonnet, Lone Horn was born into a distinguished family whose ancestors were hereditary leaders of the Minneconjous. His brother was a Shirt Wearer who was painted by George Catlin in 1832. Upon the latter's death in 1836, Lone Horn took his brother's name and became the patriarch councilor of the tribe. Lone Horn had four sons who each became leaders of Minneconjou bands. Their names were Frog, Roman Nose, Touch the Cloud (1836–1905), and Spotted Elk, the latter better known as Big Foot (1826–1890). See Hardorff, *The Oglala Lakota Crazy Horse,* pp. 27-28.

who resided on the Cheyenne Agency, which is a very old agency, being on the Missouri River. He was the chief who in Washington—when the Black Hills was raised as a question by President Grant—told him that the delegation would not consider the matter there [because] there were only a few gathered; but that if the government wanted to treat about the Hills, to come out west where all the Indians could be met and where all could take part [in the negotiations].

Touch the Cloud was in command of the Indian camp near Camp Sheridan. His father may have been and probably was living at this time.[48] Touch the Cloud was one of the Indians who held out in the north with Crazy Horse. His people were Minneconjous; and while they did not properly belong at Spotted Tail Agency,[49] yet Chief Spotted Tail[50] brought them along with him and with those who belonged to him when he came with the party that he went up north after. He did not drop or scatter these Minneconjous on the Cheyenne Reservation. The Indians composing this reservation were made up of two bands—the Minneconjous and the No Bows. These latter were so named by the early French who passed through or occupied this country. These No

---

[48]Lone Horn died of old age in his lodge on the Cheyenne River in 1875. Stanley Vestal, *Warpath, The True Story of the Fighting Sioux, Told in a Biography of Chief White Bull* (Lincoln, 1934), p. 269. According to Vestal, Lone Horn had died of shame for signing a treaty which ceded the Black Hills, which statement is contradicted by Garnett and other contemporary sources.

[49]Named after the renowned chief of the Brulés, Spotted Tail Agency was located in present northwestern Nebraska until late 1877 when it was moved to the Missouri River against the objections of the Brulé people. However, the following year they were allowed to return and they relocated their agency on present Rosebud Creek, South Dakota. For a classic study of the Rosebud Sioux, see George E. Hyde, *Spotted Tails' Folks* (Norman, 1961).

[50]Born in 1823, Spotted Tail was the head chief of the Brulé Lakotas. He was an unusually intelligent man who was respected by both Indians and whites alike. Having experienced the superiority of the whites at an early age, Spotted Tail guided his people in a dignified way on the difficult path of social reform until 1881 when an assassin's bullet ended his life. For a classic biography of this great man and a history of the Brulé people, see Hyde, *Spotted Tail's Folk*.

Bows are the Sans Arcs (Without Bows).[51] Red Bear[52] was a sub-chief under Touch the Cloud.

The [Touch the Cloud] warriors ran the first party of scouts into Camp Sheridan. The horses belonging to the scouts were put into the quartermaster's corral, and the scouts were quartered in a building where they would be protected from the infuriated braves. As the Indians belonging to Touch the Cloud's camp were coming up to Camp Sheridan—Crazy Horse among the number—the Spotted Tail Indians who were scattered in camps, and the Indian scouts who belonged to Camp Sheridan, were all gathering at this point. Just as all these different bands got there, the second party which Lieut. Clark had set off in pursuit, arrived at the camp, and the Touch the Cloud Indians made a burst for them. They were armed with guns and clubs, and one particular Indian had a mighty lance with which he made blood-curdling sweeps and passes at the scouts who had come from Fort Robinson.[53] The Spotted Tail scouts, by grand exertions, kept the Touch the Cloud Indians fended off while the assailed scouts were hurrying forward with all the speed they were able in their worried condition to make till at length

---

[51]Known to the early French as Sans Arcs, this tribe was one of the seven groups which make up the Teton Sioux. In the Lakota language, the Sans Arcs were known as the *Itazipco Oyate*, which means "No Bows," or "Without Bows." The name is said to have originated when a Sans Arc band was defeated east of the Missouri River after discarding their bows on the advice of a bardache. See Spring, *Caspar Collins*, p. 178; Hyde, *Red Cloud's Folk*, p. 147.

[52]Red Bear was a band chief who surrendered in March 1877. He enlisted with the rank of sergeant and led the Sans Arc contingent of U.S. Indian Scouts. See Nelson to Garnett, March 28, 1924, Spring Collection.

[53]Located in northwestern Nebraska near the present town of Crawford, Camp Robinson was established by Captain W. H. Jordan on July 21, 1874, to protect adjacent Red Cloud Agency and its civilian personnel. The outpost was named after Lieutenant Levi H. Robinson who was ambushed and killed by Indians near Fort Laramie on February 6, 1874. In September 1877 the garrison housed seven companies with an aggregate total of 391 military personnel, commanded by Lieutenant Colonel Luther P. Bradley, Ninth Infantry. Due to its strategic location, the post was renamed Fort Robinson in January 1878. See Olsen, *Red Cloud and the Sioux Problem*, p. 168; Grange, Jr., "Fort Robinson," pp. 198-99; Schedule "C" and "G," *Report of the Secretary of War*, 45th Congress.

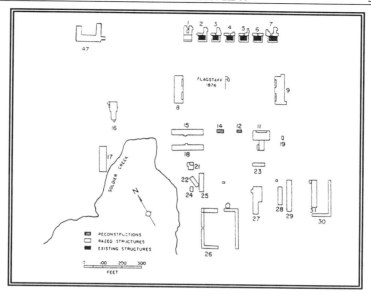

CAMP ROBINSON, NEBRASKA TERRTIORY, 1877

GARRISON BUILDINGS

1	Commanding Officer Quarter	19	Taylor & Saddler Shops
2-7	Officers Quarters	21	Bakery
8, 9	Infantry Barracks	22, 25	Quartermaster Stores
11	Cavalry Barracks	23	Carpenter & Paint Shops
12	Adjutant's Office	24	Butcher Shop
14	Guardhouse	26	Quartermaster Corral & Stables
15	Commissary Stores	27, 29, 30	Cavalry Stables
16	Hospital	28	Ordinance Stores
17	Laundresses Quarters	31	Magazine
18	Quartermaster Stores	47	Post Trader

[Adopted and revised by author from a Nebraska State Historical Society pamphlet]

they found safety from further assault at the agency to which place they had to be helped for accommodations. (See Louis Bordeaux[54] and Charles Tackett[55] at Rosebud, the interpreters, for particulars of the negotiation at Camp Sheridan.)

Next day, Crazy Horse, accompanied by the Indian Agent, his interpreter Louis Bordeaux, and a great many Indians of Touch the Cloud and Spotted Tail, proceeded to Fort Robinson, arriving late in the day, fully two hours before sunset. A scout flew from Red Cloud Agency, bearing news to the post that Crazy Horse was coming.

Crazy Horse and the party with him rode directly up to the adjutant's office. He was under guard when he arrived. It seems that Spotted Tail and, perhaps, others in conjunction, had arranged for Crazy Horse to go with some of the officers at Spotted Tail and some of his own Indians to Fort Robinson, and it was further arranged for the Fort Robinson Indian scouts to follow behind, starting a long distance behind, and gradually to draw in and overtake him and go in with him, surrounded by them as well as the guards with whom he started. He started from Spotted Tail under guard. The cavalcade halted in front of the adjutant's office on the south side of the parade ground. Dismounting, they entered the building, followed by some two dozen Indians. (Garnett was not in this conference and cannot give any account.)

At length they all went out, Crazy Horse between the officer of the day and Little Big Man, each of whom held him by the arm. As they walked toward the guardhouse, Little Big Man kept talking to Crazy Horse, assuring him that wherever he was taken to he would go with him and stand by him. It was

---

[54]For information on Louis Bordeaux see the Ricker interview hereafter.

[55]Charles Tackett was a young mixed-blood who had married Red Road Woman, the daughter of Chief Spotted Tail. He served as an interpreter at Camp Sheridan and in 1879 operated a small trade store at Rosebud Agency. Tackett spoke fluent Lakota and was well liked by the Indians. He later married Susan Bordeaux Bettelyoun whose interview follows hereafter. See Hyde, *Spotted Tail's Folk,* pp. 278-79.

about fifty feet to the guardhouse, a one-story building, having two apartments. In the west end was the room for the detention of the prisoners. This was communicated with at this time through a door entering from the east room, and this was approached from the north side where there was a closed awning, open at the east end. A military guard was pacing his beat before this entry, with bayonet fixed and his gun on his shoulder. The officer and Little Big Man, with Crazy Horse in [their] charge, passed in followed by Indians. Outside was a multitude of Indians trembling with anger, two sides, each with cocked revolvers in hand, bending and swaying like crouching tigers, ready to spring at each other's throats. Against the adjutant's office, in the space between that and the guardhouse, the adherents of Crazy Horse were lined up; opposed and against the other buildings were the scouts forming a part of the garrison. South of these immediate buildings, and toward Soldier Creek farther beyond, were, packed in and around that space and the commissary buildings occupying part of it, teams, horses and Indians in a seething mass.

A noise was heard in the building where Crazy Horse had entered. Indians came flying out, crying, "It's a guardhouse! It's a guardhouse!" There was great uproar within. Indians kept pouring out in panic. Clanking chains could now be heard. It is but a minute and prisoners from the cell are on the scene outside with balls to their ankles. Others coming out as if their hope is to escape. As the struggle in the building continues, the tumult outside increases.

When the inner door was opened to pass Crazy Horse in, it dawned on him for the first time that he was a prisoner, going into confinement. He jumped back and drew his knife to escape. Little Big Man seized him by the arms and a desperate struggle between the two ensued, the prisoner endeavoring to set himself free. At length they appeared in the open air. The two whirled into the space between the scouts and

the surging Indians on the opposite side. Crazy Horse is a small man, while his antagonist is short, thick, heavily built and weighs about 170 pounds. Indian scouts repeatedly raised their revolvers to fire at Crazy Horse. The officer of the day, moving up and down with drawn sword, forbids each successively to discharge his firearms. It sounds like a growl as Crazy Horse repeats, "Let me go! Let me go! Let me go!" Gaining an advantage for an instant, Crazy Horse twists his wrist which holds the knife and inflicts an ugly wound in Little Big Man's forearm.

About this junction, the sentenal who had been gazing at the contest, brought down his piece and extended his arms at full length as if making a thrust. At this precise instant that this was done, Crazy Horse swung himself around toward the soldier with great force in a desperate effort to break loose, and the bayonet pierced him in the side, passing nearly through his body and into both kidneys. The bayonet was instantly withdrawn. "Let me go; you've got me hurt now!" exclaimed Crazy Horse. These were his last words of which there is any account. Little Big Man was still holding on to him. Some Indian–said to be the uncle of Crazy Horse–moved by this last appeal, thrust Little Big Man in the stomach with the butt of a gun, saying, "You are always in the way!" The blow sent him backwards to the ground. As his hold was released, Swift Bear,[56] chief of the (Brulé) Corn band, and some others caught Crazy Horse. A scout, Yankton Charley[57] (also called Plenty Wolves)

---

[56]Swift Bear was the leader of the Brulé Corn Band. He was a progressive leader and, being the brother-in law of James Bordeaux, he was well liked by the whites for his friendly disposition. Swift Bear was known among the Lakotas for his ability to breed fast horses. He died in 1909. See Hyde, *Red Cloud's Folk*, p. 137; and Roberta Carkeek Cheney, *The Big Missouri Winter Count* (Happy Camp, 1979), p. 45.

[57]Known among the Lakotas as Plenty Wolves, Yankton Charley was a Dakota who had married into the Oglala tribe. In 1877 Plenty Wolves was enlisted as a U.S. Indian Scout and appears to have been quite popular with the military personnel at Camp Robinson. For his account of the killing of Crazy Horse, see Helen H.Blish, *A Pictographic History of the Oglala Sioux* (Lincoln, 1967), pp. 401-02.

leaps forward and grasps the revolver from Crazy Horse's belt. He holds it in the air and shouts that he has the revolver. The Indian who had knocked down Little Big Man jerked it from his hand. In a moment Crazy Horse sank to the ground.

The statement here made as to the bayonet performance is given without change from the personal interviews had with Chief American Horse and William Garnett, both of whom saw the particular act and are confident that the killing of Crazy Horse by the soldier was not intentional. Now occurred an incident, showing how like wild animals human beings are sometimes swayed when under excitement. The followers of Crazy Horse were now induced by someone to withdraw along the road to the Red Cloud Agency as far as Col. Bradley's residence at the northeast corner of the quadrilateral enclosing the parade ground. The scouts and the chiefs also withdrew to Lieut. Clark's residence at the northwest corner. A short consultation was had there. Crazy Horse in the meantime was lying on the ground alone in a dying condition.

At length, the two crowds started back simultaneously. On the way around in the rear of the soldiers' barracks both went to take up their old positions. The scouts gained a few steps and were on the ground a moment in advance of the others. A strong guard, several ranks deep, was thrown from the southwest corner of the adjutant's office, diagonally to the southwest, closing the space between the two buildings to all ingress by the Crazy Horse Indians so they could not occupy front ground from the rear as before. But in front of these buildings the grounds were swarming. The study now was how to avoid a conflict over the possession of the dying man's body. Chief American Horse, who was celebrated for his diplomacy (smoothness at deception), had directed the scouts when coming back to have some blankets ready to carry the wounded man into the adjutant's office; for he was going to play the other side a trick. Then, when all was ready, he stood forth and, addressing the crowd, said, "Maybe the man is badly hurt, and maybe he is not; we will take him into the same place where they had the talk, and see how much he is hurt, and probably the Indian doctors can save him. It will not do to let him lie here."

Then the blankets were spread on the ground and Crazy Horse was lifted onto them and carried into the building. When this was accomplished, American Horse, with the coolness and affrontery of the successful deceiver, came to the door and shouted: "We have the body now, and you can't have it! We've been arguing over this, but we've got him in the house now, and you can't have him!"

The soldiers in the various barracks were in great activity, getting prepared to fall into line if needed. Darkness was gathering and the crowds began to disperse. Dr. McGilly-cuddy,[58] the surgeon, was sent for. He said it was wonderful to observe the vitality which Crazy Horse displayed in living.

Crazy Horse Senior[59] came up from the camp to watch that night with his hero-son while the light of life was fading out. He brought with him his bow and arrows and hunting knife, and at Lieut. Clark's headquarters asked to be permitted to stay with him. He was told that he might, but that he must

---

[58]Dr. Valentine T. McGillycuddy was a contract surgeon who served at Camp Robinson in 1877. In 1879 he accepted an appointment as Indian agent for the Oglalas who he served until 1886. For his biography, see McGillycuddy, *McGillycuddy, Agent*.

[59]Born about 1811, Worm was one of three children of the Oglala, Makes the Song. Both he and his father were known by the name Crazy Horse, which was a family name passed on from one generation to another. Worm's sister was Rattling Stone Woman, born about 1815, who later married One Horse. Little is known about Worm's brother. Apparently, he was slain in 1844 during a raid on the Crow Indians. Worm married the Minneconjou, Rattle Blanket Woman, from which union a daughter was born about 1838, followed by a son in 1840, the latter being the renowned Crazy Horse who was killed at Camp Robinson in 1877. Upon his wife's suicide about 1844, Worm married two sisters of Spotted Tail, one of whom gave him a son named Little Hawk. This son was killed along the Platte River in 1870. After the death of Crazy Horse in 1877, Worm settled among the Brulés on the Rosebud Reservation where he passed away in 1881. See Ricker's interview with Chips, and also the Virginia Conroy letter, both published herein; *Rapid City Journal*, November 29,1986; and Hardorff, *The Oglala Lakota Crazy Horse*, pp. 28-35.

leave his arms. Then he was searched, and his bow and arrows and knife were taken and put away. The elder Crazy Horse then went down to the adjutant's office where the younger Crazy Horse was lying on a pallet on the floor. Here he waited and watched till the night had ebbed away. When daylight had come, he thought of his bow and arrows. He must have these. He went to Lieut. Clark's headquarters. In one of the rooms, William Garnett, Baptiste Pourier, Louis Bordeaux and Frank Grouard were sleeping. Under Garnett's head were two big revolvers. Under Pourrier's head were two more. Under Bordeaux's one. These three were lying in a row. Grouard was sleeping on the opposite side of the room in a corner. At Garnett's head the window was up. A hand shook him. He opened his eyes. A form standing on the outside was leaning in at the window and bending over him. It was the father of Crazy Horse. "Nephew, get up; my son is dead." Then he called for his bow and quiver and knife. These were not given to him at the time as it was not regarded as prudent to do so. When an Indian mourned for one who had fallen by a white man's hand, it was among them the proper thing to kill some white man. Therefore this precaution. Whatever the old man might have done at the moment of greatest grief, it is due to him to say that his later life and conduct showed him to be a good Indian.

That day the body of Crazy Horse was removed in an ambulance to the camp of his people at Red Cloud Agency. It had not been an easy thing to find two persons to perform this duty. At last two Indian scouts volunteered. It was feared that some outbreak in the camp might end in the killing of those who should bear the remains. On the way down, an Indian, said to be the same uncle of Crazy Horse[60] who had

---

[60]The identity of this individual has not been established. However, most scholars believe that this was Little Hawk, a half brother of Worm, although Bull Head, Ashes and Spotted Crow are also said to have been uncles of Crazy Horse. See Hinman, "Oglala Sources," p. 16.

been so conspicuous in laying out Little Big Man and in snatching the revolver away from Yankton Charley, leveled his gun at the driver who involuntarily fell over into the lap of the attendant by his side. The latter dissuaded the Indian from taking a shot, and the ambulance proceeded.

The body was taken by the Indians to Spotted Tail Agency, wrapped in blankets and deposited according to the Indian custom. A pen was built of poles around it.[61] When the Indians were removed to the Missouri River in the fall of that year, the body was placed in a cave in the butte rock, three or four miles north of the Agency and about east of where Frank N. Corn was on Beaver Creek. When the Indians were returning from the Missouri River in 1878, between the head of Wounded Knee Creek and where the beef corral is, two travois were seen moving on the road toward the east. A man was on a hill crying.[62] It was said to be the same uncle of Crazy Horse who had been so prominent at the time of his death. Some one passing at the time told others who saw the travois and heard the lamentation, that it was the body of Crazy Horse being removed. An Indian named Chips, living six miles south of Kyle, claims to have superintended all the removals of the body and to have it in his possession for sale now.

[61]The lumber for this pen was provided by Lieutenant Jesse M. Lee, military Indian agent to the Brulés, who erected the structure on September 12, 1877, to prevent cattle from disturbing Crazy Horse's remains. Sepulchered in a red blanket, the body had been placed on a scaffold on September 8, on a hill overlooking Camp Sheridan. See the extracted Lee Diary published in E. A. Brininstool, *Crazy Horse, The Invincible Oglala Sioux Chief* (Los Angeles, 1949), p. 39.

[62]See also DeMallie, *The Sixth Grandfather,* p. 204, which contains the observations of two Lakota hunters who saw the burial travois and who believe that the remains of Crazy Horse were interred along Pepper Creek, southwest of Manderson, South Dakota.

Billy Hunter Statement

INTRODUCTION

This account was obtained by Lt. George A. Dodd, Third Cavalry, at the request of Lt. John G. Bourke, and is recorded in the John G. Bourke Diaries, Volume 24, pp. 78-83, USMA Library. Billy Hunter was better known by the name of William Garnett. At the outbreak of the Civil War, Williams's father, Major Richard Garnett, offered his services to the Confederacy, and being a West Point graduate, he was promoted to brigadier general of the Virginia troops. General Garnett was subsequently killed during Picket's charge at Gettysburg in 1863. After his death, Garnett's Oglala wife, Looks at Him, married "Old Man Bouyer," a blacksmith at Fort Laramie who was known among the Lakotas as Hammering Out. From this union William Garnett's half sister Sally was born. Bouyer later remarried two Yankton Dakota sisters, one of whom was the mother of Michel Bouyer who was slain with Custer in 1876. Looks at Him eventually married John Hunter, and although the latter was killed in a gunfight near Fort Laramie in 1868, it was Hunter's last name by which William was known in 1878. By 1885, however, William Hunter had taken the name of his natural father, but when asked by the Garnett family to live on their wealthy Virginia estate, William replied that he was born and raised as an Indian, and that he would therefore die as an Indian among the people of Comes to Stand, his maternal grandmother.

THE BILLY HUNTER STATEMENT

[Fort Robinson, 1878]

In the later part of the summer [of 1877], the Indians asked for and obtained permission to leave their agency and go out on a buffalo hunt; and having no ammunition, an order was given allowing traders to sell to the Indians ammunition for hunting purposes. Shortly after this time, the delegation was forming to go to Washington, and, in a council, it was agreed to that Crazy Horse and Little Big Man should be of the number (20) to go. Crazy Horse appeared to be well satisfied before and at this time.

After the Indians had started on the hunt, a portion of the head men came back to prepare for the trip to Washington. Crazy Horse did not like this arrangement. He wanted to go on with the hunt and would give no definite reply as to whether or not he was willing to go to Washington. On account of the dissatisfaction expressed by Crazy Horse, the order allowing traders to sell ammunition to Indians was revoked.[1]

At this time, the paymaster came up to pay off the troops (including the Indian scouts), and, although Crazy Horse was

---

[1]On July 27, General George Crook approved a request for a communal buffalo hunt which allowed the Oglalas to be absent from their agency for a period of about twenty days. Accordingly, an order was issued to the Indian agent on July 28, which lifted all restrictions on ammunition sales to the Indians. Although the Military postponed the hunt on August 5, a large Oglala band finally left the agency with a cavalry escort a week later and reached Buffalo Cap on the east side of the Black Hills on August 16 on their way north to hunt buffalo. With the commencement of the hunt, the justification for ammunition sales to the Indians at the agency no longer existed. Consequently, the order was rescinded on August 13. See Bradley to Williams, telegram, August 5, 1877, and Benjamin K. Shopp to the Honorable J. C. Smith, August 15, 1877, included in the Official Documents hereafter; and also the *Black Hills Weekly Times*, August 19, 1877.

an enlisted scout, he refused to draw his pay.[2] Seeing that Crazy Horse was very much dissatisfied, the commanding officer of the post sent for him and Little Big Man to come and talk with him. They came, and the commanding officer told them that the Great Father at Washington had sent word to them that he wanted them to come and see him. Little Big Man immediately gave his consent to go, but Crazy Horse would give no satisfactory reply as to what he would do.

About three days after this time, Crazy Horse came up and selected the men that he wanted to go to Washington (selecting mostly northern Indians), but refusing to go himself.[3] At about the same time, or shortly after, scouts were enlisting to join the expedition against the Nez Perces. Crazy Horse was asked if he would go, to which he would give no reply on that day; but the next day he came up to the post, accompanied by a large number of his young men and talked very badly. He said he would not go out with the troops, but that he would move out slowly with his entire village, and when overtaken would help to fight the Nez Perces.[4]

This was merely an excuse which he thought would enable him to get away and go north, for at the same time he was doing all in his power to induce other Indians (especially the enlisted scouts) to accompany him. He did not succeed in getting away as notice was soon given that the scouts would not be required.[5] After this, all, except the northern Indians,

---

[2]Enlisting with the rank of sergeant, Crazy Horse was sworn in as a U.S. Indian Scout by Lieutenant Clark on May 12, 1877, and was discharged on September 5, 1877, with a retroactive date of August 31. See the Camp Collection, transcripts, p. 807, IU; *Cheyenne Daily Leader*, May 16, 1877; and Clark to Crook, telegram, September 5, 1877, in the Official Documents hereafter.

[3]This took place on August 18; see Clark's letter to Crook of same date in the Official Documents hereafter.

[4]This declaration of intentions by Crazy Horse was delivered on August 31; see Bradley's telegram to Williams of same date, in Official Documents.

[5]On September 1, 1877, some 150 Oglala Indian Scouts were garrisoned after the order requiring their field service against the Nez Perces was rescinded. See Sheridan to Townsend, same date, Official Documents.

wanted to move in one large village to Little White Chief Creek. They held councils, at [the] same time discussing what should be said and done by the delegation on going to Washington.

General Crook came up to Red Cloud [Agency] about this time and was to hold a council with the Indians; on the day appointed for the council, General Crook, accompanied by two or three persons, started for the Indian camp, but on the way was met by an Indian scout, Woman's Dress, who informed the General that if he went into council he would be killed, as Crazy Horse had said that if the Big White Chief (i.e. General Crook) did not talk to suit him, he (Crazy Horse) would stab him. On hearing this, the party returned to the post.

After this, and three days before Crazy Horse was killed, General Crook sent for all of the head men to come up to the post as he wanted to talk to them. They all came except Crazy Horse. The General then told them that they were being led astray by this chief (Crazy Horse) and they must take him prisoner. The Indians proposed killing him and this proposition was agreed to by the others; but General Crook told them it must not be done as it would be murder, but insisted that he must be taken prisoner.

On the next morning after the day of the council [the second morning thereafter] a party of Indian soldiers started for Spotted Tail (Agency) to which place Crazy Horse had moved some time before. They arrived at Spotted Tail and, going to Crazy Horse's lodge, informed him that General Bradley had words for him from the Great Father at Washington, and that he must come to (Camp) Robinson to hear them. He came along peaceable and, accompanied by Lieut. Lee[6] and some Indian soldiers, started in an ambulance for Camp Robinson.

---

[6]For information on Lieutenant Jesse M. Lee see the Louis Bordeaux Interview hereafter.

They arrived at Robinson about dark, but instead of stopping at General Bradley's quarters, they stopped in front of the post's guardhouse. Crazy Horse noticed this and remarked, after getting out of the ambulance, that "this is not General Bradley's quarters." He was then told that he must go into the guardhouse and, seeing himself surrounded by the guard, he left the persons who were with him and ran into the guardhouse alone, closely followed by Little Big Man and the sentinel No. 1, the sentinel remaining near the doorway.

On entering the guard room and seeing men in the cells–confined with chains on–he sprang back, saying "I won't go in there. It is the place where prisoners are kept." While moving back towards the door, he drew both his knives[7] and with one in each hand rushed toward the sentinel. Little Big Man, seeing his intention of making his escape, sprang behind him and reaching around his body, held his hands, keeping the points of his knives down. In this position, dragging Little Big Man with him, Crazy Horse

---

[7]Garnett's statement about two knives contradicts his later recollections which mention only one knife. Not withstanding, Frank Grouard also spoke of two knives, as did Dr. McGillycuddy, which agrees with the statement by Lt. Col. Thomas McArthur Anderson, who was transferred to the Ninth Infantry in 1879 and who obtained the facts from his officers who witnessed the incident. Lt. William P. Clark also wrote of "knives" in a letter to the Commissioner of Indian Affairs, September 7, 1877; but in an earlier telegram to Crook, Clark mentioned only a single knife, which observation is corroborated by numerous military and civilian eyewitnesses, as well as the Indians themselves. A possible explanation for the confusion is given by Lt. Henry R. Lemley, Third Cavalry, who stated that the second knife came from Little Big Man's scabbard, from which it was pulled by Crazy Horse during the struggle.

Witnesses describe Crazy Horse's knife as follows. According to Garnett, the weapon was a long, glittering knife, which description agrees with Lt. John G. Bourke, aide-de-camp to Crook, who wrote that it looked like a stiletto. Lt. Lemley added that the knife had originally been a butcher's knife, which had been ground to a very slender and pointed blade. This statement agrees with that of Lt. Jesse M. Lee, Indian agent, who examined the weapon and described it as a tobacco knife, ground from a butcher's knife, six inches long, and narrowed to a keen point. See the Official Documents hereafter; John G. Bourke, *On the Border with Crook* (Glorieta, 1969), p. 422; *New York Sun*, September 14, 1877, which contains Lemley's anonymous report; and Jesse M. Lee to Walter M. Camp, May 24, 1910, Camp Collection, Brigham Young University.

came up to the sentinel, who, having his bayonet "fixed," as soon as he came within reach stabbed him. He died in a short time from the effects of this stab. The points of his own knives did not touch his body.[8]

---

[8]Immediately after the stabbing of Crazy Horse a controversy arose as to whether the death wound was caused by a knife or by a bayonet. In 1881 Lt. Bourke was told by Little Big Man that he himself had caused Crazy Horse's death by accidentally forcing a knife into the latter's abdomen. Little Big Man added that at first it was thought best to let the idea prevail that a soldier had done the killing, thereby reducing the probability that he and his family would be subjected to the customary revenge demanded by Crazy Horse's relatives. Lt. Bourke stated further that he was strongly inclined to believe Little Big Man, as did Lt. Lemley who, as early as September 6, 1877, wrote the *New York Sun* that Little Big Man was responsible for the mortal wound in Crazy Horse's groin. The same belief was expressed by Lt. Clark who stated in his official correspondence that the Oglala chief was probably killed with his own knife. Significantly, on the same evening that Crazy Horse lay dying, Dr. McGillycuddy tried in vain to convince Worm and Touch the Clouds that the stabbing was caused by a knife, showing them the diameter of both the knife and a bayonet upon penetration into a piece of paper. If a cover-up was attempted, it certainly was not planned for the benefit of Little Big Man, but rather it was intended to protect the Military from any blame which would result from this bungled affair. See Bourke, *On the Border with Crook*, p. 422; Clark to Crook, telegram, September 5, 1877, Official Documents; and *New York Sun*, September 14, 1877.

American Horse Interview

INTRODUCTION

Born about 1840 near the mouth of the Grand River in present North Dakota, American Horse was the son of Sitting Bear, the leader of the True Oglalas. Nicknamed Spider, he succeeded his father as band leader and was elected to the office of Shirt Wearer in 1868. Having married a daughter of Red Cloud, he joined the latter in 1871 to become one of the Oglala agency chiefs. In 1881 the Indian agent made him the leader of the Bear People, consisting of the *Payabya,* the *Tapisleca* (Spleen Band), and the *Kiyuksa* bands. American Horse was known among the whites as a notable progressive and was quite an orator, one who had been to Washington, D.C., on a number of occasions and who had toured the entire country as a member of a Wild West show. He died from natural causes at his home near Kyle, Pine Ridge, in 1908. This interview is contained in the Ricker Collection, NSHS, reel 6, tablet 35, pp. 35-37. It should be noted that the American Horse described heretofore, who was a Southern Oglala, is not to be confused with the individual of like name who was a relative of Old Smoke. The latter American Horse, a Northern Oglala and the son of the one nicknamed Buttocks, was the leader of a very wild band of Oglalas which refused to settle on a reservation until 1877.

THE AMERICAN HORSE INTERVIEW
At Chadron, Nebr., August 18, 1906

DEATH OF CRAZY HORSE

A week before the above interview, American Horse and one of his two wives, and the daughter of this wife, having come with a large number of Indians to Chadron to take cars for Cheyenne where they were to be an attraction on Pioneer Day, took dinner at my table, and American Horse gave us a description of the killing of Crazy Horse. In the struggle to escape from his captors, he was held around the waist by an Indian who seized him from behind, while Little Big Man grasped his wrist and hand in which he held a knife. By turning his hand adroitly, he gave Little Big Man a wound in his arm which caused him to release his hold; and thereupon making a violent effort to disengage himself, he surged against a bayonet in the hands of one of the guards who was standing at a guard against infantry [?] and swaying his piece forward and backward. The bayonet entered his side below the ribs, inflicting a mortal wound.

American Horse positively affirms that the soldier did not stab Crazy Horse intentionally. He also said that he himself during the scuffle threw his gun down on Crazy Horse to shoot him, but some Indians pressed between them and prevented him from taking his life.

(So passed away one of the greatest Indian warriors of the later days.)

AMERICAN HORSE
Photo taken in Washington, DC in 1877.
Courtesy West Point Military Academy Library

Standing Soldier Interview

INTRODUCTION

Standing Soldier was a U.S. Indian Scout who later became a sergeant of the Pine Ridge Indian Police. He was a progressive leader and a member of the Oglala delegation which visited Washington, D.C., in 1906. This interview is contained in the Ricker collection, NSHS, reel 5, tablet 9, pp. 80-83.

THE STANDING SOLDIER INTERVIEW
At Pine Ridge, S.D.
November 20, 1906

He says that he was one of the scouts sent from Fort Robinson to Spotted Tail Agency to get him [Crazy Horse]. When they got over to Spotted Tail they were told that Crazy Horse had said if anybody came after him he would kill him or them. So, it was arranged for some of the Rosebud [Brulé] Indians to go out and get him, which they did, and they took him under guard to Fort Robinson. The object in taking Crazy Horse was to convey him to Washington to see the president, and the agent at Red Cloud wanted the Rosebud Indians in charge to stop with him at the agency so he could tell Crazy Horse the purpose for which he was being brought in and to have him left there; but they would not stop [at Red Cloud Agency], but went on to the fort where he was killed the same day. (I doubt whether he is correctly informed as to the object.)[1]

An officer, (and somebody else I have forgotten) and four privates went with Crazy Horse into the guardhouse, followed by an Oglala, Little Big Man, and some of Crazy Horse's friends. When inside he saw where they were taking him, and he drew his knife and began backing out. Little Big Man shouted, "Don't! Don't! Don't do that!" and seized him by the arms. Crazy Horse cut Little Big Man in the wrist. The soldiers were trying to keep him in with their bayonets; he got out of doors and the guard on the outside stepped up and thrust his bayonet into his side, low down and pretty well around toward his back. He fell and Standing Soldier raised him up, but he was soon dead. The soldier stabbed him purposely.

Crazy Horse's body was removed by the Indians to Rosebud; from there they removed his bones to the cliff on the east side of White Horse Creek, four miles above Manderson, and thence it is not known where they have been moved. (This account about the removal of his remains is apoc-

---

[1]It is quite possible that the Indians were led to believe that Crazy Horse would be taken to Agent James Irwin at Red Cloud Agency. Perhaps this impression was given by Lt. Jesse M. Lee who was uncertain as to whether to take Crazy Horse to the civilian agent at Red Cloud Agency, or to take him to the Military at Camp Robinson. So unsure was Lee that he requested additional instructions some distance east from Red Cloud Agency, prompting an immediate response to take Crazy Horse straight to Camp Robinson. See Lee's recollections in E. A. Brininstool, "Chief Crazy Horse, His Career and Death," *Nebraska History Magazine* (January-March, 1929) : 24-25.

hryphal. It is disputed by some Indians that any Indian's remains have been put up in that cliff. I cannot use the story.)[2]

---

[2]Ricker is premature in his judgement; besides, other sources confirm Standing Soldier's statement. Richard C. Stirk, who had married into the Oglala tribe, had learned from informants that Crazy Horse's body had been placed in the side of a cliff about four miles above Manderson. This hole in the wall was about fifty feet above the bottom of the cliff, in full view of the road which passed below it, the remains having been taken to this site with the aid of ladders. See the Richard C. Stirk Interview, Ricker Collection, NSHS, reel 2, tablet 8, pp. 36-37.

Chips Interview

INTRODUCTION

Chips, also known as Horn Chips, was born about 1836 and was a member of No Water's Oglala band. Chips was a cousin of Crazy Horse and is perhaps best remembered as the *Wicasa Wakan* (Holy Man) who provided Crazy Horse with a *wotawe,* objects imbued with protective power. Older Lakota traditionalists credit Chips with saving and promulgating Lakota religion at a time when it was challenged by the whites. During the reservation years Chips became known as a *Yuwipi Wicasa,* one who performs during rituals, finds lost objects, and receives answers through prayers. Chips was particularly revered on the Cheyenne River Agency because he had been able to tell through the spirits where to find the bodies of Palmer Horse Shoe's sons who became lost in a blizzard, and the location of a boy drowned beneath the ice in the Cheyenne River. Two of Chips' sons, Charles Chips and James Moves Camp, succeeded their father as *yuwipi* men. Chips passed away on January 4, 1916. This view is contained in the Ricker Collection, NSHS, reel 4, tablet 18, pp. 1-21. Throughout this interview Ricker displayed a peculiar spelling idiosyncrasy by writing his informant's name as "Chipps."

THE CHIPS INTERVIEW
Thursday, February 14, 1907
Interview with Chips, or Encouraging Bear
At his home, 8 miles southeast of Kyle, and 12 miles north-
    west of Allen
Peter Schweigerman, interpreter

ON THE SUBJECT OF CRAZY HORSE

Crazy Horse was born at the foot of Bear Butte, near the present Fort Mead, S. D., in the year in which the band to which he belonged, the Oglala, stole one hundred horses, and in the fall of the year.[1]

He was born with light hair and was called by the Indians the Light Haired Boy. His hair was always light. It did not reach to the ground as stated by Garnett, but did reach below his hips. His grandfather, Makes the Song, had a dream that Crazy Horse would be called Crazy Horse. When Crazy Horse was just twenty-one years old, the Oglalas had a fight with the Crows and Rees and others whose language they could not understand, and in this fight he counted his coup in this manner: A Shoshone lay dead on the field in a position that none would approach to strike the body. Crazy Horse's horse became unmanageable and carried his rider wildly about and up within reach of the Shoshone['s] body and Crazy Horse struck and counted coup, and from the crazy conduct of the horse the rider was dubbed Crazy Horse.[2] Chips was four (4) years older than Crazy Horse.

---

[1]Crazy Horse was born in 1840. See Richard G. Hardorff, "Stole-One-Hundred-Horses Winter: The Year the Oglala Crazy Horse was Born," *Research Review, The Journal of the Little Big Horn Associates* (June, 1987): 44-47.

[2]This would have taken place in 1861. However, He Dog, who thought Crazy Horse was born in 1838, stated that the latter was given his name when he was about eighteen years old after a fight with Arapahoes (Gros Ventres?) who made a stand on a high hill covered with big rocks, near a river. This incident may have taken place in 1857 when Lakota winter counts recorded that a war party of Oglalas and Minneconjous killed ten enemies on Captive Hill, at the head of the Moreau River, near present Spearfish, South Dakota. This same incident of tribal warfare, and the prominence displayed by Crazy Horse and his

Crazy Horse's father's name was Crazy Horse. Crazy Horse's mother was a Minneconjou, but Chips does not know her name.[3]

Crazy Horse was a man small in statue, rather light in frame and weight, [and] light in complexion. The wound [inflicted] by No Water for Crazy Horse taking his wife, did not change the color of his complexion; and this wound was in his face, the ball entering at the side of the nose, low down on the right side, and coming out at the base of the skull on the back side.[4]

---

cousin Kicking Bear, is mentioned in the Thunder Tail Narrative, Holy Rosary Mission Files, Marquette University. See Hinman, "Oglala Sources," p. 11; James H. Howard, "Dakota Winter Counts as a Source of Plains History," *Anthropological Papers*, Smithsonian Institution, Bureau of American Ethology, Bulletin 173 (Washington, 1960), p. 385; Blish, *A Pictographic History of the Oglala Sioux*, p. 117. Chips' statement may explain the cause of the name change but not the origin of the name because both Worm and Makes the Song had been known as Crazy Horse. See Hinman, "Oglala Sources," p. 11; and DeBarthe, *Life and Adventures of Frank Grouard*, pp. 179-80. For a different explanation of the name see the account by He Dog in Clark, *The Killing of Chief Crazy Horse*, p. 68.

[3]The name of Crazy Horse's mother was Rattle Blanket Woman. Born about 1815, she was a Minneconjou by birth and probably was related to the powerful Lone Horn family whose name frequents the Minneconjou winter counts. Evidence suggests that she committed suicide about 1844 due to severe mental depression caused by the death of a relative. See the Interview with Mrs. Eagle Horse, June 1918, Camp Manuscripts, IU, p. 271; Victoria Conroy to James H. McGregor, December 18, 1934, in the appendix hereafter; *Rapid City Journal*, November 29, 1986.

[4]This shooting took place on Powder River during the summer of 1870, two days after No Water's wife, Black Buffalo Woman, left her husband for Crazy Horse. The assault was accomplished with a handgun. Striking the face near the nostrils, the bullet glanced off the underlying bone structure and deflected through the fleshy layer of the gum and the cheek, fracturing the upper jaw before exiting at the neck near the base of the skull. Although Chips stated that the ball entered the right side of Crazy Horse's face, other contemporary sources strongly suggest it was the opposite side. According to He Dog, the bullet struck the jawbone just below the left nostril. This location is confirmed by George W. Oaks, a teamster, who saw Crazy Horse at Camp Robinson several times and commented that he "had quite a scar on his left cheek." William J. Bordeaux, son of Louis Bordeaux, also corroborated the location of the scar on the left cheek through information received from Crazy Horse's sister, Mrs. Joe Clown, and other contemporaries. The final corroborating evidence is provided by an unidentified reporter for the *New York Sun* who met Crazy Horse in May of 1877 and who wrote that the "bullet wound through his left cheek . . . disfigured his face and gives to the mouth a drawn and somewhat fierce or brutal expression." See Hinman, "Oglala Sources," pp. 12, 16; Ben Jaastad, *Man of the West: Reminiscences of George Washington Oaks, 1840–1917* (Tucson, 1956), p. 44; William J. Bordeaux, *Custer's Conqueror* (no place, no date), p. I; *New York Sun*, May 23, 1877.

Chips saw No Water after he had shot Crazy Horse. Little Big Man saw Crazy Horse draw his knife when No Water entered the double lodge, and he seized and held Crazy Horse, and No Water shot him, and then took his wife.[5]

Chips says that when we were young all we thought about was going to war with some other nation; all tried to get their names up the highest, and whoever did so was the principal man in the nation; and Crazy Horse wanted to get to the highest rank station.

Chips was a medicine man to Crazy Horse and gave him a feather, and he now has the feather; it is not the feather he was wearing when he was killed. Bull Head at Cheyenne River Agency has the feather that Crazy Horse wore to his honor, whatever that may be. The interpreter, Peter Schweigerman, explains that when an Indian did a brave and conspicuous deed he was given a feather.[6]

Crazy Horse never wore a war bonnet. He did not paint as the Indians usually do; but he made a zigzag streak with red earth from the top of his forehead, downwards and to one side of his nose at the base, to the point of the chin. This was done with one finger. He striped his horse with a mould from the earth.[7]

---

[5]The best description of this incident is given by He Dog in Hinman, "Oglala Sources," pp. 12, 15-18. A few months after the shooting Black Buffalo Woman gave birth to a light-haired little girl, rumored to have been Crazy Horse's daughter.

[6]Bull Head was a Minneconjou band leader and a maternal uncle of Crazy Horse.

To count coup was principally the touching of an armed enemy during a combat situation, the display of contempt being heralded by the Plains Indians as one of the most glorious acts of warfare. For an explanation of coup honors, see Royal B. Hassrick, *The Sioux: Life and Customs of a Warrior Society* (Norman, 1964), pp. 96-97.

[7]According to Garnett, Crazy Horse performed the following ritual before going into battle: "Taking some of the dirt thrown up by the pocket gophers, he would rub it on his horse in lines and streaks—not painting him, but passing this dirt over him in this way with his hand; and he would spat a little of the same on his own hair in a spot or two, and put in his hair also two, or three straws of grass, two or three inches long. As I understand it, the man from the lake [a water spirit] told him to use the straws and the dirt as described." Garnett Interview, Ricker Collection, NSHS, reel 1, tablet 1, no pagination. This ritual is also described in the Eagle Elk Interview hereafter.

Chips and Crazy Horse were raised together. The only time they separated was when Fort Fetterman was established. Crazy Horse went north and Chips came with the white people. Chips was in the Fetterman massacre. The Indians who fought there were Oglalas and Minneconjous. He says fourteen Indians were killed there. American Horse was there. American Horse did not lead the decoy party. Chips says he wants to tell the truth.[8]

Crazy Horse was not accounted good for anything among the Indians but to make war; he was expected to do that; he was set apart in their minds to make war, and that was his business.

The greatest act of personal bravery on his part was when he was fighting the Shoshones; his horse was shot under him and he sprang forward to the enemy and counted coup.[9]

Crazy Horse was held in estimation by all Indians as the greatest living warrior among the red men of the earth. He has Crazy Horse's war sack.[10]

Chips was not at the Custer battle, but Crazy Horse told him about it. Reno did not make much of a fight. There was fighting with the Ree scouts [and] they made a charge and

---

[8]The Fetterman Fight took place on December 21, 1866, near Fort Phil Kearny, Wyoming Territory, during which a combined force of Oglalas, Minneconjous and Cheyennes decoyed and killed Captain William J. Fetterman and his command of seventy-eight soldiers and two civilians. For a scholarly treatment of this battle see Dee Brown, *Fort Phil Kearny: An American Saga* (Lincoln, 1971); for a listing of the fourteen Lakota casualties, see Stanley Vestal, *Warpath, The True Story of the Fighting Sioux, Told in a Biography of Chief White Bull* (Lincoln, 1984), p. 67. According to Charles A. Eastman, the decoy party was led by Crazy Horse; see *Indian Heroes and Great Chieftains* (Boston, 1918), p. 94.

[9]This same deed of valor is also mentioned in the Thunder Tail narrative which, however, identifies the adversaries as Crows.

[10]This war sack was actually a medicine bundle, stored in a bag made from tanned animal skin, and which contained the claws and dried heart of the spotted eagle. These objects, imbued with protective powers, were part of a powerful medicine bundle given to Crazy Horse by Chips after the No Water shooting in 1870. See the Camp interview with Chips hereafter.

killed two (2) Indians. Reno did not make any fight of importance.[11]

Chips says that Crazy Horse told [him] that there were about three thousand (3000) warriors who fought against Custer. Five Ree scouts were killed—one wore a large medal suspended from his neck. Thirty-two Indians were killed in all the fighting—thirty-two on the side of the hostiles. There were quite a number wounded, but they lived through. (I do not count strongly on this statement of casualties.)[12]

He says there are two stories among the Indians—one is that Custer was killed on a hill, and the other that he was killed in a ravine. The ravine story is without [a] particle of foundation as to Custer being killed in it, or that he marched his command into it.[13]

After the Indians surrendered and got into intercourse with the whites, Gall made some notable speeches and made quite a man of himself; but he was not looked upon among the Indians as a warrior at all.[14]

Grass was a peaceable man who always lived around the

---

[11]On June 25, 1876, Major Marcus A. Reno and three companies of the Seventh Cavalry led an abortive attack on the Indian village at the Little Bighorn. Reno's conduct, like that of his superior, Gen.George A. Custer, has been the subject of considerable controversy. For a biography of Reno, see John Upton Terrell and George Walton, *Faint the Trumpet Sounds* (New York, 1966). Consisting of some twenty-five warriors, Custer's auxiliary force of Arickara (Rees) Indians may have been responsible for the deaths of as many as four Lakotas and two Cheyennes. During Reno's charge the Rees killed Swift Bear and White Bull, both Hunkpapa Lakotas. See Hardorff, *Lakota Recollections*, p. 110.

[12]Ricker is premature in his criticism because Chips' casualty count is corroborated by numerous independent sources. See Richard G. Hardorff, *Hokahey! A Good Day to Die! The Indian Casualties of the Custer Fight* (Spokane, 1993).

[13]Custer's body was found six feet southwest of the present commemorative monument on Custer Hill. However, a stone placed by the War Department in 1890 to identify Custer's kill site is actually some fifty feet from the correct location. See Richard G. Hardorff, *Markers. Artifacts and Indian Testimony: Preliminary Findings on the Custer Battle* (Short Hills, 1985), pp. 2-7.

[14]Gall was born in a Hunkpapa camp on Grand River, South Dakota, in 1840. Throughout his non-reservation life he proved himself a fierce opponent to the white aggressors. In 1867 he was bayonetted by soldiers and left for dead near abandoned Ft. Berthold. Miraculously, Gall recovered enough from the shock of his wounds to make his escape before daylight, walking twenty miles in severe winter weather to the lodge of a relative.

agency, and Chips calls him a Loafer. He was never known to do any deed of note.[15]

At the time of the fight against the Cheyennes [Dull Knife's village, November, 1876], Crazy Horse was camped on the Little Big Horn.

When the Indian scouts went out in the winter of 1876–1877 to coax Crazy Horse to come in, he was camped on a branch of the Tongue River–the Indians called the branch Otter Creek. Chips went out with the party to coax Crazy Horse to come in. He promised he would come in the spring, and Chips and others came with him as far as Powder River and there separated from him. Chips brought Crazy Horse Sr. into Spotted Tail Agency.[16]

When Crazy Horse fled from his camp below Red Cloud he went to Beaver [Creek] and came to Chips' lodge which was at the camp some three miles below Camp Sheridan. Chips went with Crazy Horse to the fort. No warriors chased the Indian scouts from Fort Robinson–nobody chased anybody.

Gall survived his ordeal and it was said that he killed seven whites out of vengeance, among whom was Lt. Eben Crosby on October 14, 1871. During the Custer Battle in 1876 Gall's family was killed. He avenged their deaths by killing and mutilating a number of Custer's troopers, and fearing reprisals, he took his band to Canada. He surrendered to the U.S. Military at Poplar Creek, Montana, in 1880. His conduct on the reservation was exemplary, and he later became a justice of the Indian Police Court at Standing Rock. Gall passed away on December 5, 1893, and lies buried at Wakpala, South Dakota. See Lewis F. Crawford, *Rekindling Camp Fires: The Exploits of Ben Arnold.* (Bismarck, 1926), pp. 166-68; Usher L. Burdick, *David F. Barry's Indian Notes on the Custer Battle* (Baltimore, 1949), pp. 33, 35.

[15]Grass was an Oglala band chief and a signer of the Ft. Laramie Treaty of 1868. A note in the Camp Manuscripts reveals that Grass once was wounded and captured by soldiers near Platte Bridge. Expecting to be killed, he was instead taken to the post's hospital and was restored to health. Grass vowed never to fight the whites again. He and his band settled near the Oglala agency and became known as *Wagluhe Oyate,* people who loafed around the forts. Grass is not to be confused with John Grass, who was a Blackfoot Lakota. Camp Manuscripts, IU, p. 275.

[16]Leading a small camp of Oglalas, the elder Crazy Horse traveled with his wife's Minneconjou relatives, Touch the Clouds and Roman Nose, to Camp Sheridan, Nebraska, where he and some 256 lodges of Northern Lakota bands surrendered to Gen. George A. Crook on April 14, 1877. See Jesse M. Lee to the Commanding Officer, Camp Sheridan, April 5, 1877, Official Documents, and the *Greencastle Banner,* April 26, 1877. For a scholarly treatment of this episode, see Harry H. Anderson, "Indian Peace-Talkers and the Conclusion of the Sioux War of 1876," in *Nebraska History* (December, 1963): 233-254.

When Crazy Horse arrived at the camp on Beaver [Creek], Crazy Horse and Chips, accompanied by a great many, went up to Camp Sheridan. When there, the officer in command asked Crazy Horse if he wanted to go back to Red Cloud [Agency], or stay at Camp Sheridan and be confined in a cellar until he would start on his way to see the Great Father in Washington. He told the officer he would like to keep his country, and [that] he would go back to Red Cloud. This was all [that] was said, and the next morning he started for Fort Robinson. Chips went with him. The Brulé agent or Spotted Tail agent (the same) (the interpreter suggests it was Major Lee) selected two Indian scouts to go back with him. When they got to Red Cloud, all the Indian scouts had their guns cocked to shoot him, but he was guarded by good boys. They went on into the fort and Crazy Horse went into the house, but Chips did not go in, and he does not know what was said. When Crazy Horse came out, an officer on one side held up his left hand,[17] and Little Big Man on the other side held up his right hand, taking him to the guardhouse. After he was taken to the guardhouse, he refused to go into the cell, but he was inside the building. Chips was inside with him—right behind him. One of the Brulés was in there with Crazy Horse, and he offered to go in and be locked up and stay with him. The Brulé was Turning Bear who offered to go in; he started ahead and the passage led down into the ground, but when Turning Bear saw where they were going, he stopped and said it was a hard place they were going into. Crazy Horse turned back to go out of the guardhouse, and the Indian scouts had their guns cocked to kill him if he refused to go into the guardhouse. The officer and Little Big Man both were still holding on to him. Crazy Horse made a grunt and struggled. He did not say a word. Crazy Horse got outside of the building. Chips did not see the

---

[17]This was Captain James Kennington, Fourteenth Infantry, who served as Officer-of-the-Day on September 5, 1877.

soldier stab Crazy Horse with his bayonet. When the soldier jerked the bayonet from Crazy Horse's body, he hit Chips in the shoulder with the butt and dislocated his shoulder, which is still dislocated. (Which I do not take great stock in.)[18]

Chips buried his body, and he is the only person who knows where it is. Crazy Horse was buried on the Beaver by the cliffs. When the Indians went down to the Missouri River his body was removed to White Clay Creek and buried; and when they returned, Chips and his brother went and took up the body to see if it had been disturbed, and finding that it had not been, they reinterred it. The burial the first time near the cliffs was in a frame house lined with scarlet cloth.[19] His body was once buried on White Horse Creek, above Manderson, but it was moved from there to Wounded Knee where it now is. Chips put the bones into a black blanket and laid them in a butte rock cave. There is no petrifaction—no flesh—nothing now but bones. The shot through the head by No Water shows in the skull.

Crazy Horse was wounded twice—once in the head and once in the calf of the leg.[20]

---

[18]Chips' statement is corroborated by Louis Bordeaux who told Ricker that the butt of the guard's rifle struck Chips' shoulder and broke the latter's collar bone. See the Bordeaux Interview hereafter.

[19]Reference is made to the cliff burial near Camp Sheridan where on September 6 relatives sepulchered the remains of Crazy Horse in a coffin draped with red blankets, on a three-feet-high scaffold. See *Frank Leslie's Illustrated Newspaper*, October 20, 1877.

[20]A *New York Tribune* reporter confirms the existence of two bullet wounds, one of which was in Crazy Horse's face, resulting in an "ugly scar." However, in an interview with Walter Camp, Chips revealed that Crazy Horse had bullet scars not only on his leg, but also on his arm. The plurality of injuries is confirmed by Red Feather who commented that Crazy Horse was wounded twice when he began his fighting career, which statement excludes the No Water wound which was sustained much later. According to Crazy Horse's cousin Eagle Elk, the arm wound was sustained during a fight with Pawnees when Crazy Horse was just a very young boy. The second scar resulted from a gunshot wound received in a fight with Utes when a bullet struck Crazy Horse in his left calf. The latter information was obtained from Owns Horn, a Minneconjou cousin of Crazy Horse. See the *New York Tribune*, May 7, 1877; the Chips Interview with Walter Camp hereafter; Hinman, "Olglalas Sources," p. 30; the Eagle Elk Interview hereafter; and the Campbell letter to Eleanor Hinman, October 13, 1932, in the appendix hereafter.

Crazy Horse killed in the Custer battle sixteen persons, and fifteen in the Reno fight. This is problematical–largely so.

Crazy Horse had one brother who was killed by a white man in a war with whites. He has no near relatives living.[21]

Chips is the one who made Crazy Horse's medicine for him. He is the one who gave him the medicine that he would be killed with a knife while his arm was held, as he sagely informed the author. Chips was the one who told him not to wear a warbonnet, nor to paint, except to use the streak down his countenance which represented the lightning. There is no truth in the story of the horseman coming out of the pond and telling Crazy Horse what to do.[22] We wear a feather to distinguish us for our deeds. Crazy Horse wore a little stone on the left side. Chips has these articles which belonged to Crazy Horse. They are different altogether. The medicine was the spotted eagle's heart, and it was the medicine of such

---

[21]The name of Crazy Horse's half brother was Little Hawk. Born about 1846, he was the only child conceived out of Worm's second marriage with two Brulé women, the sisters of Spotted Tail. Lakota elders claimed that Little Hawk exhibited traits which eventually would have made him a greater man than Crazy Horse, if not for his rashness. He was slain in combat in 1870 while Crazy Horse was convalescing from the No Water shooting. See Hinman, "Oglala Sources," p. 14

[22]Chips' answer was in reference to the following Garnett statement recorded by Ricker: "Garnett heard Crazy Horse in 1868 tell about his 'medicine.' It was up in the vicinity of the Rosebud that it occurred. Whether this appeared to him in a dream or trance or whether he was self-mesmerized, Garnett does not know. But Crazy Horse told the story that he was near a lake. A man on horseback came out of the lake [a water spirit] and talked with him. He told Crazy Horse not to wear a war bonnet [and] not to tie up his horse's tail. (The Indians invariably tie up their horses' tails in a knot.) This man from the lake told him that a horse needed his tail for use; when he jumped a stream he used his tail and [also] at other times, and as Crazy Horse remarked in telling this, he needs his tail in summer time to brush flies. So Crazy Horse never tied his horse's tail, [and he] never wore a war bonnet. It is said he did not paint his face like other Indians. The man from the lake told him he would never be killed by a bullet, but his death would come by being held and stabbed, as it actually was." See the Garnett Interview, Ricker Collection, NSHS, reel 1, tablet 1, no pagination. For another vision by Crazy Horse involving water, see the Flying Hawk Interview in McCreight, *Firewater and Forked Tongues*, pp. 138-39, in which a reference to straws of grass tends to corroborate Garnett's statement in footnote 7. In spite of Chips' denial, the water spirit did give certain instructions to Crazy Horse which, if adhered to, would apparently prevent his death. However, it was the nearly-fatal shooting by No Water in 1870 that led to Chips' eagle *Wotawe*, which made Crazy Horse bulletproof.

persons as he [Chips] gave it to; this was Crazy Horse's medicine which he rubbed on himself when he went into battle, and [which] was his protection; and when it was used before going into action no bullet would touch him. His medicine would protect him against the knife if his arm was not held; but if it was held he would not be protected.

Chips lives on No Flesh Creek; the next creek west is Little Wound Creek. The next west of this is American Horse Creek. No Flesh and Little Wound unite about one mile north of Kyle, and from the point of junction the stream is called Medicine Root.

The Second Chips Interview

This interview is contained in the Walter M. Camp Manuscripts, transcript, pp. 287-89, BYU. It took place about July 11, 1910, when Camp visited Pine Ridge to interview three elderly Oglalas.

THE SECOND CHIPS INTERVIEW
Kyle, South Dakota
[July,] 1910

Tonhcha Hansha [*Tonkce Hanska*], Long Shit or Long Turd, was Crazy Horse's medicine man at the Little Bighorn. Big Road[1] was a sub chief; Black Twin[2] was a sub

---

[1]Big Road, or Wide Trail, was a *Wicasa Yatanpi*, a Shirt Wearer, and the leader of a *Oyuhpe* band of Oglalas. He was an intelligent but unreconstructed man who preferred exile in Canada in 1877 rather than face reservation life at one of the Missouri River agencies. See Hinman, "Oglala Sources," p. 11, and DeMallie, *Lakota Society*, p. 21.

[2]Black Twin, also known as Holy Bald Eagle, was one of the last elected Shirt Wearers of the Northern Oglalas. He was a man held in high esteem by the older tribesmen who described him as a traditionalist who bitterly exposed white encroachment on Lakota lands. He was an older brother of No Water, the leader of the Badger Band of the *Oyuhpe* Oglalas. Black Twin had a twin brother named Holy White Buffalo who, it was said, was of a lighter complexion and was nicknamed the White Twin. Although George Hyde stated that Black Twin died on the reservation in 1877, Lakota sources indicate that he passed away on Powder River in 1875, in one of the camps of the Northern Oglalas. His twin brother, Holy White Buffalo died several years later in Canada during his exile with Sitting Bull. See Hinman, "Oglala Sources," pp. 11, 16; DeBarthe, *Life of Frank Grouard*, p. 54; Hyde, *Red Cloud's Folk*, p. 306.

chief, but [he was] not [present] at the Little Bighorn.
Hunkpapas had the most teepees at the Little Bighorn.[3]

Crazy Horse, in camp, one time had forbidden Little Big
Man to sleep with one of the squaws. They got into a fight
over it and were never friends after that. Low Dog died many
years ago.[4] He was an Oglala. At the Little Bighorn thirty-
odd [Indians] were killed.

German, Wouptucha [*Woptuh'a*] is Chips' name.[5] Crazy
Horse never had his photo taken. Chips is seventy-four years
old in 1910. Crazy Horse was five years younger than Chips.
If [he were] living in 1910, Crazy Horse would be sixty-nine
years old.[6] He was killed when thirty-six. Chips was a cousin
of Crazy Horse.

Crazy Horse's body was first buried on a scaffold at Spotted Tail [Agency] in a coffin. A house was then built over this
scaffold. When we moved to the Missouri we took the body
and unjointed the legs so as to get it into a small space,[7] and
Chips and Old Man Crazy Horse carried it to above the head

---

[3]For a study of the Indian population at the Little Bighorn see John S. Gray *Centennial Campaign: The Sioux War of 1876* (Fort Collins, 1976), pp. 346-57, and Robert A. Marshall, "How Many Indians Were There?" The Little Big Horn Associates' *Research Review* (June, 1977): 3-12.

[4]Born about 1847, Low Dog was an exceedingly brave individual and the leader of an Oglala band which fought Custer in 1876. He surrendered in May 1877, but becoming dissatisfied with the prospect of continued reservation life, he fled to Canada several months later. Low Dog returned to the United States in 1880 and settled among the Minneconjous at the Cheyenne River Agency. He died in 1894. See William A. Graham, *The Custer Myth: A Source Book of Custeriana* (New York, 1953) p. 75-76; Camp Manuscripts, p. 233, IU.

[5]The Lakota word *woptuh'a* means wood or horn chips. The use of the word "German" in this sentence is not quite clear. The Lakota word for German is *Iyasica*, which is derived from *iya* 'to speak' and *sica* 'bad or incomprehensible.' Chips was a Holy Man, one who spoke *wakaniye*—sacred language which was not understood by common Lakotas. The possibility exists, therefore, that *iyasica* had reference to Chips' ability to converse in sacred language.

[6]Crazy Horse was born in the fall of 1840. The interview took place in June 1910.

[7]This statement is corroborated by Black Elk in John G. Neihardt, *Black Elk Speaks: Being the Life Story of a Holy Man of the Oglala Sioux* (Lincoln, 1961), pp. 147-48, although the original transcripts fail to reveal this information. See DeMallie, *The Sixth Grandfather*, p. 204.

Wooden structure surrounding the tentative
sepulcher of Crazy Horse's remains on the bluffs
overlooking Camp Sheridan in 1877.
Courtesy West Point Military Academy Library

of Wounded Knee (not on the creek), and buried it in the
ground in a box. Old Man Crazy Horse and Chips are the
only ones who knew where [it was] buried in a box. Later on
Chips and Chips' brother (Crazy Horse)[8] took up and buried
[the remains] in another place in a blanket–buried under a
bank and [then] covered the bank in. Later on Chips and his
wife and another buried the remains in another place.

[8]Among the AGO records in Washington is an enlistment document for an individual
named Crazy Horse, Jr. who enlisted as a U.S. Indian Scout at Camp Sheridan on April 15,
1877. Since Chief Crazy Horse enlisted at Red Cloud Agency on May 12, 1877, the earlier
record probably refers to Chips' brother who surrendered at Camp Sheridan on April 14,
and was sworn in as a scout the next day. See the Camp Manuscripts, p. 807, IU; the *Greencastle Banner*, April 26, 1877.

Later on Chips took up and buried [the remains] again, and he is now the only one who knows where. This [last] time [the remains] were buried in a rawhide sack. This was twenty-seven years ago or 1883.[9] The reason [why I] don't tell where the bones are is because the Sioux depended much upon Crazy Horse as a fighter; but just before [he was] killed, many of the Oglalas turned against him and were jealous of him and told lies bout him. Little Big Man was[one of] the principal enemies of Crazy Horse.[10] Crazy Horse wanted peace. All the stories [then told] about him were false.

---

[9]In 1883, or 1884, an old trapper named White brought a skull to the Wounded Knee trading post which he had found with some bones and a set of travois poles in the Bad Lands, somewhere between Wounded Knee Creek and Porcupine Creek. This skull showed a bone deformity in the upper jaw below the corner of the nose, and a second deformation between the cheekbone and the eye cavity. Several old Indian women who examined it, and who had known Crazy Horse, stated that it was definitely the skull of the renowned Oglala. One of these women, Louise Pourier, who was a relative of Crazy Horse, took the skull to her cabin and kept it hidden in a closet for several years. One day she wrapped the skull in a piece of blue woolen blanket and, after crushing the skull with an axe, she buried the remains in her backyard near present Rockyford, South Dakota. See the Lone Eagle Statement, part II, box 28, Mari Sandoz Collection, University of Nebraska.

[10]The extent and duration of animosity between Little Big Man and Crazy Horse was probably considerably less than what Chips makes it appear to be. If any friction existed, it did not occur until after their surrender in 1877. It is true that Little Big Man was involved in the 1870 wounding of Crazy Horse, but only to the extent that he prevented Crazy Horse from stabbing No Water. Significantly, this interference averted an unlawful act by Crazy Horse which would have violated his oath as a Shirt Wearer. Nonetheless, the adulterous affair with No Water's wife led to Crazy Horse's resignation as a Shirt Wearer. This incident did not strain the relationship between Crazy Horse and Little Big Man, who were cousins. In fact, it was Little Big Man who served as intermediary between Crazy Horse and the Chief Society when Crazy Horse returned his scalp shirt and other Shirt Wearer paraphernalia. During the 1860s and 1870s, Little Big Man was a close ally of Crazy Horse, both being actively involved in raiding the Platte Valley. During these years Little Big Man stayed in Crazy Horse's camp, and he surrendered with him in 1877 as one of the six principal men of Crazy Horse's Northern Oglalas. Prior to that time, Little Big Man had violently opposed the white invaders, his explosive nature being particularly noted by the Allison Commission in 1875 during its negotiations with the Lakotas to purchase the Black Hills. Upon the surrender in 1877, Little Big Man's ideology changed sharply from that of Crazy Horse's, and their ways separated when they enlisted as U.S. Indian Scouts. It was noted that Little Big Man executed his new responsibilities with great zeal, while Crazy Horse displayed only apathy. It was during this period that rumors began to circulate among the Oglalas that Little Big Man was acting against the good of his own people. These accusations were further fueled by his controversial involvement in the slaying of Crazy Horse,

When Crazy Horse surrendered he was dressed up in a war bonnet and had two guns. He rode up, dismounted and sat down and handed his two guns to an officer in uniform called White Hat (Philo Clark). Crazy Horse handed White Hat his guns and put part of his war toggery on White Hat and said: "I have been a man of war and have always protected my country against invaders. Now I am for peace. I will look at the ground and fight no more. I will settle down and attend to my own business.[11]

Crazy Horse was born at a small butte near Bear Butte on Bear Creek, a tributary of the Cheyenne River.

Crazy Horse was a very brave man and this was the reason why he was made a warrior chief. He seemed to bear a charmed life, and no matter how near he got to his enemy they could not hit him. Crazy Horse put great confidence in his medicine. His particular medicine was an eagle's feather and eagle claws and a small medicine bag, and also the feather he wore on top of his head.[12]

Crazy Horse was a quiet fellow who attended councils and listened, but [who was] not much of a talker on such occasions or at any other time.

---

which may explain why Little Big Man refused to flee to Canada with the other Northern Oglalas in the fall of 1877. For the charge of adultery, see Hinman, "Oglala Sources," pp. 12, 17, which accusation was made by He Dog who himself was a Shirt Wearer. Little Big Man became the custodian of Crazy Horse's scalp shirt and later sold it to Lt. John G. Bourke. See *On the Border with Crook*, p. 415. For evidence of Little Big Man's unpopularity among the Northern Oglalas, see the Richard Stirk Interview, Ricker Collection, NSHS, reel 2, tablet 8, pp. 36-37, and also the Garnett Interview, Ricker Collection, reel 1, tablet 2, p. 104.

[11]Chips is mistaken. Crazy Horse did not wear a warbonnet and he did not give anything to Lt. William P. Clark. In fact, Crazy Horse stated to Clark, "I have given all I have to Red Cloud." In addition, Crazy Horse presented not two but three Winchester rifles during the arms surrender. It was He Dog who presented Clark with a warbonnet, a scalp shirt, a ceremonial pipe, a buffalo robe, and a pony. See the *Chicago Times*, May 7, 1877; and the *New York Herald*, May 7, and May 28, 1877.

[12]Crazy Horse's eagle *wotawe* included two bilateral tail feathers of the spotted eagle. One feather was worn upside down in the loose hair, while the other one was laced to a rawhide skin which covered a little round stone. See the Eagle Elk Interview, and also the He Dog interview with Mari Sandoz, both hereafter.

Crazy Horse [was of] medium height and was slender. [He had] light hair and light complexion and [had a] full face. [He was] a full-blood Oglala.

American Horse was the son of Ass (Winchonze [*Win-conze*]).[13] There is a current story that Chips wanted to sell Crazy Horse's bones. Chips says the story is false. He has never tried to do it and has never offered them for sale.[14]

Crazy Horse was once shot in the leg and in the arm fighting Sissetons,[15] and through the face in a scrap over taking a fellow Oglala's wife away from him. After this Chips fixed him up with the medicine described above and Crazy Horse had no more trouble from wounds in battle.

His favorite enemy was the Crows with whom he had many battles.

---

[13]Ass, or Buttocks, may have been the nickname of Old Smoke, the patriarch leader of the Smoke People. He died at Fort Laramie in the fall of 1864. See Hyde, *Red Cloud's Folks*, p. 115.

[14]Crazy Horse's brother-in-law, Red Feather, was implicated by similar rumors. A map drawn by Red Cloud in 1895 bears a notation in Lakota that Red Feather would not reveal the burial location of Crazy Horse's bones unless he was given some money. See the Red Cloud map in the Frank F. Aplan Collection, Manuscript 479, NSHS.

[15]The Sissetons were a Dakota-speaking tribe of the Santee, the eastern division of the Sioux. Although occasional clashes had taken place between the allied Sioux tribes, by 1850 such incidents had ceased to occur. It seems unlikely, therefore, that Crazy Horse had fought the Sisseton tribe. The Dakota word *sisseton* is derived from *sinsin* 'to smell like fish,' and *tunwan*, which means 'village'. It is quite probable, therefore, that Chips merely stated that the attack had been made against a village which smelled like fish, and not necessarily the Sisseton tribe, as was inferred by the interpreter. We know that the Winnebagos occupied a small agency along the Missouri River in northeastern Nebraska. They were fish eaters, calling themselves the Big Fish People, who originally lived in the Green Bay area of Wisconsin, and who may have been the people referred to by Chips. Support for this belief comes from He Dog who stated that Crazy Horse had raided the Winnebago people at an early age and that he had slain one of their women. See Powers, *Oglala Religion*, p. 22; Paul Radin, *The Winnebago Tribe* (Lincoln, 1990), pp. 4, 5; and Hinman, "Oglala Sources," p.9.

Baptiste Pourier Interview

INTRODUCTION

The son of Joseph Pourier and Marie Aubuchon L'Arbe, Baptiste Pourier was born in St. Charles, Missouri, on July 16, 1842. At age fourteen he found employment as a teamster and moved with Indian traders into the country west of the Mississippi. In this capacity he gained a thorough knowledge of the country and the Sioux Indians, eventually marrying Josephine Richard, an Oglala mixed-blood of French extraction. Pourier's expertise was fully recognized by the military authorities in 1869 who employed him as a scout, guide, and interpreter for many years. Baptiste Pourier passed away on his Wounded Knee ranch near Manderson, South Dakota in 1932. For a Biography of this humble man see Hila Gilbert, *"Big Bat" Pourier: Guide and Interpreter, Fort Laramie, 1870–1880* (Sheridan, 1968). Although Gilbert states that Big Bat was born on October 5, 1841, an affidavit by the latter lists the date as July 16, 1842. See the James McLaughlin letter dated August 30, 1920, in the South Dakota Historical Society, to which is appended Pourier's affidavit of August 26, 1920. The Pourier Interview is contained in the Ricker Collection, reel 3, tablet 13, pp. 19-25, NSHS.

THE BAPTISTE POURIER INTERVIEW
A[t] Baptiste Pourier's
March 6, 1907

CRAZY HORSE

Bat Pourier says: He was in Lt. Clark's quarters at the northwest corner of the square when Crazy Horse was wounded, and did not see the tragedy. He says that he himself and Touch the Cloud, Dr. McGillicudy, one soldier on guard, and the father of Crazy Horse (whose name was also Crazy Horse) were with him that night of his death until he died. Bat was the first to discover that Crazy Horse was dead. He remarked to the doctor that he was dead. The doctor said he guessed not, but on feeling of him found it was so. Then they feared to announce it to Crazy Horse Sr. on account of his grief. So Bat suggested giving him a drink of grog which was done, Bat getting his portion also. The old man expressed his satisfaction, saying it was good. Calling Bat his son, which he usually did, he said, "It was good, that will open my heart." Bat says: "Don't take it hard; your son is dead." The old man's outburst of grief and remorse was explosive. His expression: "Hengh" (a grunt like a bear when he seizes and squeezes, and is just an exclamation.) "Micinci watoye sni te lo." ("My son is dead without revenging himself!") Crazy Horse died at 4 o'clock a.m.[1]

Bat says: Crazy Horse was wounded this way (although he did not see it:) When Crazy Horse entered the guardhouse, Touch the Cloud was the first to speak and warn him that he was going into confinement–that he was in the guardhouse, as he saw and heard balls and chains. Crazy Horse sprang back

---

[1]Pourier is mistaken. Crazy Horse died at 11:40 P.M., Wednesday, September 5, 1877. See Lt. William Clark's telegram to Gen. Crook, September 6, 1877; Col. Luther P. Bradley's telegram to Gen. Sheridan, September 6; Gen. Alfred H. Terry's telegram to Col. Miles, September 7; and Lt. Clark's letter to the Commissioner of Indian Affairs, September 10, 1877, Official Correspondence. The monument on Crazy Horse Mountain in South Dakota erroneously lists the date of death as September 6.

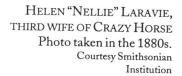

HELEN "NELLIE" LARAVIE,
THIRD WIFE OF CRAZY HORSE
Photo taken in the 1880s.
Courtesy Smithsonian
Institution

and drew his knife; Little Big Man seized him, but Crazy Horse cut him across the base of the thumb and base of the forefinger–a slight wound only–but Little Big Man howled and cried and acted the baby as though he was half killed.

Bat says that when Crazy Horse was wounded there were orders to take him to Laramie in an ambulance, and from there to Omaha. Bat was to go with him, also Yankton Charlie and No Neck, and another, and an escort of [an] officer and soldiers.[2] Bat's understanding is that Crazy Horse was purposely stabbed.

Crazy Horse was a slim, light man; weight about 140 pounds. Little Big Man was very short and stout, weight in his prime was about 140. Bat says Crazy Horse was as fine an

[2]The third Indian Scout was Little Big Man. No Neck was a respected Oglala band leader. After enlisting as a U.S. Indian Scout he resided on No Neck Creek, Pine Ridge, where he died in 1887. The escort consisted of Company E, Third Cavalry, commanded by Second Lieutenant Henry R. Lemley. Lemley had received orders from Gen. Bradley to escort Crazy Horse to Fort Laramie by ambulance and from there to Cheyenne, where a train was to be boarded for Fort Marion, St. Augustine, Florida, where Crazy Horse was to be imprisoned. See H. R. Lemley to John G. Neihardt, March 5, 1920, Neihardt Collection, University of Missouri; Captain H. R. Lemley, "The Passing of Crazy Horse," *Journal of the Military Service Institution of the United States* (May-June, 1914): 321.

Indian as he ever knew. When Crazy Horse stole two blooded mares from him at Fort Laramie (when Billy Garnett was herding his horses for him), Bat went to him and asked for them, and Crazy Horse told his wife to get them, but she did not want to do it–did not want to give them up–but he ordered her again to get them, saying they belonged to Bat, and she delivered them. Bat says he [Crazy Horse] was the only Indian who would have given them up. Crazy Horse fought only for his country, and was not a bad man at all. He was slow of speech. Bat says that Crazy Horse's second wife was the daughter of Joe Larrabee, and that Lieut. Clark had gotten Crazy Horse to take her as his wife, thinking that this chief would regard it as a favor and that it would have the effect to mellow his feelings and make him more kindly disposed toward the whites.[3] There may be a mistake about this. (When Crazy Horse fled to Spotted Tail Agency he took his original full-blood wife and left the Larrabee woman, Bat says.)

Bat says it was bad policy to arm Crazy Horse and some of his men as scouts. When Lt. Clark wanted him to go against the Nez Perces, Crazy Horse taunted him by saying that he [Crazy Horse] had given up his arms as an act of peace, and "now," he says, "you put arms into my hands again to go to war!"

Bat does not know anything about the councils between Gen. Crook and the Indian scouts over the Agency question.[4]

Bat says that Garnett is in error about his being in the room with him at Lt. Clark's headquarters on the night of Crazy Horse's death, and being awakened in the morning by Crazy Horse Sr. Bat sat up that night with Crazy Horse.

---

[3]For a discussion of this matter, see Eleanor Hinman to Mari Sandoz, December 7, 1947, and the latter's reply, December 10, 1947, both in the Hinman Collection, University of Nebraska, and the Tom Laravie Interview, undated, in William J. Bordeaux, *Custer's Conqueror* (Sioux Falls, no date), no pagination.

[4]One of these councils took place at Camp Robinson on May 25, 1877, during which session, in a very rare display of public speaking, Crazy Horse briefly addressed Gen.Crook on the issue of a Northern Oglala agency. See the *Chicago Times*, May 26, 1877.

Louis Bordeaux Interview

INTRODUCTION

Born near Fort Laramie in 1849, Louis Bordeaux, was one of seven children of William J. Bordeaux and a Brulé woman. After receiving a formal education in Hamburg, Iowa, Louis returned to Dakota Territory and became a government interpreter, accompanying the first Sioux delegation to Washington in 1869. He was known among the Lakotas as Louis Mato (Bear), the last name having been given to his father on account of his boisterous voice and mannerisms. In later years Louis Bordeaux established a ranch in present Todd County, South Dakota, which he successfully operated until his death in 1917. For additional information on the Bordeaux family, see Virginia Cole Trenholm, "The Bordeaux Story," *Annals of Wyoming* (July, 1954) : 119-27, and the Susan Bordeaux Bettelyoun manuscript in the NSHS. The Louis Bordeaux Interview is contained in the Ricker Collection, reel 3, tablet 11, pp. 61-95, NSHS. For additional accounts by Louis Bordeaux, see the publication by his son, William J. Bordeaux, *Custer's Conqueror,* pp. 75-90, and Bruce R. Liddic and Paul Harbaugh, *Camp on Custer: Transcribing the Custer Myth,* pp. 137-151.

THE LOUIS BORDEAUX INTERVIEW

Interviewed at his house, six miles north of Georgia, Nebraska, on the Northwestern RR, Friday, August 30, 1907.

FRAGMENT OF THE HISTORY OF CRAZY HORSE

Mr. Bordeaux is of French and Indian descent, and the Sioux language is his mother tongue. He is in stature a short, thick, heavy man, of very dark complexion, the two strains of his blood showing with prominence in his color.

At the time of the Crazy Horse episode he was the official interpreter for the Spotted Tail Agency and Camp Sheridan. The Agency was three-quarters of a mile above Camp Sheridan on Beaver Creek.

Major Burke[1] was the officer in command at Camp Sheridan. Lieutenant Lee was the Acting Agent at Spotted Tail Agency. He was called Major because he was an agent.

It was in the fall of 1876 that the Indians went to the Indian Territory to view the territory and to decide whether to move there. These were chiefs and sub-chiefs, a lot of them; they went to Sidney by horseback etc.; there they went by rail as far as they could and then finished by horses etc.

Lieut. Jessie M. Lee[2] [was] an army officer.

---

[1]Captain Daniel W. Burke, Fourteenth Infantry, commanded Camp Sheridan. The garrison consisted of C Company, Fourteenth Infantry, and M Company, Third Cavalry, an aggregate total of seven commissioned officers and 106 enlisted men.

[2]After serving honorably through the Civil War years, Jesse M. Lee received a commission of second lieutenant in the Thirty-Ninth Infantry on July 28, 1866. He became first lieutenant on January 7, 1867, and served as regimental adjutant until April 20, 1869, when he was transferred to the Twenty-Fifth Infantry. On December 31, 1870, Lee was assigned to the Ninth Infantry, serving as its regimental adjutant from March 1878 to May 1879. Lee was promoted to captain on May 1, 1879, and to major on April 26, 1898. He was appointed colonel of the Tenth United States Volunteer Infantry on May 31, 1898, and was honorably discharged from volunteer service on July 8, 1898. On August 7, 1900, he was transferred to the Fifteenth Infantry, but was transferred once more two months later to become lieutenant colonel of the Sixth Infantry. On November 8, 1901, Lee obtained the colonelcy of the Thirtieth Infantry. He was promoted to brigadier general on June 17, 1902, and retired eventually with the rank of major general. In regards to his service in 1877,

Mr. Bordeaux says that when Crazy Horse went down to Touch the Cloud's camp from his own near Red Cloud Agency that the Indian scouts who followed him from Fort Robinson were afraid of him; that they went to Camp Sheridan with word that Crazy Horse had quit his own camp and was in the camp below, which was Touch the Cloud's at the confluence of the Beaver and the fork of the Beaver (it was not at the mouth of the Beaver, but was in the vicinity of Corn's). These Indian scouts went into the barracks at Camp Sheridan. They were careful to keep well concealed inside; but it is not true that the Indians pursued them and that they sought safety in flight and escaped to the barracks. The Indian warriors, Touch the Cloud's, numbered about 300 and were in overwhelming force against not only the scouts from Fort Robinson, but [also] the regular garrison of troops which consisted of only two companies.

When the scouts arrived from Fort Robinson, Mr. Bordeaux was up at the Agency. He was sent for. He and Major Burke and Acting Agent Lieutenant Lee and Joe Marrivaill[3] (who was a Mexican mixed blood; I think Charley Marrivaill said he was French; ask Mary Ann) started down to the camp where Crazy Horse was.

Corrected: Before Crazy Horse started to come up to Camp Sheridan, Joe Marrivaill, scout and interpreter, and [of] mixed French and Spanish blood (Marrivaill is a French name, [and] the Spanish probably came through the mother,

---

records reveal that on May 14, Lee commenced to serve a special assignment as acting Indian agent at Spotted Tail Agency. His account of the killing of Crazy Horse may be found in the *Journal of the Military Service Institution of the United States* (May-June, 1914): 323-340. This same article, along with a few extractions of Lee's diary and his wife's recollections of the slaying, was later published by E. A. Brininstool in *Crazy Horse, The Invincible Oglalla Sioux Chief* (Los Angeles, 1949). After reading Lee's writings, one cannot escape the impression that Lee felt personally responsible for Crazy Horse's death. These haunting feelings of guilt became even stronger later in life.

[3]The last name of this individual is variously recorded as Marrivaill, Merivale, Merriville, and Maraville.

says Bordeaux. Marrivaill was a light man in complexion, [and] would be called a white man.) and Charley Tackett (Bordeaux says this name was *not* Taggart but Tack*ett*)–these two had gone down to Touch the Cloud's camp to see if they could get Crazy Horse to come up to the Post. Tackett was a Sioux mixed blood and [a] scout and interpreter. They had been sent down after the Indian scouts had come from Fort Robinson with a letter telling of Crazy Horse's flight and asking that Crazy Horse be arrested and sent back, and offering a reward of $50 to anyone who should arrest him.[4]

White Thunder,[5] a sub-chief and principal scout for the government, belonging at Camp Sheridan, and Black Crow,[6] a sub-chief and right bower of Spotted Tail, had also gone down, and with these were coming back Crazy Horse, Touch the Cloud and a large band of Indians. Marrivaill and Tackett had been first upon returning, and they said Crazy Horse was coming.

Some of these were in a four-mule ambulance: namely Major Burke and Lieut. J. M. Lee and one or two other officers.[7]

On the way down, they met Crazy Horse, Touch the Cloud, White Thunder and a lot of Indians, some of them in

---

[4]The reward was $200, quite large when compared with an enlisted soldier's annual pay of $150. See Clark to Crook, telegram, September 4, 1877, and Lee's account in Brininstool, *Crazy Horse*, p. 28.

[5]White Thunder was the leader of the Brulé Loafer Band. He had an excellent reputation as a brave and honest man who was regarded as a progressive leader during the reservation years. Elderly Brulés credit him with the slaying of Capt. W. D. Fouts on Horse Creek in 1865. In 1884 White Thunder and his old father were assassinated by Young Spotted Tail after an incident involving the stealing of White Thunder's young wife. See Hyde, *Spotted Tail's Folks*, pp. 104, 289, 305; Hyde, *A Sioux Chronicle*, p. 168; and Paul Dyck, *Brulé: The Sioux People of the Rosebud* (Flagstaff, 1971), p. 172.

[6]Black Crow was the leader of a Brulé band. He was an ambitious man who had married Spotted Tail's daughter and who was later implicated in the 1881 assassination of his father-in-law. See Hyde, *Spotted Tail's Folks*, pp. 287, 289, 301.

[7]In addition to Capt. Burke and Lt. Lee, only one other officer was present, Dr. Egon A. Koerper, Assistant Surgeon, U.S.A., attached to Camp Sheridan. See Lee's account in Brininstool, *Crazy Horse*, p. 25.

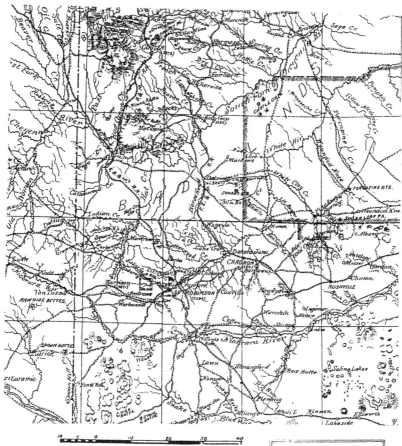

Scale of Miles.

Section of a 1890 military map showing Fort Robinson and adjacent territory, compiled and drawn under direction of 1st Lt. Chas. A. Worden, 7th Infantry, Acting Eng. Officer, Department of the Platte.

EXPLANATIONS.

Indian Agencies ....
Military Posts ....
Capital Cities ....
County Seats ....
Towns, Post offices &c ....
Boundaries of States ____ __ _
    • Indian Res's
    Indian Camps ▲
Rail Roads:
Wagon
— ABBREVIATIONS USED —
Ci. ... City | R.R. Rail road
Res ... Reservation | Rcn ...
Mt. ... | Pk ... Peak

warbonnets and fighting attitude, coming up to Camp Sheridan. Major Burke and other members of the party shook hands with Crazy Horse who was friendly, though he was not a man to talk. The party turned about and started to return. They had not gone but a little way when White Thunder approached Mr. Bordeaux and told him to tell his party to make better time and get back as soon as they could, for he was not sure but there might be trouble; he did not know what some of the Indians who were the friends of Crazy Horse and were exited, might do. (Touch the Cloud's and Crazy Horse's Indians were northern Indians of the same band of Sioux.)[8]

The officers had met Crazy Horse about a mile and a half below Sheridan. The Indian camp was two miles or a little more below. They accelerated their pace and when within a mile of the camp, White Thunder told Bordeaux to hurry his party back, as stated above. Mr. Bordeaux himself kept along with the Indians until within half a mile of Camp Sheridan when he hastened forward and reached there ahead of the Indians. Crazy Horse and his followers rode into the quarters of Camp Sheridan where Major Burke and Lieutenant Lee tried to talk with him, but he would say nothing. The Indians were numerous and swarming.

The officers made effort to get something out of him; they told what was required of him; that he must go back to Fort Robinson; that he would not be hurt; [and] that he should be protected etc.; but he refused to speak.

Spotted Tail was present at the Post (he did not go down toward the Indian camp with Major Burke's party) and he took up the conversation with Crazy Horse, telling him that he (Crazy Horse) was under his (Spotted Tail's) control; that this was his (Spotted Tail's) Agency, and that he did not want him to come there to make trouble; that his Agency was a peaceable place and had the name of being so, and that he did not want

---

[8]The Northern Indians were of different Lakota bands: Touch the Cloud led the Minneconjous, while Crazy Horse led the Oglalas.

any disturbance. He asked Crazy Horse if he would go into the Adjutant's Office and converse with the officers. He replied, "I will." These were the first words he had uttered.

One of the episodes of the excitement when this strain was at its height was the entrance onto the scene of an Indian named Buffalo Chips who had a long braid of hair down his back. He came up to Crazy Horse and addressed him, saying that he was afraid to die; that he was a coward, and then to Spotted Tail he said in the same spirit of denunciation, "You are a coward!"[9] Crazy Horse said nothing. Spotted Tail answered him with a pleasant laugh. Then Buffalo Chips addressed the officers and told them to hang him (Buffalo Chips) and let Crazy Horse live a hundred years, for he was a coward; and to let Spotted Tail also live a hundred years, for he was a coward too. Chips took hold of Burke's coat when he was talking to him. Major Burke laughed and said to Chips, "We don't want to hang you; we don't want to hang anybody." The Indians were quiet but were swarming around by the hundreds, surrounding these six men, namely, Major Burke, Lieut. Lee, the military surgeon (name forgotten),[10] Louis Bordeaux, Chief Spotted Tail and Joe Marrivaill. Then Buffalo Chips, turning to Major Burke, told him to hang him (Buffalo Chips) and to let Crazy Horse and Spotted Tail live a hundred years, as more correctly stated above.

Crazy Horse, with a few of his friends, went into the Adjutant's Office, and here he was asked why he had left his camp at Red Cloud. He explained that he saw a great force of soldiers and scouts coming to his camp, and he did not want trouble, so he came down to Touch the Cloud's to avoid disturbance. He said that when he came in from the north and

---

[9]According to Lt. Lee, Buffalo Chips had stated: "Crazy Horse is brave, but he feels too weak to die today. Kill me—Kill me!" In this version, neither Spotted Tail nor Crazy Horse were called a coward by Buffalo Chips, which is a preposterous accusation in view of their fearless reputations. See Lee's account in Brininstool, *Crazy Horse*, p. 27.

[10]Dr. Egon A. Koerper.

met the officers and others on Hat Creek, he presented the pipe of peace to the Great Spirit there and said he wanted peace and wanted no more war, and promised that he would not fight against any nation anymore, and that he wants to be at peace now; but only a day or two before this he had been called into a council at Fort Robinson with the officers, and they had asked him to go out and fight the Nez Perces; that he did not want to do that, for he remembered his promise to the Great Spirit not to fight anymore; but nevertheless he said he would go and camp beside the soldiers and fight with them till the Nez Perces were all killed. (Nez Perces, pronounced Nez Perces, says Bordeaux, and means "pierced noses." Nez Perces is French.)

It is here explained by Mr. Bordeaux that Grouard was the interpreter at that council, as Billy Garnett [had] said when he met him coming away and Grouard told him it was too hot for him there, so he left.

Bordeaux says that Grouard willfully misinterpreted Crazy Horse's words. He represented him as saying that he would not go out to fight the Nez Perces, but that he was going back to his country in the north and would take the warpath and fight the soldiers till they were all killed.

Bordeaux says Grouard was afraid of Crazy Horse, after having lived among his band for years as a refugee from trouble on the Missouri where he killed a schoolmate, and had killed, as Crazy Horse told Bordeaux, mail carriers and robbed the mail and carried letters into the Indian camp and read them to Crazy Horse, the contents disclosing information as to the whereabouts and movements of the soldiers, in all of which the Indians were keenly interested.[11]

---

[11]A nearly similar charge was made by Money, an Oglala woman better known to the whites as Nettie Goings. She, like others, maintained that Grouard's last name was Brazeau, or Prazost, an erroneous identification disproven by historical evidence. See the Nettie Elizabeth Goings Interview, Ricker Collection, reel 3, tablet 13, pp., 107-09, NSHS, and Hardorff, "The Frank Grouard Genealogy," pp. 123-33.

I have told Bordeaux what Billy Garnett told me, as I recollect, about Crazy Horse refusing to go against the Nez Perces and threatening to go off north to hunt. He says it may have been so, but he remembers that Billy told him that he (Billy) was not in that council; that Grouard interpreted on that occasion. Billy may be mistaken and stated to me what he learned from Grouard. I am satisfied that Crazy Horse's statement was as Bordeaux says, as reason for so thinking will appear farther on. Garnett was speaking only of what he had been told that Crazy Horse had said; he was not present when Crazy Horse said it, but Grouard was.

Mr. Bordeaux says that Crazy Horse was slight in form, tall, very light in complexion, hair long and hung down to his hips.

Lieut. Lee was a sincere and warm friend of the Indians; had their highest good at heart; treated them upon the principle that they were men; trusted them; considered their claims and wishes, and yielded to them no doubt far beyond his instructions, because he understood them and it was the better way. It was better than government by headquarters—by directions from distant headquarters.

When Crazy Horse was explaining why he came down to Touch the Cloud's, he also said that the Spotted Tail Agency had the reputation of being a peaceable place, and he wanted to come there and have his band transferred to that Agency.[12] Mr. Bordeaux explains that when an Indian presents the pipe to the Great Spirit it is the holy pipe; to the wild Indian this act and vow was in the nature of an oath, as such obligations are among civilized peoples; to the Indian it is a holy, sacred act, solemn and to be kept with honor.

---

[12]Blaming Red Cloud and his agency Oglalas for the slaying of his son, Worm refused to live among them any longer and instead settled among the Brulés on the Rosebud Reservation in 1878. Worm died here in 1881. Although little is known of his descendants, one of them, Black Bull, his grandson, later became a member of the Rosebud Indian Police. See Hyde, *Spotted Tail's Folks*, pp. 254, 255; the Susan Bordeaux Bettleyoun Recollections hereafter; and the Camp Manuscripts, p. 384, IU.

Mr. Bordeaux says that when the council was held at Fort Robinson and Crazy Horse was asked to go against the Nez Perces, Touch the Cloud, and High Bear[13] who belonged to Touch the Cloud's band and was a sub-chief in it, were present at that council. These two latter came home. Grouard was the interpreter at the Fort Robinson council. He was sent, after the council was held, from Fort Robinson with a letter to the commanding officer at Camp Sheridan, and Major Burke, Touch the Cloud, High Bear, Spotted Tail and other chiefs were brought into council at Sheridan. Bordeaux was present as interpreter. Here it was told by Touch the Cloud in High Bear's presence without contradiction just what Crazy Horse had said; that on Hat Creek he had promised not to go on the warpath any more etc., but now the same men who had desired to have this pledge from him were urging him to go killing men again (but this time it was to do it for them); however, he would do it; he would go and camp beside their soldiers and fight with them till all the Nez Perces were killed.

Mr. Bordeaux states that this occurred three or four days before Crazy Horse came down to Touch the Cloud's camp. In the conference in the headquarters at Camp Sheridan Crazy Horse repeated the same thing exactly. Grouard was present in the former council and heard Bordeaux's translation of what Touch the Cloud said when telling what Crazy Horse had said, and Grouard called Bordeaux down, saying he was not correctly interpreting Touch the Cloud, accusing him of not being familiar with the northern dialect. Bordeaux told him he could out teach him his mother tongue, and that he (Grouard) was not well enough versed in the three Sioux dialects, namely, the Teton which Bordeaux

---

[13]High Bear, also known as Tall Bear, was the leader of a small band of Northern Sans Arcs. He was a close ally of the Minneconjou, Touch the Cloud, with whom he enlisted in the U.S. Indian Scouts in 1877. High Bear passed away at the Cheyenne River Agency in 1910.

HIGH BEAR
Photo taken in Washington, DC in 1877.
Courtesy West Point Military Academy Library

speaks and which is the prevailing speech west of the Missouri River, and the Santee which uses the d̲, the Yankton
which uses the n̲, and the Teton which uses the l̲, etc., etc., to
understand him or be an interpreter. Major Burke interposed
and said to Grouard that Bordeaux could not be impeached if
the testimony of other interpreters of reputation could be
relied on, for they all, without exception, gave him the com-
mendation of being an accurate and brave interpreter–brave

meaning that he interpreted just what a man said without change or modification. Grouard had no more to say.

In this council at Camp Sheridan Crazy Horse stated to Major Burke that he wished to have his band transferred to Spotted Tail Agency where there would be a better opportunity to live in peace, and Burke and Lee both told him to go back to Fort Robinson and have a talk with the officers there; that no harm would come to him; that he would be protected; and that they would exert their influence to have him and his band transferred. On these promises Crazy Horse consented at once that he would go back. He was going back with Touch the Cloud to his camp, and Major Burke privately told Touch the Cloud that he would hold him personally responsible for Crazy Horse; that he must not let him escape in the night. The chief said he would not let him get away.

Next morning, early, Bordeaux came down from the Agency and met Crazy Horse and Touch the Cloud and a few others at the Post already there.

It should be noted here that Crazy Horse Senior was at the camp of Touch the Cloud, having come from the north ahead of his son, and was down there. He must have gone to Fort Robinson with some of those who went that fatal day.

I have omitted in the proper place to say that when Major Burke and Lieut. Lee were riding back to their camp, returning from their trip down the creek to see Crazy Horse, as they sat in the ambulance, they were discussing the qualities of Crazy Horse as they looked back at him following behind. They agreed that he was an able young man, destined, if no ill fortune prevented, to become great among his people; that he was not trained like the old chiefs in speaking and in diplomacy; he was not spoiled by any acts to gain advantage, but was straightforward and meant what he declared and could be depended on to perform what he promised.

Touch the Cloud was an honorable and peaceable Indian, a man of good character, a very fine man [who] deprecated hostilities and [who] was a peacemaker.

The night before, Major Burke turned Crazy Horse over to Touch the Cloud for safe keeping.

After arriving at the camp, Crazy Horse concluded that he must go back to Touch the Cloud's camp and get a saddle, he having come from his camp at Red Cloud on his horse bareback, and he was allowed to go. But Good Voice[14] and Horned Antelope, Indian Scouts at Camp Sheridan, were sent down to watch him and not let him get away. The two scouts were told if he attempted to escape to shoot his horse; if he resisted to kill him.

White Thunder was the principal scout who brought Crazy Horse up from Touch the Cloud's camp to Camp Sheridan. Good Voice was the principal scout who was directed not to let him escape from Touch the Cloud's camp, and if necessary to shoot his horse or kill him.

Major Burke and Charley Tackett followed these; a little later Lieut. Lee, Louis Bordeaux, Swift Bear,[15] a sub-chief, and Black Crow went down together in the ambulance to Touch the Cloud's camp. They found Burke and Tackett around Touch the Cloud's tepee. On arrival of Lee, Burke told Lee to get Crazy Horse if he could and go right on towards Fort Robinson; in the meantime he would return to Camp Sheridan and get the Indian Scouts, so that if so obliged, they could take Crazy Horse by force.

Lieut. Lee was in a small tepee and he sent Bordeaux in to

---

[14]Good Voice was the leader of a band of *Wajaje* Brulés and a member of the Brulé delegation which visited Washington in 1877. He enlisted in the U.S. Indian Scouts in 1877 and later became one of the first on the reservation to adopt the white man's dress. See Hyde, *A Sioux Chronicle*, p. 207; and Dyck, *Brulé: The Sioux of the Rosebud*, p. 148.

[15]Swift Bear was an uncle of Louis Bordeaux whose mother, christianized Marie, was Swift Bear's sister.

get Crazy Horse, but just at that moment Crazy Horse was invited into Touch the Cloud's tepee to have breakfast of bread, meat and coffee, and Crazy Horse asked Bordeaux to come and breakfast with him, which he did. After the repast, Bordeaux asked him if he was ready now to go. Crazy Horse replied that he was; but he said, ["You go on and I will come after you."] Lieut. Lee said to Bordeaux, "Let us go and cross Beaver Creek, and if he does not come we will come back here again and wait till Major Burke comes with the scouts;" so they went on and crossed the creek and stopped. Bordeaux looked back and saw Crazy Horse coming with the two scouts aforementioned and nine or ten of Touch the Cloud's men with him. Touch the Cloud and High Bear were in the ambulance with Lieut. Lee; they had come down with the officer from Camp Sheridan.

Lieut. Lee now proceeded slowly on the way. Crazy Horse overtook the ambulance. When these two got to Little Bordeaux Creek, about fifteen miles from Camp Sheridan, scouts overtook them. When they got to about Chadron Creek more Camp Sheridan scouts overtook them, and later they were joined by more Camp Sheridan scouts till there were some sixty of these in all.

None of the Fort Robinson scouts showed up on the march to Fort Robinson, but Bordeaux says he saw some of them at the Fort after he got there.

There was no trouble on the road with Crazy Horse; but once Major Burke and Bordeaux, who had had no sleep the night before, fell asleep both at the same time for a brief nap; when they woke up, Crazy Horse was gone; they asked for him and were told that he had gone on ahead. Scouts were ordered to bring him back, which they did; and then he was kept in rear of the ambulance the rest of the way to the Fort.

Arriving at the Fort, the occupants of the ambulance alighted and Crazy Horse dismounted. Little Big Man (who was jealous of Crazy Horse) came up, and taking him by the arm, told him, "Come along, you are a coward."[16]

They all went into the Adjutant's Office. Bordeaux acted as interpreter. Lieut. Lee told Bordeaux to call Swift Bear out of the office. Lee said to Swift Bear, "I have done all I can for Crazy Horse. The Big Chief (meaning the commanding officer at the Fort) will take care of him tonight." Swift Bear said that was alright. Lee then told Bordeaux to call Touch the Cloud and High Bear, and he told these the same that he had [told] Swift Bear, and in addition that the officers would take care of Crazy Horse that night and have a talk with him in the morning. Bordeaux went back into the office, and the Officer-of-the-Day came in and took Crazy Horse by the hand and raised him up and Crazy Horse started with him, and Little Big Man stepped to his side and took him by the other arm—the left arm. They moved to the guardhouse, some Indians preceding them into the building. Lieut. Lee and Bordeaux followed outside; Lee said to Bordeaux that Crazy Horse was turned over and they had nothing more to do with him, and cautioned Bordeaux not to get into any trouble on account of Crazy Horse, and as he said this he turned away towards the officers' quarters. Just then a tumult was heard in the guardhouse and the Indians came out, among them Crazy Horse and Little Big Man, struggling. Bordeaux saw Little Big Man let go and then blood flowed from his wound instantly.

Crazy Horse was seized by Swift Bear, Black Crow and others, friendly Indians from the Camp Sheridan scouts.

---

[16]Bordeaux' recollection of Little Big Man's alleged statement has to be viewed with definite skepticism. According to Red Feather, who was Crazy Horse's brother-in-law, Little Big Man's words were advisory and conciliatory—"We'll do whatever White Hat [Lt. Clark] says"—promising Crazy Horse "to stay by him all the time." Red Feather's statement is corroborated by Garnett who recalled that Little Big Man assured Crazy Horse that "wherever he was taken to, he would go with him and stand by him." See Hinman, "Oglala Sources," p. 27; and the Garnett Interview heretofore. Further evidence that Louis' recollection of this incident had erred may be found in his embellished account in *Custer's Conqueror*, p. 87-88.

The military guard thrust Crazy Horse with his bayonet and inflicted his death wound. While this scene was in progress, the Officer-of-the-Day was crying, "Stab the son-of-a-bitch! Stab the son-of-a-bitch!"[17] The soldier made another thrust and grazed the door casing of the guardhouse;[18] as he jerked back his weapon, the butt of his piece struck an Indian, Chips, Crazy Horse's medicine man–Chips says he was the one struck and knocked down–and broke his collar-bone. The Officer-of-the-Day was vigorously exerting himself to stab Crazy Horse with his sabre, but he could not reach him, as so many Indians were around the Chief.

Crazy Horse sank to the earth. Charley Roubidoux,[19] a mixed blood scout, was near him and he told Bordeaux that he did not hear Crazy Horse say anything while the scene was transpiring. Swift Bear also said Crazy Horse did not say a word; but Standing Bear said that as he was sinking he

---

[17]Born in Ireland, James Kennington served in both the Second and Eleventh Infantry from October 1851 to December 1862, during which period he received promotions up to the rank of commissary sergeant. On November 26, 1862, Kennington obtained a commission of second lieutenant in the Eleventh Infantry and was promoted to first lieutenant on May 5, 1864. Having been unassigned from April 14, 1869, to December 31, 1870, he was subsequently attached to the Fourteenth Infantry of which he became a captain on December 10, 1873. He retired on June 15, 1887. In 1862 Kennington received a brevet of first lieutenant for gallant and meritorious service in the battle of Fredericksburg, Virginia, and in 1865 he was awarded the brevet of captain for general good conduct in the field. Kennington was known for his blind devotion to duty, evidenced by the literal and unquestioning way in which he obeyed orders. He died on April 22, 1897. See the Thomas McArthur Anderson Manuscript, Western American Collection, Yale University, which contains a chapter on the Crazy Horse killing and Anderson's evaluation of Kennington. For confirmation of Kennington's order to "Stab the-son-of-a-bitch!" see Lt. Lee's account in Brininstool, *Crazy Horse*, p. 33.

[18]This statement is confirmed by Lt. John G. Bourke who obtained this information from Little Big Man in 1881. However, according to Private George W. McAnulty, Ninth Infantry, the bayonet thrust did not miss Crazy Horse but "went clear through his body and pinned him against the log building!" See Bourke, *On the Border With Crook*, pp. 422-23; Brininstool, *Crazy Horse*, p. 86.

[19]Charles Roubidoux was a mixed blood of French and Brulé parentage. One of his relatives, Louis Roubidoux, lived at the Jordan Trading Post at the Brulé Agency where he was employed as the official interpreter around the turn of the century. See Dyck, *Brulé*, p. 8.

made some remark like that he was going to die.[20] He was removed into the Adjutant's Office.

Bordeaux went to the Commanding Officer's (Col. Bradley's) Office, and from there to Lieut. Clark's office, and from there he was sent to the Adjutant's Office, where Crazy Horse was lying, and where he then went on duty, watching with the wounded man. He was relieved about twenty minutes before twelve o'clock at night.[21] Touch the Cloud, Crazy Horse's father and two doctors, Dr. McGillicuddy being one of them—a contract doctor—were there when Bordeaux left.[22]

Quite a while before Bordeaux's departure, Crazy Horse, Sr., said, speaking to his son: "Son, I am here." Crazy Horse, Jr., said: "Father, it is no use to depend upon me; I am going to die." The old father and Touch the Cloud both cried. Then Crazy Horse said to Bordeaux: "No white man is to blame for this; I don't blame any white man; but I blame the Indians. I don't wish to harm anybody, but one person; he has escaped from me."[23] Evidently he referred to Little Big Man.

---

[20]This was probably the Brulé, Standing Bear, a member of the Wears Salt Band which was led by Lip. Standing Bear was a mixed blood who operated a store on the Rosebud Reservation in the early 1880s. He died on Pass Creek in 1898. Standing Bear was the father of Henry Standing Bear whose account follows hereafter.

Standing Bear's recollection is corroborated by William Garnett who recalled that Crazy Horse's words were, "He has killed me now," while He Dog remembered the words as, "They have stabbed me." He Dog recalled further that Crazy Horse was moaning, but that it was more from anger than from pain. Woman's Dress, who also was a witness to the stabbing, added that Crazy Horse, when he was lying on the ground and was suffering from his wound, kept repeating the words, "Father, I want to see you." See the Garnett Interview heretofore; Hinman, "Oglala Sources," p. 20; Clark, *The Killing of Chief Crazy Horse*, p. 66; and James H. Cook to John G. Neihardt, March 3, 1920, Neihardt Papers, University of Missouri.

[21]Since Crazy Horse died at 11:40 P.M., Bordeaux must have left the Adjutant's Office prior to that time.

[22]The second doctor was Capt. Charles E. Munn, U.S. Medical Department, who was the post surgeon at Camp Robinson.

[23]Although Bordeaux provided the translation, the words spoken by Crazy Horse were actually addressed to Lt. Jesse M. Lee who had been asked to come to the Adjutant's Office by Touch the Cloud, the uncle of Crazy Horse. Since Bordeaux was Lee's interpreter, both men probably went to the Adjutant's Office together, arriving at about 10 P.M. See Lee's account in Brininstool, *Crazy Horse*, p. 34.

This was the last he said. Bordeaux knew he was dying. He was growing cold. Injections in his arm by the doctors revived him for a while.[24] He was restless and turned in great pain. McGillicuddy said he could not last till midnight.

Big Bat came and relieved Bordeaux who went to headquarters for rest. In a short while, Big Bat returned to headquarters, saying that Crazy Horse was dead. Lieut. Clark who had been out came in and asked: "How is my friend, Crazy Horse, getting along?" Big Bat said: "He is dead!" [Clark said:] "Impossible that he is dead. He ought not to die." He turned to go; but painfully, unwilling to believe the cruel fact, he wheeled back and asked again: "Is it true that he is dead?" Bordeaux answered, "Yes, Lieutenant, when Pourier relieved me he was dying; I know he is dead." Clark, who was a man of great humanity, could not restrain the tears as he said: "It is a shame! It is a shame! He ought not to die." He meant that he ought not to have been killed. That was the truth of the case.

Next morning his body was delivered by ambulance to his friends at Red Cloud. Next [time] that Bordeaux saw his body was down at Camp Sheridan. Bordeaux is very certain that Crazy Horse was killed in October, 1877.

Bordeaux says he has been told by the brother of an officer who claimed to know, that orders had been issued for Crazy Horse to be taken East and held a prisoner indefinitely.

As soon as this tragedy was committed and before Crazy Horse had breathed his last, the false word was dispatched to Camp Sheridan that he had accidently stabbed himself.

---

[24]Crazy Horse's vital signs began to weaken about 10 P.M. When Dr. McGillycuddy attempted to revive him by giving him some brandy, Worm objected, stating in sign language that the liquor would only make his son's "brain whirl." McGillycuddy then administered several hypodermics of morphine to Crazy Horse, which seemed to ease the pain, but which did not prevent his death which followed shortly thereafter. This sudden death, occurring after the injections, immediately aroused Worm's suspicion that his son was poisoned. See McGillycuddy to Garnett, May 10, 1926, and June 24, 1927, in Clark, *The Killing of Chief Crazy Horse,* pp. 117-18, 126; and Hinman "Oglala Sources," p. 31.

Henry Standing Bear Interview

INTRODUCTION

Henry Standing Bear was the son of the mixed-blood Brulé, Standing Bear, having been born from his father's second marriage with the two daughters of One Horse and Rattle Stone Woman, the latter a sister of Worm. Henry's half brother was Luther Standing Bear (1863–1936), author of *My People the Sioux* and several other books on Lakota life. Being a maternal cousin of Crazy Horse, Henry Standing Bear successfully persuaded the renowned sculptor Korczack Ziolkowski to carve a commemorative monument of Crazy Horse in the mountains of the Black Hills, a gigantic task which Ziolkowski finally accepted in 1947. The Henry Standing Bear Interview is contained in the Walter Mason Camp Manuscripts, transcript, pp., 816-18, IU. This interview was probably conducted in July 1910 when Walter Camp visited Pine Ridge to interview several elderly Lakotas.

THE HENRY STANDING BEAR INTERVIEW
Told by Standing Bear

[Pine Ridge Reservation, circa 1910]

THE KILLING OF CRAZY HORSE

While Crazy Horse was in camp after his surrender, many rumors were floating around among his people and some of his personal enemies to the effect that he had taken such a prominent part in the recent war that the authorities in Washington would hold him responsible and probably deal with him severely. Finally, it was reported that he was wanted in Washington, and he left and went over to Spotted Tail Agency. These false rumors worried Crazy Horse a great deal and he did not know first how to understand them. At length he consulted Turning Bear[1] and asked what he had better do. There was now a demand that he go to Ft. Robinson, and Turning Bear advised him to go and said he would accompany him. An ambulance had been sent to take him to the fort, but he gave up willingly and rode his own horse all the way, Turning Bear going with him.

When they arrived at the fort they were escorted into a room which led into another, and from there into the guardhouse. When Crazy Horse espied the guardhouse his suspicions were aroused and he said to Turning Bear: "What kind of a place is this they are taking us into? It looks to me like a prison." Turning Bear said: "Yes, I believe it must be a prison. Let us go back." At this both of them started back, and when

---

[1]Turning Bear was a prominent Brulé leader who enlisted in the U.S. Indian Scouts in 1877. In 1880 he was indicted for the killing of a Nebraska citizen, but was released because civilian authorities did not have legal authority over Indians. It is further known that he took a leading part in the Ghost Dance hostilities which broke out in 1890. Turning Bear was killed by a train in 1912 while waiting for his son's arrival from Carlisle Institute at the railroad station in Valentine, Nebraska. See Dyck, *Brulé*, pp. 96, 98; Cheney, *The Big Missouri Winter Count*, p. 45.

they got outside they were met by soldiers trying to force them to return, whereupon Crazy Horse, not understanding the situation and thinking he was about to be killed, pulled out his knife and was immediately seized by Little Big Man by the wrist, in an endeavor to wrest the knife from him. In the struggle which followed, a soldier pressed him lightly with his bayonet two or three times and told him to drop the knife; but he [Crazy Horse] did not understand what was said, and the soldier then thrust him hard with the bayonet, inflicting a mortal wound.

After Crazy Horse was killed, his body was given to the custody of his father who took it to Wounded Knee. Soon after this the Indians broke camp and moved away, but the father of Crazy Horse remained three days with the body and finally carried it away. When he came up with his people he had disposed of the body, and when questioned about it [he] said he had buried it in [the] dead of night and would not tell where. The old man never told and the secret died with him. Thus the [burial site] of Crazy Horse is not known. His likeliness was never photographed or sketched, although false photos have been published.[2] The true features of the great warrior chief of the Oglalas will never appear in history.

---

[2]Contemporaries of Crazy Horse–Oglala tribesmen, military personnel and civilians alike–have repeatedly stated that he refused to have his "shadow" captured on a photograph. For that reason, published pictures of Crazy Horse have to be viewed with considerable skepticism. However, the Oglala, Short Buffalo, claimed to have seen several photographs which he thought were images of Crazy Horse–one showing him on a pinto pony which he rode in the Custer fight. See Hinman, "Oglala Sources," p. 39. For a photographic essay of unauthenticated portraits of Crazy Horse see Kadlecek, *To Kill an Eagle*, pp. 72-74.

HE DOG
Photo taken in Washington, DC in 1877.
Courtesy West Point Military Academy Library

He Dog Interview

INTRODUCTION

The son of Black Rock and Blue Day Woman, He Dog was born in an Oglala camp near Bear Butte, South Dakota, in 1840 and grew up in the powerful Smoke band which later became known as the Bad Faces. He Dog had a reputation of being a brave man, respected by all for his undisputed valor and leadership abilities. In recognition of these qualities, the Chief Society elected him as *Wicasa Yatanpi,* a Shirt Wearer, one of four praiseworthy young men who were entrusted with the welfare of the Oglala tribe. In 1870 the powerful class of warriors elected him to lead the Crow Owners Society. For the next six years He Dog not only fought enemy tribes, but also resisted white encroachment, culminating in 1876 with the Indian victory at the Little Bighorn. However, realizing that further resistance to the whites would be futile, He Dog surrendered his band to the U.S. Military at Camp Robinson on May 6, 1877. Although reservation life must have been stifling to him, He Dog nonetheless became a progressive leader. His high moral standards earned him a position of judge to the Pine Ridge Court of Indian Offenses in the 1890s. He served this post for many years until advanced age and failing sight made further service impossible. He Dog passed away in 1936. This interview is contained in the Mari Sandoz Collection, Part II, Box 31, University of Nebraska Library. In addition to making a few minor changes in grammar and spelling, I have also deleted several paragraphs of unrelated material. See also Hinman, "Oglala Sources," pp. 9-24, which contains two additional interviews by He Dog, given on July 7 and July 14, 1930. Clark, *The Killing of Chief Crazy Horse,* also contains a He Dog interview, which will be discussed in more detail in the Eagle Hawk Narrative hereafter.

INTERVIEW WITH HE DOG
by Mari Sandoz
Interpreter: John Colhoff
Oglala, South Dakota
June 30, 1931

•   •   •

Q. Was Long Joe the same as Joe Larrivee [Laravie]?
A. Long Joe was the father of Crazy Horse's last wife, a half-breed Frenchman–he stayed along the Platte and Fort Laramie. I did not know him much.[1]

•   •   •

Q. Was this last wife [Nellie Laravie] any relation to Louis Richard or Reshaw?[2]

---

[1]Joseph Laravie was a mixed-blood French trader among the southern tribes of the Sioux and the Cheyennes. His first wife was a Southern Cheyenne woman who bore him four daughters, of which the second daughter was Helen Laravie. Upon his wife's death, Joseph married Susan Metcalf, which union resulted in the birth of six sons. With the removal of the Indians from the Platte Valley, Laravie followed the Sioux to their new agency on White River in 1873 and eventually settled on Larrabee Creek, just south of the Nebraska-South Dakota border. See the Tom Laravie Interview in Bordeaux, *Custer's Conqueror,* no pagination.

[2]Subject to French pronunciation, the name Richard sounded like Reshaw, which became its phonetical equivalent. Born in 1849, Louis Richard was the mixed-blood son of John Richard and Mary Gardiner. Although the Richard family was described as a "hard lot," Louis was said to have been a fine man who was well respected by everyone who knew him. For biographical data on the Richard family, see Gilbert, *"Big Bat" Pourier.* Pourier was married to Josephine Richard, a sister of Louis.

A. No. I know Joe Reshaw [Richard]–Frenchman, no connection. (He Dog says there was at least none he remembers.)

Q. Relatives of Crazy Horse?

A. Don't know; relations all mixed up. Clinchers and Iron
White Man[3] are related to Crazy Horse, [but I do] not know
relationships. Horse Stands in Sight was an early name for
Crazy Horse, [who was also] nicknamed Yellow Fuzzy Hair,
as a little chicken is yellow and fuzzy haired.[4] Crazy Horse's
father had two wives. He [Crazy Horse] had a half brother
who took the name of Horse Stands in Sight after Crazy
Horse was given his later name. This half brother was killed
by white men near Chimney Rock.[5]

·   ·   ·

Q. Were Club Man [who married Crazy Horse's sister]
and Young Man Afraid [of His Horses] related?

---

[3]Lack of biographical data makes further identification of these two individuals impossible. One of the Sans Arc bands was led by a man named Iron White Man who was held in
considerable esteem. Perhaps he may have been the individual referred to by He Dog. See
Hardorff, *Lakota Recollections*, p. 108.

[4]He Dog's interview in Clark, *The Killing of Chief Crazy Horse*, p. 68, reveals some additional nicknames such as Crushes Man, possibly a reference to his dexterity with the club,
and Buys a Bad Woman, a reminder to his ill-fated affair with Black Buffalo Woman. It is
of interest to note that Crazy Horse's boyhood name was rendered in Clark as Horse Partly
Showing, in the Sandoz interview as Horse stands in Sight, and in the Hinman interview as
His Horse on Sight, which deviations are probably the result of typographical errors and the
translator's degree of expertise.

[5]Of reckless nature, Little Hawk was killed during the summer of 1870. According to
He Dog, Little Hawk had ventured on a war expedition south of the Platte River and never
returned. See Hinman, "Oglala Sources," p. 14. See also Charles A. Eastman, *Indian Heroes
and Great Chieftains* (Boston, 1918), p. 90, who stated that Little Hawk was killed while
trying to stampede some horses from a frontier post, which seems in agreement with Hyde,
Red Cloud's Folks, p. 147, who reveals that Little Hawk was slain by troops in 1865. Hyde
may have obtained the erroneous date from the New York *Tribune*, May 7, 1877, which
printed that the killing took place at Fort Laramie in 1865. According to the Oglala, Flying
Hawk, Little Hawk was slain near the present state of Utah during a skirmish with some
settlers. However, Worm stated in 1877 that his son was killed fighting the Shoshones, thus
disputing all other sources, which identify the adversaries as being whites. See McCreight,
Firewater and Forked Tongues, p. 139; *New York Sun,* September 14, 1877.

A. Club Man and Man Afraid called each other brothers. Man Afraid was a Minneconjou, [but] I don't remember the relationship–probably on their father's side.[6]

Q. Were Chips, the medicine man, and Red Feather related?

A. Probably no blood relationship. Chips belonged to the No Water crowd, and Red Feather to Big Road's. Sometimes some of them were orphans, and were taken by other families. Woman's Dress and Iron Hawk[7] are related–all from one family, but fathers [had been] killed and children [had been] taken here and there.

Q. Was this the Chips who had given Crazy Horse his medicine?

A. Chips made medicine for Crazy Horse [and gave him] a sort of black stone–like a good-sized marble–covered with buckskin and with one of the two center feathers of an eagle.[8]

---

[6]Club Man was a Minneconjou who surrendered with Crazy Horse at Camp Robinson in 1877. After enlisting in the U.S. Indian Scouts, he and several other Oglalas were assigned to General Phil Sheridan's party which visited Custer's battlefield in July of 1877. It was rumored among Sheridan's escort that Club Man had played a prominent part in the defeat of Custer's battalion the previous year. Club Man was married to Crazy Horse's sister by whom he had eight children. Although Club Man's brother, Little Killer, told Eleanor Hinman that the entire family had passed away by 1901, one of Club Man's daughters was still living as late as 1917. She had married a Brulé named Eagle Horse and resided at the Lower Brulé Agency on the Missouri River–far away from her Oglala tribesmen with whom her grandfather, Worm, had broken ties so many years ago. See Hinman, "Oglala Sources," pp. 42, 43; Camp Manuscripts, IU, p. 271.

He Dog's memory is in error regarding the tribal origin of Young Man Afraid of His Horses. The latter was born in a highly respected Oglala family whose first-born males had long been hereditary leaders of the Oglala *Payabya* Band. Like his father Old Man Afraid of His Horses, Young Man Afraid was known among the Oglalas as a *Wicasa Itancan,* meaning 'leader of men.' See Powers, *Oglala Religion,* pp. 30, 40.

[7]Iron Hawk was a respected elderly Oglala. He is not to be confused with a Hunkpapa namesake who, although a Custer Battle veteran, was only fifteen years old in 1877.

[8]The stone spoken of by He Dog was a *wasicun tunkan,* a sacred stone, perhaps one of the small, translucent, hemispherical stones found near anthills. Invested with a protective spirit helper, such stones were placed in a small buckskin bag. In the case of Crazy Horse, this bag was laced with a rawhide string which was worn over the right shoulder, suspending

(Each eagle has two exactly-matched feathers in his tail, bilaterally placed.) The other feather he wore in his hair in battle. His eagle wing-bone flute (from same eagle) was made to wear over his neck on a rawhide string. All the medicine, head feather and flute were from the spotted eagle.[9]

Q. Where did this eagle come from, and who caught it?

A. I don't remember.

Q. What became of Crazy Horse's medicine?

A. It was buried with Crazy Horse.[10]

---

the stone under his left arm. See Powers, *Oglala Religion* p. 216; Hinman, "Oglala Sources," pp. 12, 30. Although He Dog spoke of a black stone, Red Feather recalled it as being white, which may suggest translucency.

[9]It was said among the Oglalas that a spotted eagle—a war eagle—descended from the heavens every night to walk about on Crazy Horse's scaffold while his remains were sepulchered near Camp Sheridan. See Hinman, "Oglala Sources," p. 29.

[10]He Dog is mistaken. Crazy Horse's *wotawe* was *not* buried with him. Upon Crazy Horse's death, the eagle *wotawe* was returned to Chips whose mediation had given it its power which now had ceased to exist. The sacred stone, however, was given to Red Feather; whose son, Stanley Red Feather, still had it in his possession as late as 1930. See Hinman, "Oglala Sources," p. 30.

Susan Bordeaux Bettelyoun Narrative

INTRODUCTION

Born near Fort Laramie in 1857, Susan Bordeaux was the daughter of James Bordeaux and a Brulé Indian woman. Throughout her life Susan Bordeaux was sympathetic to the plight of her mother's people, which feelings come to expression in her correspondence and manuscripts housed at the Nebraska State Historical Society. The bulk of this material was written in the 1930s with the help of her friend, Josephine Waggoner, to whom she entrusted her recollections and dictated her letters. Among these items is the Crazy Horse manuscript which is contained in the Susan Bordeaux Bettelyoun Collection, Box 2, Folder 3, NSHS. In addition to making some minor changes in grammar and spelling, I have also deleted several paragraphs of unrelated material.

THE SUSAN BORDEAUX BETTELYOUN NARRATIVE
Checked and corrected by Mrs. Waggoner
May 16, 1936

CRAZY HORSE, OR TA'SUNKE WITKO

I was living at Camp Robinson in 1877, when several chiefs and their bands, about two hundred in number, were to be sent out to get Crazy Horse. They were ordered to make a peace treaty and to get his consent to a surrender. White Thunder, Spotted Tail, Swift Bear, Black Crow, High Bear, Touch the Cloud, Good Voice, Horned Antelope and many others were in this peace envoy. When they started in December, 1876, winter had already set in severe[ly]; the snow was bad. Spotted Tail and Swift Bear turned into the Black Hills to hunt with their bands; so they were left behind and never did reach Crazy Horse's camp to talk with him. White Thunder, Touch [the] Cloud, Good Voice, High Bear, Black Crow and others went on with the interpreters, Bushay,[1] Tom Dorian[2] and Chas. Tackett, my first husband.

Now, Touch [the] Cloud and Crazy Horse were great friends. After the pipe of peace was accepted by Crazy Horse, it settled the matter. He, by smoking with the envoy, was at peace for once and forever. The peace pipe was considered such a sacred pact that no one ever broke its law. If they did, they came to grief, brought on by their own untruthfulness, for breaking the law of truth. All that was unclean was never practiced with the peace pipe. The white people, [having] little understanding [of] the power of the pipe as something sacred and holy, doubted the veracity of the peace made with the peace pipe. It is often laughed and jested about by them. The peace pipe, like the white man's sacrament, was a symbol

---

[1] This was probably F. C. Boucher, a trader.

[2] This may have been Tom Dorion, a descendant of a French trader named Pierre Dorion who had married into the Yankton Sioux tribe. See Gordon Speck, *Breeds and Half-Breeds* (New York, 1969) which contains several chapters on the Dorion family.

of truth and inward grace. Its laws were spiritual and not to be desecrated.[3]

When Crazy Horse listened to the promises and words of peace, he had set aside all animosity—he had given up fighting as all the rest of his people had done. He knew he and his little handful of followers would not win. It was not because they lacked courage and bravery; they also knew they were in the right and had a just cause. He knew he was outnumbered by the millions. These people were intelligent human beings, who had the mind to think and to act according to their own interests. They did not want to supinely lay down and be trampled over by another race. For years they had been fighting for their territory and had won it from other tribes who were in possession [of it] in the days when bow and arrows were used. Now it was guns and gun powder, and these had to be gotten from the white man.

Swift Bear ['s] and Spotted Tail's band came back from the Black Hills in the spring when the snow went away. They had been living good in the Hills on elk, bear and deer meat, for in those days there was plenty. The peace envoy returned the first part of May, and two weeks later Crazy Horse came in with his band, consisting of about five hundred souls.[4] They were poor and destitute from having to give up their lodges and camp equipage so many times to the soldiers [by whom they had been attacked].

I have been told many times about how they had to maneuver to escape contact with the pursuing army. At times they had to follow the streams to hide their trails. Other

---

[3]For an authoritive work on the rituals of the pipe and its spiritual powers, see Joseph Epes Brown, *The Sacred Pipe: Black Elk's Account of the Seven Rites of the Oglala Sioux* (Norman, 1963).

[4]A census of the hostiles with Crazy Horse on May 6, 1877, revealed a total of 145 lodges and a population of 899 people, consisting of 217 men, 312 women, 186 boys, and 184 girls. See the report of Lt. Charles A. Johnson to the Hon. J. Q. Smith, June 4, 1877, Official Documents.

times they put their lodge poles across the backs of two horses so as not to leave any trail, for it was the camp they [the soldiers] wanted to capture.

All through the summer, Crazy Horse's camp was perfectly contended and satisfied. They were well treated and received rations from Agent [James J.] Saville, who was there at that time. Wooden Knife's band had been with Crazy Horse. His camp was [on the river] below, at Camp Sheridan, [and] not very far.[5]

My husband, Chas. Tackett, was a scout, but when he was not on duty, he clerked in Jewett's store, and [he] had waited on Crazy Horse. My mother-in-law and I drove up to the store one day when Crazy Horse was there; she pointed him out to me. He was a very handsome young man of about thirty-six years or so. He was not so dark; he had hazel eyes, [and] nice, long light-brown hair. His braids were wrapped in fur. He was partly wrapped in a broad-cloth blanket; his leggings were also [of] navy-blue broad-cloth, [and] his moccasins were beaded. He was above the medium height and was slender.

He had two wives. His oldest wife that he had lived with for ten or twelve years was the sister of Red Feather, who was a very noted man at that time. The last wife, a concubine to the elder wife, was a half-breed woman, her last name being Larrave [Laravie]. It was this last woman who took sick and had to be taken to Spotted Tail Agency. At Spotted Tail there lived a medicine man who could cure ailments.[6] To this place Crazy Horse went, not thinking there would be any trouble.

---

[5]Wooden Knife was a renowned Northern Brulé leader who maintained strong ties with the Northern Oglalas. It is quite possible, therefore, that he or his relatives settled on allotments on the Pine Ridge Reservation. Although I have been unable to confirm any genealogical ties, a Wooden Knife family presently operates an Indian frybread company near Interior, South Dakota, one of the very few Lakota-owned businesses. See Hyde, *A Sioux Chronicle*, p. 180.

[6]Susan Bordeaux is mistaken. It was Black Shawl who became ill and who was taken by Crazy Horse to Spotted Tail Agency, perhaps to be treated by Chips. See the Garnett Interview and the Eagle Hawk Narrative herein.

When Scout Frank Grouard knew that Crazy Horse had come in, he left Camp Robinson and went to Camp Sheridan to take refuge there under General [Lt. Jesse M.] Lee. He knew he had done treachery and he feared for his life, though no one had said anything. He gave false interpretations and was lying to the officers who questioned him in regard to Crazy Horse. He wanted to see Crazy Horse put out of the way so he could be free from the fear of losing his life. He succeeded, and it was found out too late.

When Major [Lt. William P.] Clark asked Crazy Horse if he would fight the white people any longer, he replied he would not—that he was through. Frank told Major Clark and the staff of officers just the opposite. Touch the Cloud reprimanded Frank Grouard about this and called him a liar. Everyone knew that Spotted Tail and Red Cloud were jealous of Crazy Horse and wished him out of the way.

When Crazy Horse was taken to the garrison to make a speech, he did not have much to say; he only told the people [that] if they were going to smoke the peace pipe [they were] not to break the laws, but [to] carry it out according to the sacred traditions. Spotted Tail then made a speech. After this came to pass, Crazy Horse was led to the guardhouse. At the guardhouse, Turning Bear stopped to tell Crazy Horse that it was a guardhouse to which they were leading him. The guard, with his bayonet, stabbed him through the side in a downward glance—through his left kidney, downward to the right groin. Little Big Man, a scout, struggled with Crazy Horse, which made matters worse.

The body was given back to the old parents. They sat on the hill opposite the garrison [at Spotted Tail Agency] for two or three days. When the orders came from the [Interior] Department to move the Indians to the Ponca Agency [on the Missouri] so annuities could be issued to them, the journey was started. The soldier escort went first, and the Indians in their travoys and the half-breed families in their wagons followed. Stops were made every ten miles. It took about a month to reach Ponca Agency. It was getting cold then.[7] Crazy Horse's body was carried on a travoy till a certain butte was reached. Crazy Horse's niece, Mrs. De Noyer, told me he was laid [to rest] in the cliffs under the ledges of Eagle Nest Butte.[8]

The old father and mother came with the rest of our people back to Rosebud in the spring [of 1878]. They lived with the Salt Users,[9] who camped two miles northwest from the [Spotted Tail] Agency. Here the old mother died in two years after Crazy Horse's death,[10] and Old Man Crazy Horse died three years after his son's death.[11] They were both buried there, along the banks of the Rosebud. It has been said that the bones of Crazy Horse were brought back and buried beside his parents.

---

[7]The Brulés commenced this journey on October 29, 1877. For an account of this shameful affair, see Hyde, *Spotted Tail's Folks*, pp. 254-62.

[8]Eagle Nest Butte is located between Bear in the Lodge Creek and Eagle Nest Creek, near the present Indian community of Wanblee, Pine Ridge Reservation.

[9]The Wears Salt Band was a small subdivision of the Brulé Lakotas. According to Luther Standing Bear this band was led by his father, Standing Bear the Elder, who had married two daughters of One Horse and Rattling Stone Woman, the latter a sister of Worm. In 1877 Rattling Stone's husband had died and she was then living with her two daughters in the Salt Wearers camps. This may explain why Worm brought his own camp to the Brulés and eventually settled near the Wears Salt Band at the confluence of Rosebud Creek and White River on the Rosebud Reservation. See Luther Standing Bear, *My People, The Sioux* (Lincoln, 1975), pp. 84, 87, 100; Hyde, *Spotted Tail's Folks*, pp. 255, 256.

[10]She would therefore have died in 1879. However, according to Jake Herman, a member of the Oglala Sioux Tribal Council, Worm's wife passed away in 1884, several years after Worm had died. The 1884 date receives validity from the fact that in her final years Worm's wife was being cared for by Felix Bald Eagle, a relative. To complicate matters more, a diary entry made by Lt. Jesse M. Lee on September 13, 1877, reveals, "Crazy Horse's wife died, and her body was placed on the platform beside his body." Since the deceased could not have been Black Shawl, I venture to state that it probably was one of the two Brulé wives of Worm. See the Sheridan *County Star*, April 15, 1954; James M. Robinson, *West from Fort Pierre: The Wild World of James (Scotty) Philip* (Los Angeles, 1974), p. 53; Brininstool, *Crazy Horse, The Invincible Ogalalla Sioux Chief*, p. 40.

[11]Worm would therefore have died in 1880. However, George Hyde discovered that the old man was still alive as late as 1881 when he headed a camp at Spotted Tail Agency called the Northerners. See Hyde, *Spotted Tail's Folks*, p. 255.

After Crazy Horse was wounded, he lived till after midnight. My brother, Louis Bordeaux, stayed with him all night and made hourly reports to General Jesse Lee. The old parents were also allowed to stay with him till he died in the morning, when the roosters were crowing at 1 o'clock.

Crazy Horse was resigned to his fate. He was a warrior and had expected to die in battle sooner or later. He saw the littleness, the jealousy, and the aspirations of personal aggrandizement of the chiefs, especially Spotted Tail and Red Cloud whom he thought were easily bought, and from whom he had expected more.

YOUNG MAN AFRAID OF HIS HORSES
Photo taken in Washington, DC in 1877.
Courtesy West Point Military Academy Library

Eagle Hawk Narrative

INTRODUCTION

Born in an Oglala camp about 1870, Eagle Hawk was the son of He Dog, a respected Shirt Wearer among the Northern Oglalas. After the surrender of the hostiles in 1877, Eagle Hawk was enrolled at the government Indian school at Carlisle, Pennsylvania, from which he later graduated. He was known to the whites as Joseph Eagle Hawk and, like his father, he was eventually appointed as judge to the Court of Indian Offenses at Pine Ridge. In later life, he became devoted to Protestant church affairs, and having been ordained, he became known on the reservation as Reverend Joseph Eagle Hawk.

The Eagle Hawk manuscript was once part of a collection owned by C. D. Leedy, a prominent citizen of Rapid City, South Dakota. Sometime prior to his death in 1951, the manuscript was acquired by Historian Agnes W. Spring who eventually deposited it in the Western History Research Center at Laramie, Wyoming. The manuscript consists of eight pages of typescript, of which the first page bears the notation, "Copy," and, "Mss in possession of Eddie Herman." Herman, a mixed-blood of German descent, was a relative of Jake Herman, a member of the Oglala Tribal Council in the 1950s. Apparently, Eddie Herman had obtained the manuscript from Reverend Eagle Hawk.

The date of origin of the manuscript is not known. A second and more recent account by Eagle Hawk was published in Clark, *The Killing of Chief Crazy Horse*. However, unlike this modern version, the older account is unique in that the narrative is based on a series of twenty-one pictographs. Most likely, these pictographs had been drawn by He Dog himself to serve as a memory aid in the narration. Unfortunately, the whereabouts of these drawings are no longer known, so that only the context is produced herein, modified by some minor changes in grammar, spelling and punctuation. The Eagle Hawk Manuscript is contained in the Eddie Herman Collection of Transcribed Letters, Agnes W. Spring Collection, University of Wyoming Library.

THE EAGLE HAWK NARRATIVE
Told to Eagle Hawk [by He Dog]
[Circa 1940]

HISTORY OF CRAZY HORSE

This history is something about He Dog also, because Crazy Horse and He Dog were always together . . . during their lifetimes, up to the time that Crazy Horse was killed. There are some old pictures [pictographs] that go with this story that were drawn at the time that He Dog was living. Of course, the pictures are a little bit worn out now, but I think I can manage to use them, and they illustrate all of the things that he had done while he was living; and I will have to number each picture—like one, two, three, and so on down—to correspond with what he has done while he was on earth.

[Pictograph] 1

The person on the right in this picture (in the black shirt) is He Dog. The people [shown here] are He Dog, Crazy Horse, [Young Man] Afraid of Horses, and American

Horse. This is the time when they were initiated to get the appointment as chiefs. The tents are all in a circle, and this lodge in the center . . . is where all the appointments of those four chiefs took place. The one [figure] on the left is a chief by the name of Smoke, and the one on the right is Chief Red Cloud, the old man himself, and he is giving the four young chiefs, as they were given the war shirts, . . . instructions as to how to perform chieftainship in the future; and the two down below [in the pictograph] are what you might call the Masters of Ceremonies—they have the pipe of peace, which they all have to smoke after they get their instructions.[1]

After giving [them] these war shirts, or scalp shirts . . . , He Dog and Crazy Horse were to go north with their bands, and Young Man Afraid of His Horses and American Horse were to go south with their bands; so the two bands split up that day, one going north and the other going south. The two fellows sitting around the circle [in the pictograph] are chiefs also, but the younger chiefs were to take charge of the bands, one to go north and one to go south.

[Pictograph] 2

The one on the right is Crazy Horse, and this one on the left, on a black horse, is He Dog; and this hill (mountain) represents the Black Hills, what was called at that time the Heart of the Earth. That's what they called it at that time,

---

[1]The ceremony spoken of was that of the *Wicasa Yatanpi* when the chiefs selected and appointed four praiseworthy men to serve as Shirt Wearers of the Oglala tribe. According to William Garnett, who witnessed this event as a thirteen-year-old, this ceremony took place in 1868, although other sources list the date as about 1865. The presence of Smoke in the drawing is incongruent with either date because of his reported death at Fort Laramie in 1864. Although Garnett gives the names of the four Shirt Wearers, he does not mention He Dog, but he instead lists Man Who Owns A Sword, whose appointment is confirmed by Black Elk, Thunder Bear and Caligo, all Oglalas. See the Garnett Interview, Ricker Collection, reel 1, tablet 1; Hinman, "Oglala Sources," pp. 11, 18, 47, note 9; and DeMallie, *The Sixth Grandfather*, p. 322.

and they were to guard this place because there were buf-
faloes, antelopes, and elk, and all kinds of game there in the
Heart of the Earth.

. . . The ones with the yellow bands are He Dog's orderlies,
and the ones with the red bands are Crazy Horse's. And they
are to protect the Black Hills on account of its minerals—gold
and silver—and animals. The one in red is In Front of Horn,
and the one in green is Black Moccasin. The other[figure] is
Eagle, and the other one is Squirrel. These two orderlies
were killed here.

[Pictograph] 3

There was a big battle that took place in the north here. He
Dog and Crazy Horse were protecting the Black Hills, and
they had a battle [along the Little Bighorn River on June 25,
1876]. American Horse and Afraid of His Horses were then
friendly chiefs, and they were on the side of the whites. After
the battle, American Horse and Young Man Afraid of His
Horses went out to meet the two warring chiefs, Crazy
Horse and He Dog, . . . and they took some presents—two
blankets and horses—and each made a special talk to Crazy
Horse and He Dog. [They told them] to surrender and live
in peace with the whites; that they wanted to have their children learn the white man's way and go to school; and they
wanted peace between the Indians and the whites, and for
that reason brought the presents and these horses. So Crazy
Horse said he would [make peace], and the others who were
sitting down on the ground were all in favor of it also. He said
he would take the pipe of peace and smoke, and he said the
reason he was at war was that he [had been] protecting the
Black Hills, because there was a lot of riches in the Black
Hills . . . , but he said, "Now I will smoke, and everything will
be in peace henceforth."

And He Dog reported the same as Crazy Horse: that he
would lay down his arms and be for peace henceforth.

[Pictograph] 4

After they made peace with Crazy Horse and He Dog, this [pictograph] represents them all going to what they call the Red Cloud Agency near Ft. Robinson. They are on their way to the agency, and the one with the green shirt (on the red horse) at the left, is He Dog, and the other one, riding a spotted pony on the right, is Crazy Horse. Both are in the lead, and the other six men are what you might call orderlies; and those horseback-riders are Indian soldiers, He Dog's and Crazy Horse's. And the advisors are walking. The soldiers are Kicking Bear, Black Fox, Charging, Two Lance, Little Shield,[2] Good Weasel,[3] Hard to Hit, Iron White Magpie, Thunder Iron, Looking Horse,[4] Kills Alone–these are the Indian soldiers that belong to the two leaders, crazy Horse and He Dog.

[Pictograph] 5

This is part of those on their way into Red Cloud Agency. Their packs [are] on the trail, poles on each side of the horses, their stuff on the end of that pack of the horse. On the way toward Red Cloud Agency on a peace mission.

[Pictograph] 6

This represents [the occasion] after they got to Red Cloud

---

[2]Little Shield was a younger brother of He Dog and a close ally of Crazy Horse. See Hinman, "Oglala Sources," p. 47, note 15.

[3]According to Short Bull, Good Weasel was "a kind of lieutenant for Crazy Horse" being "always with him." This statement suggests that this man perhaps may have been a minor war chief of one of the warrior lodges, possibly of the Last Child Lodge which was led by Crazy Horse. This close association is born out by Good Weasel's presence when Crazy Horse led a very small war party in the fall of 1870 during which fight Hump, a renowned Minneconjou relative of Crazy Horse, lost his life in the Wind River Mountains of Wyoming. See De Barthe, *Life of Frank Grouard,* p. 348; and Hinman, "Oglala Sources," pp. 14, 35.

[4]Looking Horse was a Northern Oglala who surrendered in 1877. He was a member of the Last Child Society, and although he enlisted as a U.S. Indian Scout, his loyalties remained with Crazy Horse. Looking Horse resided for many years at the Cheyenne River Agency. See Clark, *The Killing of Chief Crazy Horse,* p. 82.

Agency. They searched their tents, and the one[figure] in the upper end there is Crazy Horse, and the one below here is He Dog; and these are soldiers and officers and an interpreter, coming to look the village over. This is Lieutenant W. P. Clark, the English called him "White Hat," who went to greet Crazy Horse and stuck out his hand, but Crazy Horse wouldn't greet him . . . , nor would he shake hands with him. So he [Clark] comes on down the line to where He Dog was, and He Dog made a bow to him and he shook his hand, and He Dog said [that the] only way to get along is to greet one another with respect. The interpreter was Billy Garnett. The square beneath the tent is a flag that represents peace—a white flag with two pipes like "X" there. [Clark] handed this to He Dog, and said, "I am coming out again with soldiers with the peace flag, and so you can hold a council; and when I come I want you to take this white flag—this peace flag—and fasten it onto my left shoulder when I come to your camp tomorrow."

[Pictograph] 7

This represents the soldiers, and this represents White Hat, and he advances toward He Dog, and He Dog approaches and fastens this peace flag on his left arm as [Clark] suggested; and the one to the left, on the spotted horse, is Crazy Horse, and in the lower picture is He Dog. And after he [He Dog] pinned this peace flag on the arm of the lieutenant, Crazy Horse says, "That's all right; I am satisfied with what you have done."

. . . [Turning to He Dog and Crazy Horse] he [Clark] said, "The soldiers want four different things from you." Well, they asked the interpreter, Billy Garnett, to explain what those four different things were that he mentioned, [but] the interpreter said, "That's all I can tell you because that's all he [Clark] told me to say." Of course, they began to contradict between them. The two, He Dog and Crazy Horse, tried to figure out what the [next] move would be. They were kind of anxious to try to solve the problem of what he meant.

[Pictograph] 8

This represents the camp, and they could not make out what that officer meant by "two or four things" that they wanted; so they all broke camp and they all moved off to another place; and in the meantime He Dog and Crazy Horse remained on the ground that was . . . [vacated] by the campers. They lit their pipes and smoked, [but they] could not understand what he meant by it, and they were sitting there smoking, trying to find out just what it was [that Clark] wanted. Of course, they asked Old Chief Red Cloud if he could solve the question. He said he did not understand it either. He made inquiries, but he got the same answer; so they [He Dog and Crazy Horse] were feeling pretty bad, [more so] because they had to go back to camp on foot. . . . They were discussing the question, but they could not solve the question; so finally Crazy Horse said to He Dog, "I am going back to Lame Deer–I am going to get my men and go back to Lame Deer!"[5] He Dog [however] said, "I have already given my word of honor with this pipe of peace, so I am going . . . to the agency."

---

[5]It seems almost incomprehensible that the military authorities did not state the articles of the surrender to the hostile Indians at that time. Judging from the reaction of the Indians, it appears that the lack of communication and adolescent treatment by the U.S. Military resulted in suspicion which nearly led to the departure of Crazy Horse's band and the renewal of hostilities.

Lame Deer was a Minneconjou leader who was killed on May 7, 1877, by troops under Gen. Nelson A. Miles on present Lame Deer Creek, Montana. After the battle one of Lame Deer's three surviving sons, Flying By, returned to recover his father's body, but found it decapitated, the trunk containing seventeen bullet wounds. For an excellent review of this minor engagement, see Jerome A. Greene, "The Lame Deer Fight: Last Drama of the Sioux War of 1876–1877," *By Valor and Arms* (No. 3, 1978): 11-21.

[Pictograph] 9

This represents all the soldiers and scouts that came up this hill [for the] general council. He Dog [still] could not figure out what this officer meant by wanting "two or four things." But later on he figured out what he [Clark] wanted. One [Indian] fellow had an army horse, an army saddle, an army gun, and an army pistol. So he thought that [that] was what he [Clark] wanted.[6] So he went to work and gave the party that had the army horse and other army accouterments two horses (He Dog gave this), and then, [when] they met here, he [He Dog] claimed they were throwing reflections of mirrors at one another. [After] they met on the flat [two miles north of Red Cloud Agency], He Dog presented the army horse, the gun, the pistol and saddle to Lieutenant W. P. Clark, or White Hat. He [also] turned over to him his lance, his war bonnet, his war shirt and his shield, and he put them on this officer, and he gave his honor and pledged himself that he was at peace; while he had been wearing what the lieutenant had on there, he [He Dog] had been at war; but now he had taken them off and had given them to Lieutenant Clark. And each had their war charms on top of their heads, which protected them, and [He Dog] said, "We have been in a bloody war, but this day we will make peace;" and, of course, this council took place soon after the Custer Massacre, and everybody, as well as the soldiers, was on their nerve yet. So he [He Dog] delivered this [speech] to them, and told them that there would be no more bloodshed, no more scalps to be found up on the prairies, and that they would live in peace in the future. In the picture here is Old Red Cloud himself. It

---

[6]This statement shows the absurd misconception held by the Indians of the military demands. The four conditions spoken of by Eagle Hawk probably stated that the hostiles were to surrender their arms and ponies; that they were to remain peaceful and take up farming; that they were to remain on the reservations; and that they were to send their children to Indian schools.

seems that Red Cloud was given this shirt by the whites; and the one facing left is Crazy Horse. Crazy Horse goes to work and gives Red Cloud this horse and blanket; Red Cloud is on the right.

Crazy Horse said, "Red Cloud, I want my children and the women to be protected, and for that I am giving you this horse and blanket which is trimmed with porcupine work." This officer, White Hat, held up his hand toward the sky and was offering a prayer. . . . After he got through, they asked the interpreter what he had been saying, and he [Garnett] told them that he [Clark] wanted the Almighty God to have mercy on all of them; that this day we were going [to have peace forever] and all our wars and bloodshed would end; and that we will dig a hole and cover up all what has taken place [in the past] . . . , and from this day forward we will live in a peaceful way. That's what the lieutenant said in a prayer.

After the lieutenant got through with his prayer-offering to the Almighty God, He Dog took his pipe of peace and held it up toward the sky, and he also asked the Great Spirit to have mercy on him; [he said,] "The four of us have been foes, and we have caused a lot of other people and horses to be killed upon earth–us four men: He Dog, Crazy Horse, Red Cloud and White Hat–but this day we will bury all the past, and live in peace from this day henceforth in brotherly love for each other." So He dog, after he got through, held the pipe up to the sky. "Now, if you are in earnest," he said, "I want you to take a puff of this pipe of peace," which White Hat did. He took a puff and blew some smoke out of his mouth, and he rubbed the smoke on his body and his cloths to show that he meant what he said.[7]

After He Dog got through, White Hat told Crazy Horse, "There are four places that you can go and be at peace;" four

---

[7]The accuracy of Eagle Hawk's narration is born out by the newspaper dispatches of the surrender. See, for example, the *Chicago Times* of May 7, 1877.

places: . . . the commanding officer's house; the store man (they use to call it the suttler's store), which was run by a man by the name of Cut Foot or Frank Yates; and there was a minister at a house there; and the agency office—those four places they could make up their minds to go into if they wanted to live in peace henceforth. So they wanted to know which one they should go to [first], and the officers told them, "You are men and you ought to know what is best for you, and [thus] you ought to know what place to go to [first]."

[Pictograph] 10

Crazy Horse and He Dog came up and were talking between themselves which place they should enter first. Crazy Horse said to He Dog, "Well, you better go ahead in suggesting—you suggest what place we shall enter," and He Dog said, "If we go to the military man[first], maybe the agent won't like it, and if we go to the agent [first], maybe the military man won't like it." Crazy Horse said, "The first time we ever meet any white men who are friends of ours and whom we shook hands with, we go in there first; we will enter the other three [places] later on." They got off their horses and went into Cut Foot's store, and sure enough, he gave them blankets and gave them other presents. From there they went to the other two buildings—the red building, was the headquarters of the army officer, and the yellow house was the agent's house—and the white church; the pastor to that church was W. P. Cleveland.

[Pictograph] 11

This represents where they were surrounded by the soldiers on the right, and on the left by the Indian . . . [Scouts who] were then dressed up in civilian clothes, but they still retained their long hair; and above [in the pictograph] is the

Indian Scout, and then Lieutenant White Hat, and in the middle are guns. White Hat said, "I want you all to surrender your guns that you have, and your horses;" so the horses were all rounded up, and they all put their guns in a pile. . . . This officer told them, "Now, I want you all to be peaceful, and I want you to learn to put in farms, and send your children to schools, and not to go off the reservation any more."

And he also told Crazy Horse and He Dog, "You can go and make a visit to the Great Father, and then, after you return from Washington, you will be chiefs." . . . So they said, "Alright. We will go and pitch our tents on the flat [near present Crawford, Nebraska], and later on we will take a visit to see the Great Father."

[Pictograph] 12

The tents on the left are those of He Dog, and in those days they had all kinds of designs painted . . . on their teepees. When it came time to make this visit to the Great Father in Washington, and after Red Cloud had heard that he [Crazy Horse] was going to be the big chief, they began to discourage him from going to Washington. They told him, "If you go to Washington, they are going to kill you when they get back–they are going to stuff you in the mouth of a cannon and kill you; that is what they are going to do with you." [As a result of] these agitators telling him that, he refused to go to Washington, as he had promised; so after he refused . . . , He Dog dissolved partnership with him, and he moved back to the [Red Cloud] agency.

After He Dog came back to the agency, he enlisted as a scout and was a high corporal, and he went back to try to persuade his friend, Crazy Horse, to go to Washington, but every time he was unsuccessful. He went there again, and Crazy Horse's father came out and told He Dog that Crazy

Horse wasn't home; so He Dog came back again to Crazy
Horse's teepee, which was located somewhere in the [pre-
sent] town of Crawford . . . and found the old man, Crazy
Horse's father, and told him, "Hear your friend He Dog out
here." This, after he had made several other visits to his tent.
So finally, he [Crazy Horse] invited him into the teepee; so
he went in and . . . [Crazy Horse] showed him two pocket
knives—one with a red handle and one with a blue
handle—and he said that two white men who had large stomachs had come to his tent. [They] claimed [to be] from Crow
Creek (Cheyenne, Wyoming) and presented these two
knives to him. And, of course, they [Crazy Horse's inform-
ers] claimed that it was bad luck, and that it meant death by
these two men that presented him these pocket knives. . . .

[Pictograph] 13

[Several days before] Crazy Horse stampeded from his
camp, Red Cloud, some of his band, and other bands all
threw in with the military, and all were given instructions to
go and capture Crazy Horse. Three Bears with a bunch [of
Scouts] took to the northern track [along White River], and
He Dog and American Horse were to take the middle. So, on
the north was Old Three Bears, and on the southern route
was Young Man Afraid of His Horses. Of course, there were
scouts [watching] the movement. By chance they run into
Looking Horse, who was one of Crazy Horse's protectors or
soldiers, and when he met this squad [of Scouts] he told
them, "You people are all Indians! Why don't you have pity
on one another!" He was angry because they were taking the
side of the white men instead of taking Crazy Horses' side; so
he got real mad and began to call them all kinds of names,
and he insulted them. [One of the Scouts,] Buffalo Head,
said, "I don't allow any one to come in front of me when I am
going anywhere!"—and he went to work and shot Looking

Horse's horse, and took the butt end of his gun and beat up Looking Horse. After he was knocked down, his brother, White Cow Killer, who was in the party to capture Crazy Horse [led by] Afraid of His Horses, came and took his brother, Looking Horse, and dragged him to a tree and left him there, and went on with the party.

While they were on their way to get Crazy Horse, they met one of Crazy Horse's soldiers [Black Fox], and he got off his horse and said, "Is He Dog in the party? If you are, come down." So He Dog got down off his horse, and sat down along side of him, and Black Fox said, "Is American Horse in the party?" So they got off their horses and he said that it was always customary when you are on a trip to always take a smoke, and then to go on; but from the position he was sitting in, He Dog noticed–and so did American Horse–that he [Black Fox] was going to stab [either] one or the other. He had a knife handy while they were smoking the pipe of peace; . . . [but the other scouts] all moved up to where the two others were sitting. He had in his mind to stab either American Horse or He Dog, sitting pretty close to him, [but he] couldn't get at his knife very well. . . .

[Black Fox told them] that Crazy Horse and his wife [had left] and had gone to [Spotted Tail Agency at] Beaver Creek. [Number "14" is lacking in the sequence.]

[Pictograph] 15

This represents where [Crazy Horse] leaves the camp. He has his packhorse and his wife. His wife's name is Black Shawl. He had two wives, but he took Black Shawl down in the tent; that's where he makes his getaway toward Beaver Creek.

[Pictograph] 16

This represents where Crazy Horse got to Spotted Tail's village, and they called a council with the other chiefs around in a circle. Standing up is Crazy Horse [on the] left; [on the] right is Spotted Tail. Spotted Tail told them he didn't want any bloodshed in his village; he says, "You ought to go to your own village! I would if I were you. Now," he said, "we don't want no blood shed in this village, so we are going to take you back where you came from in a peaceful way;" and he gave him a horse. Crazy Horse said, "Alright, I will go. I know I won't be able to do any harm, but I will be killed [anyway]."

[Pictograph] 17

This is an escort, taking him back to Fort Robinson. Yellow Horse[8] and Swift Bear were scouts for Crazy Horse [who went] back to Fort Robinson, following the ambulance of He Dog. He [He Dog] comes over and gets the escort, and he is all prepared for any engagement that might take place. He took off his leggings and his shirt, and he put his medicine charm on top of his head; and he advanced toward Crazy Horse, and the escort told him to keep back, but he didn't pay any attention to the orders and went up to Crazy Horse, and said, "My friend, you ought to listen to me and go back with me to Washington. You ought to take that trip to Washington now [that] you are in a jam. I knew this was coming; that's why I always asked you to go to Washington with me." And he asked him if he had any weapons; and, of course, He Dog had a shotgun with him and a blanket. [Note: number "18" is lacking in the sequence.]

[Pictograph] 19

[This pictograph represents] the guardhouse. Oglala Indians were there and, of course, the [Brulé] escorts. They were dismounted from their horses, and they were now taking

---

[8]A Santee by birth, Yellow Horse was a U. S.Indian Scout who had married a daughter of Chief Red Cloud. See Helen H. Blish, *A Pictographic History of the Oglala Sioux* (Lincoln, 1967), p. 401.

LITTLE BIG MAN
Date and origin of studio portrait are unknown.
Courtesy Little Bighorn Battlefield National Monument

Crazy Horse to the jail. . . . They are going to hold a council
inside the jail with Crazy Horse. That's why [they] are
escorting him into the jail. At that time, they had a stockade
all around [the military buildings], and [there was] only one
gate to the stockade because there were thousands of Indians
on the outside. . . . The escorts are the only ones that got in
through the gate.

[Pictograph] 20

He Dog dismounts his horse and goes into the stockade, and as he gets inside he heard a commotion . . . [after] Crazy Horse refused to go in[to the jail]; and a little short man, they call him Little Big Man—the fellow in the red shirt (an Indian)—grabbed him, and Crazy Horse had a butcher knife in his hand [and he] pulled off the ornaments around his [Little Big Man's] hair. Crazy Horse pulled them off, and Little Big Man said, "I wouldn't do that!" [While Little Big Man] hung onto one arm, an officer was holding the other arm, and at that time his [Crazy Horse's] blanket fell off his back, and [revealed] he had a revolver—a white-handled revolver —strapped to him. By that time, an Indian scout by the name of Plenty Wolves came from some direction, and he saw this white-handled pistol strapped around him. So he went up [to Crazy Horse] and grabbed the pistol out of the holster, and said, "Go ahead! Do whatever you want with him! I have got the weapon—the gun!" Plenty Wolves said [this].

[Pictograph] 21

During the scuffling and wrestling with the officer and Little Big Man, there was a sentry who was marching up and down the beat; and he saw it, and he went into the prison room, and [when] he came out he started for the scene. When he got there he put the bayonet to him [Crazy Horse], but it slid and tore his shirt on the first lunge. He made a second lunge and struck him over the kidneys.[9] Crazy Horse staggered backwards and finally fell. He told Little Big Man, "Let me go! Let me go! I want to get revenge—let me go!"

---

[9]Indian informants have stated consistently that Crazy Horse was confronted by two guards, one of which circled to Crazy Horse's rear to deliver the fatal bayonet stroke. White informants refer to these two guards as Sentenal Number One and Sentenal Number Two, implicating Sentenal Number One as the possible killer. The identification of this latter guard; the question whether the stabbing was intentional or not; indeed, the question whether the bayoneting actually took place, are matters which have been the subject of continued speculation.

On September 5, 1877, the guard at Camp Robinson was commanded by Captain James Kennington, Officer-of-the-Day. Also reporting to him was Lt. Henry L. Lemley, Officer-of-the-Guard, who, with E Company, Third Cavalry, was to escort Crazy Horse to Ft. Laramie for imprisonment out East. It is further known that Kennington had posted two guards outside the guardhouse during the second shift from 1700 to 1900 hours, the time frame during which Crazy Horse was stabbed.

The regular garrison guard consisted of sixteen soldiers, which included one sergeant, one corporal, one bugler, and thirteen privates. One of these privates was assigned as orderly to Kennington, while the remainder was divided into three details which each worked four two-hour shifts called "reliefs" during a twenty-four-hour period. These details were assigned to the quartermaster building, the ordinance storehouse, the cavalry stables and hay corral, and the guardhouse.

The names of the garrison guard were recorded in a Guard Report Book, which report, dated September 5, 1877, was signed by Kennington. The Nebraska State Historical Society owns a Camp Robinson Guard Report Book for the period September 1877 to July 1878; unfortunately, it commences with September 15, ten days after Crazy Horse was killed. I have not actually examined this ledger, but it appears from the photocopies that a number of pages have been removed from the front of the book, most likely the pages which covered the events around September 5th.

Although we do not have the guard report to assist us in the identification of guard personnel, we do have testimony that reveals the names of several guards and which implicates more than one individual with the killing of Crazy Horse. One of the informants was Private Edwin D. Wood, B Company, Third Cavalry, who wrote his father in September of 1877 that he knew the man who bayonetted Crazy Horse. Unfortunately, Wood failed to identify him by name. This was not the case with Sergeant William F. Kelley, Fourteenth Infantry, who stated many years later that only he and one other man, probably Private Wood, saw the stabbing and identified the guard as Private William Gentles, a member of Kelley's own regiment.

During the turn of the century, Walter Mason Camp of Chicago, an indefatigable researcher of the Indian Wars, sought to confirm Gentles' involvement in the slaying by contacting some of the surviving individuals who were at Camp Robinson in 1877. One of his correspondents was Col. Charles F. Lloyd who was a lieutenant in 1877, assigned to B Company, Fourteenth Infantry. Asked to review the Kelley article, Lloyd stated that it was historically correct in most of the particulars, except the identification of the guard who did the killing. Although Lloyd was unable to recall the guard's name, he stated it was not Gentles, but remembered that the man was a member of B Company rather than Company F. The identification of Gentles as the killer is brought to further doubt by J. J. Boesl, a civilian employee at Camp Robinson, who recalled that the name of the guard was Tom Todd. To complicate matters even further, Walter Camp, who was a meticulous researcher, reached the conclusion that the guard was not a member of the fourteenth Infantry at all, but that he belonged to the Ninth Infantry!

Other than the information provided by J. J. Boesl, there exists no evidence to implicate Tom Todd in the slaying—indeed, we do not know whether he was even present when the slaying took place. This is not the case with Gentles. Army records indicate that Gentles was court-martialled on August 13, 1877, for unauthorized absence from his company, for which he was sentenced to twenty days of hard labor and forfeiture of one month of pay, amounting to twelve dollars. These records establish Gentles' whereabouts until September 3, and it is quite possible, therefore, that he was subsequently assigned to guard detail to serve on September 5.

(footnote 9 continued on following page)

All that time Little Big Man was trying to pacify him. He [Crazy Horse] staggered back a couple of times, then he fell, and by that time He Dog went up to him and wrapped him up. Crazy Horse said, "See where my wound is." So he pulled his shirt, and where the first lunge was made there was a scratch, but on the second lunge they had struck him right in the kidney.[10] A little blood was running out of his nostrils.

The evidence cited heretofore in reference to Gentles is not sufficient to identify him as the killer. However, there is one more source that warrants consideration. Although Col. Lloyd recalled that the killer was from Company B, General Thomas McArthur Anderson flatly contradicted Lloyd. Anderson, who served in both the Ninth Infantry and Fourteenth Infantry from 1879 until 1900, learned from his subordinates and civilian witnesses that the guard who bayonetted Crazy Horse came from F Company, Fourteenth Infantry, to which Gentles was assigned. See Fort Robinson Records, series VII, Item 18, Guard Report Book, NSHS; Edwin D. Wood to Francisco Wood, *New York Times*, September 28, 1877; Statement by Sergeant William F. Kelly, *Crawford Tribune*, June 26, 1903, clipping in the Fort Robinson Museum Files, Crawford, Nebraska; Walter M. Camp to Col. Charles F. Lloyd, April 9, 1910, and Lloyd's reply, undated, and also Camp to Pauline Delaney, February 24, 1919, Camp Collection, BYU; J. J. Boesl to Camp, April 22, 1912, Robert S. Ellison Collection, Denver Public Library; Camp Robinson Records, General Order No. 60, August 13, 1877, NARS, Record Group 393; Col. Thomas M. Anderson Manuscript, William Robertson Coe Collection, Yale University Library; and also Ephriam D. Dickson III, "Crazy Horse: Who really wielded [the] bayonet that killed the Oglala leader?," *Greasy Grass* (May 1996) : 2-8.

[10]Reports are contradictory as to the location and number of stab wounds found on Crazy Horse's body. According to William Garnett, the bayonet thrust was delivered to the left side of Crazy Horse's body, which same location is also identified by Judge Noah Bad Wound and Charles P. Jordan who both witnessed the incident. However, Lt. Jesse M. Lee recalled that the blade entered the victim's right side, which observation is confirmed by the attending physician, Dr. Valentine T. McGillycuddy. Corroborating testimony about the location of the wound on the right side was given by He Dog and also the *Chicago Tribune* of September 11, 1877, the latter source reflecting the observations of a number of military personnel.

According to McGillycuddy the stab struck Crazy Horse above the hip, which is confirmed by the *Chicago Tribune* dispatch and also by Jordan, who specified that the penetration was just below the lower ribs. However, none of these sources agree with the observations of He Dog who was asked by Crazy Horse to examine the wounds moments after the stabbing took place. He Dog recalled that the penetration had occurred between the lower ribs in the back, to the right of the spine column. His description reveals further that the blade of the bayonet had traversed diagonally through the body, and that hemorrhaging had caused a lump to rise under the skin just below the heart.

He Dog also discovered a second wound in the small of Crazy Horse's back. This wound was also caused by a bayonet which, he thought, had penetrated both kidneys.

Although Eagle Hawk described this second wound in nearly identical terms, he only briefly mentions the first wound, which he identified as a flesh wound–a scratch, or cut in the skin. Nearly all testimony that I have examined refers to this second wound, the so-called abdomen or kidney wound. This makes me believe that most witnesses were unaware that more than one wound was inflicted on the victim's body. These sources state that the bayonet had traversed the abdomen and, according to Private McAnulty, went clear through the body, pinning the victim momentarily against the log building. Although no other witness corroborated McAnulty's observation, the evidence of bayonet damage to the guardhouse door is silent testimony that more than one attempt was made to disable Crazy Horse.

In the evaluation of evidence, the question arises whether any of Crazy Horse's vital organs were damaged. Asked to describe the wounds, Garnett stated that the bayonet went through both kidneys, and that the point of the blade nearly exited below the ribs on the opposite side. Although he added that he received this information from Dr. McGillycuddy, the latter contradicted Garnett's recollection by stating that the bayonet did *not* penetrate the kidneys, but that it traversed the length of the bowel mass which lay in the front of it.

Although I do not intend to question McGillycuddy's medical observations, his statement does not explain the trauma observed by He Dog upon his examination of Crazy Horse's wounds. According to He Dog, blood was dripping from the mouth and nostrils, suggesting that one of the lungs had been pierced. Internal hemorrhaging was filling the lung cavity with blood, which fluid was draining through the nasal and oral passages with each exhalation of breath. McGillycuddy knew about this trauma condition because he later spoke of the froth which had formed around Crazy Horse's nose and mouth, a telltale sign that the lungs were affected. McGillycuddy's description of the trauma, therefore, lends credence to He Dog's assertion that more than one stab wound was inflicted upon Crazy Horse's body.

After evaluating all the evidence, I have come to the conclusion that Crazy Horse was stabbed twice. Although the remote possibility exists that one of the wounds was caused by his own knife, the presence of a jagged bayonet hole in the guardhouse door convinces me that the stabbing was intentional and not accidental as was alleged by some witnesses. The first stab entered the body diagonally at a posterior position near the right hip, the blade of the bayonet slicing upward to pierce the left lung. The second stab entered the soft tissue at the right hip and traversed the abdomen toward the left hip. Both wounds caused internal bleeding which, linked with the limited knowledge of trauma treatment, proved to be fatal a century ago. See the William Garnett Statement herein; the Judge Noah Bad Wound Statement, December 3, 1931, William C. Brown Papers, Box 11, Folder 4, University of Colorado; Charles P. Jordan to Duane Robinson, June 26, 1902, Duane Robinson Papers, SDHS; McGillycuddy, *Agent,* p. 83; Clark, *The Killing of Chief Crazy Horse,* p. 66; Brininstool, *Crazy Horse, the Invincible Oglala Sioux Chief,* pp. 33, 86; Hinman, "Oglala Sources," pp. 20-21; Bourke, *On the Border with Crook,* 422-23; the William Garnett Deposition, August 19, 1920, Sioux Ethnography File, Hugh L. Scott Papers, Smithsonian Institution; Walter M. Camp Manuscripts, transcript, pp. 226-27, and James N. Gilbert, "The Death of Crazy Horse: A Contemporary Examination of the Homicidal Events of 5 September 1877," *Journal of the West* (January 1993): 5-21.

He was in agony. His friend [He Dog] went to work and took his blanket and threw it over him, and took Crazy Horse's blanket and made a pillow of it. . . . By that time, American Horse came in and wanted to put his blanket over him, but He Dog said, "No! I wouldn't have anything to do with him." Then Red Cloud came in, and he told them, "There is nothing to do [anymore]. You fellows . . . [wanted it] this way, and now it happened." And [Red Cloud] said, "Now, I advised you, but you did listen to the agitator [instead], and there is no one around [now] to assist you."

So they took him [Crazy Horse] into the hospital [Adjutants Office], and he lay there until some time of the early part of the morning, when he died. The officer came, and Clark and he wrote some[thing] on a piece of paper. And he [Clark] told this officer . . . , "We [once] had a council and we pledged between the two of us that there would be no more bloodshed, and that we would cover up all the [bad] blood that had been [between us]."

Eagle Elk Interview

INTRODUCTION

The son of Long Whirlwind and Pretty Feather Woman, Eagle Elk was born near the confluence of the White and Missouri rivers in the fall of 1851. He grew up among the *Oyukpe* Oglalas, a powerful band of the Smoke People. In addition to the customary confrontations with enemy tribes, Eagle Elk participated in many of the fights with the whites, among which were the Fetterman Battle of 1866 and the Custer Battle a decade later. In 1871 Eagle Elk married a Sans Arc woman, and after the surrender of the Sioux in 1877, his family settled down in the Wounded Knee District on Pine Ridge Agency. In 1944 Eagle Elk granted an interview to Dr. John G. Neihardt. This interview was recorded by Neihardt's daughter Hilda whose transcript totals some forty-nine pages. The Eagle Elk manuscript is contained in the John G. Neihardt Collection, Joint Collection University of Missouri Library and State Historical Society of Missouri, Columbia. The material dealing with Crazy Horse is here reproduced by special permission from the John G. Neihardt Trust.

THE EAGLE ELK INTERVIEW
Told by Eagle Elk
[Pine Ridge, 1944]

HISTORY OF CRAZY HORSE

. . . My father was already related to Crazy Horse's father. They were cousins. He [Crazy Horse] choose to call me "cousin" from the marriage of his mother. Many times on war campaigns that I was in, he was always in that same party; he was a very brave man. He does not attack the enemy . . . [for the purpose of counting] coup as many times as he can. He does not count many coups. He is in front and attacks the enemy. If he shoots down an enemy, he does not count coup. He drops behind and let others count three or four coup counts. He takes the last coup. . . . I often wondered why he did that. He had such a reputation that he did not have to get more of that. My father married Crazy Horse's aunt.[1]

Crazy Horse had an organization. I refer to a sort of organization where they don't feast and dance, but they were just followers of [him and consisted of] more than forty selected warriors. This organization was called the Last Child [Society] (Ho-ksi-ha-ka-ta) [Hoksi Hakata].[2] They were all very brave warriors and always went out with him and fought with him. He picks the last child in the family. If they did great deeds or something very brave, then they would have greater honor than the first child. They were always making themselves greater. I had three older sisters, an older brother and a younger brother. The older brother was killed in a war.

One day a crier for the Last Child came around and picked

---

[1]This kinship can not be established. Eagle Elk's mother was of Yankton stock, while Crazy Horse's mother, Rattle Blanket Woman, was a Minneconjou by birth. Perhaps the kinship was derived from Crazy Horse's stepmother, although she was a Brulé.

[2]*Hoksi Hakata*, derived from *hoksila*, meaning 'boy', and *hakakta*, meaning 'last born child'.

EAGLE ELK
Photo taken by John G. Neihardt at Pine Ridge in 1944.
Courtesy Hilda Neihardt Petri and the
John G. Neihardt Trust

certain people from different families. The crier called my
name, but I did not know it [then]. That is how I joined the
Last Child.

Crazy Horse was not a tall man—not too small a man
[either], but just above a small man. His hair was not so dark
as the other Indians; it was rather brown. His complexion
was not so dark [either]. He was a very good looking man; his
face was fine. His hair was braided down on both sides. That

is how he wore his hair all the time.[3] He wore a strand of braided buckskin; at the lower end was something like medicine, tied up in the buckskin. He had an eagle-wing whistle tied on. He had it with him all the time. Just before the start of a battle . . . he got off his pony and got a little dirt from a molehill and put it between the ears of his horse, and then he took some [more] and got in front of the horse and threw it over toward the tail, and then he got around behind the horse and threw some toward his head. Then he went up to the horse and brushed it off and rubbed it in. Then he rubbed a little on his hand and [brushed it] over his [own] head. Then he took a spotted eagle feather and put it upside down on the back of his head instead of standing up, as most [warriors] did. He wore moccasins. He generally wore just a shirt and breechclout, taking off his leggings. He did not paint [himself].[4] Chips was the one who directed Crazy Horse to do these things, so he would not be hurt.

There were five ponies that he rode at different times in battles. One was shot twice and died the second time. The second pony was shot, but did not die. The other ponies were shot from under him and died.[5] Crazy Horse was never hit in battle.[6]

One time we had a fight with the Utes. . . . One [of them]

---

[3]According to White Bull, Crazy Horse wore his hair loose in combat. See the Campbell letter in the appendix.

[4]Eagle Elk is mistaken. In preparation of combat Crazy Horse painted his face with the powerful symbols of the Thunder Beings —a red zigzag line to represent lightning, and random white dots representing hail. Ritually applied, these painted images were part of the *wotawe* which made Crazy Horse bulletproof. See the Chips interview with Ricker herein.

[5]However, Red Feather recalled that as many as eight ponies had died, the last one having been killed in the skirmish with Gen. Nelson A. Miles and the Fifth Infantry near the mouth of the Little Powder on January 2, 1877. It was said among the Oglalas that the sacred stone worn by Crazy Horse made him very heavy and that this was the reason why his war ponies would not last very long. See Hinman, "Oglala Sources," pp. 30, 36; and DeMallie, *The Sixth Grandfather*, p. 203.

[6]Eagle Elk is mistaken. Prior to receiving his bulletproof *wotawe* in 1870, Crazy Horse had received bullet wounds in the leg, arm, and face. See Hinman, "Oglala Sources," p. 30.

was a good shot; he came forward and no one could go up against him. Then Crazy Horse went for him and shot down the Ute. He rode right up to him. The Ute fell, and Crazy Horse called for his younger brother to come and get his first coup. His brother was dressed up beautifully and rode a good horse. Crazy Horse himself did not get fixed up like that.

Crazy Horse was wounded through the arm once. Many people [still] talk about him. He went with some others to the Pawnees, and they attacked the Pawnees. He took the lead, although he was just a very young boy. He was making a dash to coup an enemy. From that time on he was talked about.

[Once] several bands got together, and there was news that soldiers were looking for the Sioux. . . . There were some soldiers located near Powder River. The news spread among the tribes. All the warriors got together and came to look for the soldiers. They found them in rough country and started to fight them. But the Indians could not do much because the soldiers had sought shelter in the rough country. Pretty soon a man came around, saying, "Let's draw them out of that country by making them believe we are ready to run away." They went out on the flat country and the soldiers followed. Then the Indians attacked and the soldiers went back into the rough country. The man who suggested it was Hump. . . . Then Crazy Horse came along. He said, "Just keep away for a little while. These soldiers like to shoot. I am going to give them a chance to do all the shooting they want to do. You draw back and I will make them shoot. If I fall off, then you can do something if you feel like it; but don't do anything until I have run by them." The first time he ran by them they shot at him many times and he passed by safely. He rested a little while and then came again, this time closer to the soldiers. He was not hurt. The third time he rode still closer to the soldiers. They started to shoot, but [then] stoped shooting at him. He rode close, but they did not shoot [anymore]. . . .[7]

After this battle Crazy Horse went over the Rockies to his people who were there at the time. After a little time there he came back again. At that time there were a bunch of warriors who were going out on the warpath. A lot of them got together and started off. When they did, Crazy Horse eloped with the wife of another Indian named No Water. She went with him on this war party. No Water followed the tracks of the war party, [taking] with [him] his gun. He was following Crazy Horse and hiding all the time. He overtook them at some point where, at a late hour after dark, he slipped up to the war party. He was laying for Crazy Horse, who showed up. He was unaware that No Water was laying for him. He took aim at Crazy Horse and shot him through the head below the eye.

At that time I was with the other parties on the other side of the Rockies. We were looking for the Shoshones, but could not find any. Finally we located some and a battle took place. While we were there, somebody came and . . . brought the news that Crazy Horse was shot. It took some months for him to get over it. Just about that time when we were fighting the Utes, his brother was killed. His horse was a beautiful horse. When Crazy Horse was well enough, he went to where his brother['s remains] were and shot the horse over the grave of the brother. On the return he came across a number of soldiers, and he attacked them and killed two of them himself. As he came across the country, he again met a number of soldiers, and he chased them and killed two more. Those are the things that aroused the people. . . .

---

[7]For examples of other deeds of valor by Crazy Horse, see McCreight, *Firewater and Forked Tongues*, p. 139; Eastman, *Indian Heroes and Great Chieftains*, pp. 90-91; Hinman, "Oglala Sources," p. 32; Hardorff, *Lakota Recollections*, 87-88; and the Thunder Tail Manuscript, Marquette University.

Official Documents

Headqrs., Camp Robinson, Neb.
March 3d. 1877.

Lieut. J. G. Bourke,
    A.D.C.

Sir:

I have the honor to report that this morning five Indians of Colonel [Julius W.] Mason's party returned and reported that on leaving here they went direct[ly] to the Belle Fourche, taking the trail north of the Black Hills. At the creek a party of hostiles was met and was supposed to be a war party. They [Mason's scouts] continued on to the Little Powder River, and after going down this stream for some distance, quite a large trail was discovered leading to the right.

One of them [Mason's scouts] followed it and soon overtook about forty lodges of Indians, saying they were going to the Agencies, and so he continued with them.

On reaching Cheyenne River, some twenty-four lodges, mostly Sans Arc and Minneconjoux went down that river to the Cheyenne Agency. The remaining sixteen lodges (Ogallalas) skirted along the base of the Black Hills, and at Rapid Creek [they] met Spotted Tail who advised them to go to his Agency, which they did—or were very near there yesterday when left by this Indian [scout].

The remainder of Colonel Mason's party continued on down Little Powder River, and when near its mouth [they] met three Indians who told them that Crazy Horse was encamped some little distance above on Powder River, and that Sitting Bull was just below the mouth of Little Powder. They then went up Powder River till they struck Crazy Horse's camp, who had only ten lodges with him at the time. They [Mason's scouts] were kindly received, a "feast" [was] given them [and] a council [was] called, and [whereupon] they informed the hostiles of the object of their visit.

Their speeches were not responded to. Soon [there]after another council was called and Crazy Horse said: "[that] the smoke was good. He did not commence the war. His relations were at the Agencies; he could send for all the [hostile] Indians and let them decide what they would do; that if he told them to stay they would do so, even if they were to die, but he would let them say."

The large camp at [the] forks of Tongue River had been broken up a little before this time, and runners were sent to the different bands and villages. Crazy Horse started in the direction of the head waters of Little Powder – lodges joined him en route, so that when these Indians [Mason's scouts] left, he had about one hundred and twenty lodges with him, mostly Ogallalas and Cheyennes. This party was only five nights coming from Crazy Horse's camp, and [they] brought with them one Sioux Indian and his two squaws. (I neglected to mention that the hostiles gave them [Mason's scouts] a fresh mount, and modestly requested that beef, rations ect. might be sent out to meet them at Hat Creek.)

The Indian brought in was [among those] in the main village at [the] forks of Tongue River when it was broken up. He states that most of the Uncpapas went down to join Sitting Bull, as well as some Minneconjoux and Sans Arcs; that some of the Indians went over the mountains to Greasy Grass Creek [Little Bighorn River] ; [and] that the bands scattered in consequence of having but little to eat. It was understood that Sitting Bull had sent word back to Crazy Horse that he was going north to the British Possessions. Buffalo[es] are and have been for some little time in the vicinity of Crazy Horse's present camp, and they have recently had two "surrounds." Most of the ponies are reported as thin and weak.

I am sir, very respectfully, Your obedient servant,
(signed) W. P. Clark
1 Lieut. 2d. Cavalry.

[Copy]   [April 5, 1877]

(Through Comd'g Officer, Camp Sheridan, Neb.)

Sir:

I have the honor to report that Spotted Tail with two or three other Indians has just arrived and in the presence of the commanding officer [of] Camp Sheridan stated the following:

"I have come in in a hurry so as to see General Crook before my people (meaning the northern Indians) arrive here.

"I have left them three (3) nights ago at the Belle Fourche. They will try to come in as quick as they can.

"When I left with the big village–below the mouth of Little Powder River–to come in, I had one plug of tobacco left. I sent it to the Ogallallas who were camped at Bear Lodge, and told them not to come in unless they brought their women and children—that they must bring their wives and children with them. I sent them word that this was all the tobacco I had, and it would be a great thing for them that they should come in.

"It was impossible for me to see Sitting Bull. Last summer he went to British America—he left some of his people in British America and came back for the balance of the Uncpapas. The last I hear of him he was across the Missouri River and I don't know where he is.

"I can't say any more now. The people (meaning northern Indians) are very anxious to see General Crook—they want to see him as soon as they come in. They want to talk with him.

"Crazy Horse's father is coming. Crazy Horse was out hunting by himself—[I] could not find him. [I] sent one of my young men with a Red Cloud Indian with tobacco, but they did not find him. His father says that Crazy Horse, though not here, makes peace the same as if he were here, and shakes hands through his father the same as if he himself did it.

"Crazy Horse's father gave a horse to [Joe] Merrival as a token that Crazy Horse makes peace.

"The Indians will reach Cheyenne River in eight (8) or nine (9) days. If all of them had lodges there would be about three hundred (300) lodges. There are three hundred families and about as many to a family as among my people here.

"General Crook sent me out for these people—he is the only man that sent me. I went our for him and have brought the people in. I want to see General Crook and talk with him."

The foregoing is an exact report of what Spotted Tail communicated to Col. [Anson] Mills and myself.

I started rations of hard bread, sugar and coffee this morning to meet the Indians at Cheyenne River.

[I] shall start 60 head of beef tomorrow. Spotted Tail seemed too tired and exhausted to be very communicative. I think by tomorrow or next day he will be sufficiently rested to give more particular details.

A full report of which I shall promptly forward.

I am, Sir,

Very respectfully,

Your obedient servant,

(signed.) J. M. Lee,

1st Lieut. 9th Inf'ty.

Copy Telegram

Chicago, Ills., April 8, 1877.

Genl. W. T. Sherman
        Washington, D.C.

General [George] Crook informs me that fifteen hundred (1500) hostile Minneconjoux, Uncpapas and Two Kettles are on their way to surrender and were last heard from at Bear Butte Creek on the Fort Pierre route. They were accompanied by Spotted Tail and Joe Merriville [Maravale], a scout who sent this information to Captain [Peter D.]Vroom, Third (3d.) Cavalry, at Deadwood City. Crazy Horse with the Cheyennes, Ogalallas and Arapahoes are coming in on the West side of the Black Hills. Sitting Bull with his small party were followed to the mouth of Powder River, but could not be communicated with, and he has gone towards British Columbia. If all this proves true, it will only change the character of the contemplated operations in the Department of the Platte. There will be no change of those contemplated in the Department of Dakota.

(sd.) P. H. Sheridan
Lieutenant General

Copy Telegram.

Headqrs., Army of the United States
Washington, D.C., April 9, 1877.

General P. H. Sheridan
Comdg. Military Division of the Missouri
        Chicago, Illinois

Your dispatch announcing the coming in of the Indians is received and fulfills your predictions. Now, will there not be too many Indians at Red Cloud and Spotted Tail Agencies to be fed & guarded economically[?] Ought not these Agencies to be moved right away to the neighborhood of Fort Randall [on the Missouri River], where one dollar will go further towards feeding them than three or four dollars will at the present Agencies [?] Besides, these two Agencies are in Nebraska and must be moved sooner or later.

(sd.) W. T. Sherman
General.

Red Cloud Agency, Neb.
June 4th, 1877.

Hon. J. Q. Smith
 Commissioner Indian Affairs
  Washington, D.C.
Sir:

I have the honor to make this my report for month of May.

On the 6th [of] May, Crazy Horse arrived with 145 lodges of Indians, numbering 217 men, 312 women, 186 boys, [and] 184 girls, being a total of 899 people. They turned over to the military their arms and horses, the latter being returned to them.

On the 15th [of] May, 14 lodges of Cheyennes under Medicine Wolf arrived; they numbered 14 men, 19 women, 13 boys, [and] 11 girls, [in] total 57 [people].

On the 25th [of] May, Genl. Crook held a council with the Indians. They all spoke in a very friendly manner, stating that hereafter they intended to do whatever the Great Father wished. The substance of their talk was that they wished an agency established near to Bear Buttes.

On the 28th [of] May, Lieut. H. W. Lawton of the 4th Cavalry took charge of the Cheyenne Indians and started with them to the Indian country [Oklahoma]. I turned over to him a registered list of all the families; about 130 [Cheyennes] remained here, being transferred to Arapahoe and Sioux bands. The Cheyennes who left with Lieut. Lawton numbered about 980.

On the 29th [of] May, 2 Indians arrived from [the] north and reported that Sitting Bull had been whipped by Genl. [Nelson A.] Miles' command. Rumors state that some of these Indians will soon surrender here.

Very respectfully
Your obt. Servt.
C[harles] A. Johnson
1st Lieut. 14th Infty., Actg. Ind. Agt.

Copy

Camp Robinson,Nebr.
July 13th., 1877.

Adjutant General
 Department of the Platte,
  (Thru Headqrs. Dist. Blk. Hills.)

Sir:

I have the honor to report that I returned to-day from Spotted Tail Agency, having completed the enlistment of Indian Scouts at that place, having secured with the exception of Spotted Tail–who is employed as guide–all the principal men or head-chiefs of the different bands there.

They are beginning to appreciate the benefits that accrue to them through the enlistment, and to understand that the Scouts are to look out for their own interests as well as those of the Government, and in conducting their affairs in a quiet and orderly way at their agency they are performing an important and necessary duty.

The rumors and reports that small bands of Indians are leaving the agencies are utterly without any foundation in fact.

The census of the Indians is frequently taken, and there are many other and even better checks taken to guard against anything of the sort, so that I have no hesitancy in positively stating that no such parties have left.

Small scouting parties have been sent out from both Agencies to look up the remnants of Lame Deer's band, and one such party is still out from Spotted Tail Agency with instructions to follow them [to] wherever they may be, even if they have gone to some agency on the Missouri river, which I consider as very probable.

Indian affairs at both Agencies are in a satisfactory condition, the influence of the Agency Indians over those who have recently come in from the North is particularly good.

I am sir, Very respectfully,

Your obedient servant,

(sd.) W. P. Clark,

1st Lieut. 2d. Cav., Comdg. Ind. Scouts.

Red Cloud Agency, Neb.

July 26, 1877.

To the Hon.

    Commissioner of Indian Affairs

      Washington, D.C.

Sir,

I have the honor to state that in taking charge of this agency I am at a loss to know what the plans of the goverment are and how to conduct matters to meet issues of which I am not informed. Are preparations to be made for wintering here or not, is a question of importance. If not here, are there preperations being made elsewhere[?]

I came to this agency determined to steel my heart against all sympathy for my old enemies against whom I have skirmished on this border for twelve long years, and simply attend to my duties. But when I was called into their council and heard their simple tale of wrongs and their earnest appeal for the goverment not to move them to the Missouri River where they would not live, and as long as they were peaceable to let them stay where they are, I could not help feeling that justice should not overreach itself in dealing with these troublesome people, and I am forced to the conclusion that since they (Ogalallas and Brules) have yielded and promised to be peaceable, it is not only policy but justice to yield a little to their wishes if it is apparent to the proper authorities that it will not militate against the public interest.

I have told them that I believed they could not stay here—that they were in the land of Nebraska and would have to move off. And why do you wish to stay here [?] You tell me you want to learn to farm and I believe it, for I see [that] a good many have little fields planted. I have rode [sic] around to see them, and the things you have planted look badly because they are parched up and you have not enough water to irrigate, and there is not farm land enough to amount to anything. They agreed to all this, but say it is still worse on the Missouri River, and that thieves, gamblers and whiskey dealers will take all they have and cause bloodshed and riot among them; that their young men will not stay there, and there will be trouble as heretofore, and they have no heart to go there.

Perhaps I could suggest a remedy that has not been presented to the department. That is, to move th Red Cloud and Spotted Tail Agencies to or near the mouth of the south fork of the White Earth River, from seventy-five to one hundred miles from the Missouri River, and in Dakota Territory. From all the information I can gather there is a beautiful country there—broad and fertile valleys, easy to irrigate and plenty of water, an almost inexhaustible supply of oak and pine timber, the latter of good quality, and the hills and valleys covered with grass.

If this point was selected for the agencies, I could promise to take them there willingly and indeed gladly, and I also promise that with proper assistance they will go to farming in good earnest. They will do their own transportation from the river if supplied with a few wagons and work cattle.

The principal necessity of soldiers would be to protect us from out-siders. Give us a fair chance with a <u>prospect</u> <u>in</u> <u>the</u> <u>future</u>—<u>something</u> <u>to</u> <u>live</u> <u>for</u>—<u>an</u> <u>aim</u> <u>in</u> <u>life,</u> without which no human being will ever amount to any-thing. By introducing proper discipline it would be much easier to keep whites and Mexicans away from the agencies—with their tale bearing and detraction-whiskey and other deteriorating habits and influence—than it would be up on the Missouri River where all the offals of the river [and] mountains will congregate, and where the east side of the river would be an open sepulcher. The Indians' roving disposition can not be checked nor any progress made in civilizing them until they have an opportunity to become interested in farming and stock raising. Therefore, the necessity of selecting a good place to teach them useful labor and economy; and further more, the people have become tired of supporting ten or fifteen thousand idle Indians and keeping up a little army to manage them, and the dissatis-faction will be still greater if the Sioux are taken up the Missouri River where they will not stay, but wander about in a semi hostile attitude. I hope to be excused for the liberty I have taken and that this matter be duly con-sidered. I would go down and see the country mentioned, if desirable, and make an official report.

The Indians have had an intimation that some of them could go to Washington and talk with the President. I would respectfully recom-mend that they have a patient hearing on the matters now pending.

Very respectfully

Your obdt. servant

James Irwin

U.S. Indian Agent

Red Cloud Agency, Neb.

August 4, 1877.

Hon. J. Q. Smith
Commissioner of Indian Affairs
   Washington, D.C.

Sir,
   I have the honor to receive office letter of the 21st inst., marked "C", relating to the peace attitude of the Indians at this agency and others.

I would respectfully state that after I had been here a few days I felt misgivings in the matter referred to, but through the respect for the opin-ions and operations of those having this matter under their special charge, and not being so presumptuous as to suppose I could see further in a few days than men more competent in months of experience at this agency, I have kept quiet, not willing to cause divisions or in any way obstruct the efforts being made by the Military Department to restore peace and order in this country.

It now appears that Crazy Horse has not been acting in good faith with the Army. He has all the time been silent, sullen, lordly and dictatorial . . . [illegible] with his own people and other bands of Sioux at this and Spotted Tail Agency. He indicates the place for his agency up north and says he is going there; [he] refused to sign receipts for his goods and made some other demonstrations about the agency, which I reported to the commander of the post and it was hardly credited as the military still had faith in Crazy Horse. Now, however, he comes out boldly and refuses to go as delegate to Washington; [he] objects to the Indian enlisted men going out to [the] Big Horn [country] to meet Joseph's band, and says he is going to take his band and go north. [All] this has caused exitement among all the other bands, although I do not think any of them side with him as bands. I think the most if not all the difficulty arose from a misconception of Crazy Horses' character.

Taking the Indian soldiers north, the encroachment of the Nez Perces, the moving of the agency, and the visit to Washington, together with the talks and actions of Crazy Horse, has disturbed and excited the Indians; but I do not think it will amount to an outbreak. I have made arrangements to meet the chiefs in a quiet way and talk the matter over and will report tomorrow.

Very respectfully, Your obdt. servant
James Irwin
US. Ind. Agent

Telegram.   Camp Robinson, Neb., Aug. 5, 1877.

General Williams.

I think there will be no trouble about postponing the hunt. Will try to have Crazy Horse go to Washington, but he refuses now. Can delegation be increased to 25? Would like to know soon.

Bradley, Lt. Colonel.

Copy.   Camp Sheridan, Neb., Aug. 8th, 1877.

My dear Clark.

The Indians here are very anxious to have more go to Washington than seems to be the intention to let go. They would like that three should go from each band, and I think that two at least should be allowed. Do you think that there is any prospect of having the number increased? There are five different and distinct bands here [at Spotted Tail Agency], viz: the Brules, Loafers, Wazazies, Minneconjous and Sans Arcs. Taking two from each would make but ten from here. Please arrange to have that number go if you possibly can. They also want one interpreter. Everything remarkable quiet here.

Very Truly Yours,
(Sd.) Burke.

Washington, D.C.
August 15th, 1877.

Sir:

In reply to your verbal inquiry of this date as to the general condition of affairs at the Red Cloud Indian Agency I have the honor to report:

Dr. [James] Irwin had recently been taken from the Shoshone Agency and had assumed control of this [agency] about one month ago [as of July 1, 1877]. He retained in office the same clerk who had been employed by his predecessors–Lieut. [Charles A.] Johnson and Mr. [James S.] Hastings. The books of account having been irregularly kept under the administration of the other agents, Dr. Irwin had instituted measures to have the accounts more accurately and systematically kept, in order that full facilities might be afforded for determining the condition of their supplies and containing such other information as might be demanded.

On Friday the 27th of July ult. an Indian council was convened at the agency to listen to a message from Genl. Crooke [sic], U.S.A. About seventy warriors had assembled, including the celebrated chiefs Red Cloud, Crazy Horse, Little Big Man, Young Man Afraid of His Horses, Many Stars, and others. A lieut. from Camp Robinson (adjoining the agency) read the message which was substantially this: Genl. Crooke had promised that the Indians should go on a buffalo hunt. He was about to redeem that promise, and all who wished to might start as soon as they could make the necessary arrangements and be absent about 20 nights, then to return to the agency. He would exact from them, however, certain terms. They were to go on the buffalo hunt, conduct themselves peaceably, and all [were to] return at the time agreed upon. Permission had also been obtained from the Hon. Secretary of the Interior for 18 Indians to visit Washington, D.C. with a view of presenting their grievances as to the contemplated change of the Indian agency to the vicinity of the Missouri River. They should select their best and strongest men for this mission and not go for their own gratification merely, but for the protection of their interests, and seek an interchange of views as to what would ultimately result to their good. They were expected to be in readiness to leave there by the 15th of September next.

An opportunity was then given for an expression of their views, either approving or disapproving the order, but no feelings of disapprobation were manifested. During the reading of the message or the delivery of the "talk" or explanations of the Lieut., they were apparently pleased.

A feast had also been promised to them as was customary on the assembly of councils. Young Man Afraid of His Horses suggested that the feast be had at the lodge of Crazy Horse and his partner, Little Big Man. No oral objections to this proposition were made, although Red Cloud and one or two others left the room. Dr. Irwin promised to issue an order giving them three cattle, together with some coffee and sugar, as soon as they should determine to whom it was to be issued. The council then adjourned.

About ten o'clock that evening, while I was engaged with Dr. Irwin, two Indians came to see him and were exceedingly anxious that he should send for an interpreter at once. He told them that he attended to no business at such a late hour and begged them to call in the morning. They refused to leave. An interpreter was sent for and upon his arrival they all engaged in a long and earnest conversation regarding the council and the proposed feast. These Indians represented Red Cloud and several other bands, and said that there was considerable dissatisfaction among them as to the proposition to hold the feast with Crazy Horse. He having but lately joined the agency, it was but right and a matter of courtesy for him to come to them, and they were not disposed to go to him, as such action indicated a disposition to conciliate him. He had always been regarded by them as an unreconstructed Indian; he had constantly evinced feelings of unfriendliness towards the others; he was sullen, morose and discontented at times; he seemed to be chafing under restraint; and in their opinion was only waiting for a favorable opportunity to leave the agency and never return. The time had now come. Once away on the hunt, he with his band of at least 240 braves, well armed and equipped, would go on the warpath and cause the goverment infinite trouble and disaster. The other Indians [whom] these men represented had no confidence in him. He was tricky and unfaithful to others, and very selfish as to the personal interests of his own tribe. The ammunition that would be furnished to them would be used for the destruction of the whites, against whom they seemed to entertain the utmost animosity.

These Indians told Dr. Irwin that they came with no lie–they simply presented a true story. They were pleased with the agent. He had yean [?], and they respected him. He issued orders and they cheerfully obeyed them, and should an outbreak occur, he could rely upon the hearty and undivided co-operation of Red Cloud and the other tribes.

Dr. Irwin afterwards freely expressed to me the opinion that Crazy Horse and his band were not in a friendly attitude towards the goverment really, although nominally they were, and were regularly receiving their rations without complaint, and he shared in the belief that trouble was to be apprehended from them on their expedition.

On the following day an order was received from Genl. Crook directing the agent to remove all restrictions as to the sale of ammunition to Indians. The post trader took a copy in my presence for his protection. All of us expressed surprise at the order, but believed that it was only issued after a careful study of the probably results. I notice, however, that this order has been rescinded within the last few days.

But in my opinion all others on the reservations should be prohibited from selling either arms or ammunition to any of the Indians, and not limit the sale to the trader. I was informed that an Indian a few weeks ago exchanged four ponies for an ordinary rifle. They seemed determined to secure arms at all hazards, and will exchange property of great value for them. These sales are generally conducted secretly, either by freighters and others unconnected with the agency.

The unfriendly disposition towards the goverment evinced by Crazy Horse convinced me of the importance of having the Commissioner of Indian Affairs fully apprised of his recent acts, and to take such prompt and effective measures to secure the protection of the goverment as the emergency might require. To this end, I respectfully suggest that Dr. Irwin be requested to communicate with the department from time to time, and especially to submit a statement at once as to Crazy Horse, his whereabouts, and any other information he may possess of value concerning him.

It would not be improper in my opinion to require each agent to forward to the department monthly a detailed statement of their transactions, the supplies received and furnished, amounts remaining on hand, whether any irregularities have been detected in the transportation of goods, whether an inferior quality has been received or not, when barrels, packages or sacks containing Indian supplies are received having no brand thereon to indicate a proper inspection by a military officer, to at once report the fact, and in all cases to keep accurate books of account to show at a glance the exact condition of such agency.

I am also informed that all the tribes located at this and at Spotted Tail Agency were unwilling to leave their present reservations for the Missouri River. Spotted Tail, White Thunder and others at the latter agency express the hope that the goverment will permit them to remain there, but at the same time say that whatever the Great Father, at Washington, in his wisdom may indicate, they will cheerfully acquiesce. All the Indians here too, so far as I could learn, entertain the same ideas about the unfriendliness of Crazy Horse etc. and are willing to render any assistance to the goverment that they can.

Very Respectfully
Benj. K. Shopp, Special Agent

Hon. J. Q. Smith,
 Commissioner of Indian Affairs,
  Washington, D.C.

Copy.   Camp Robinson, Neb., Aug. 18th 1877.

Dear General [Crook].

I write you an outline of [the] affairs here so that you may know that everything has been done that could possibly bring about the very desirable object of having Crazy Horse go on [to Washington] with the other head men. During the summer, I feared this result and thought I had worked matters so that it would certainly be avoided. I cultivated the friendship and confidence of all the northern Indians and Crazy Horse in particular and succeeded in getting on excellent "dog-eating" terms with them and him, but it is impossible to work him through reasoning or kindness.

When the first telegram came, I read it in council and afterwards explained it kindly and fully to him and his head men, and afterwards to each of the latter at my home and their own lodges. He was not pushed for a decision, hoping that the influence of his head men might be sufficient. Frank [Grouard], since his return, has also done what he could. The other Indians at the Agency have no influence whatever with him. The Agent has also done his best.

Yesterday your telegram came, requesting him particularly to go: it was read in council at the Agency to all. The Agent gave him two beef cattle and I bought a lot of things of Commissary and gave them for a feast, to talk over the matter and decide. I explained to him that in addition to the other interests involved, you wished him to come on [to Washington] with the others and work with you in regard to their Agency and, if possible, prevent any undesirable change. That the President wanted him to come and you were anxious to have him go; that it was important and necessary for us all to work earnestly and honestly together in this matter, ect., ect.

Today, he came up, said he would not go himself, but brought up the men he had selected to go; wanted Spotted Tail, Little Wound, Red Cloud and the rest thrown away and only the men he had picked out, sent on; [he] had already said where he wanted his Agency, and if they wanted to know anything more, these men could tell them, ec. I kindly, but firmly, told him that the head men were going, and this was a matter he could only decide for himself and Band; that the men who went would not only be considered but would be the chiefs of the bands; he had been asked if he would work with the President and yourself in this matter and I wanted to know if he would do so. He replied by stating that "he had already stated he was not going."

Force is the only thing that will work out a good condition in this man's mind; kindness he only attributes to weakness. His head men are all right and dead against him in this matter. Extremely reticent, very brave and generous, he has had a large reputation and influence, but this power could be easily broken at the present time—and I believe it necessary. I am very reluctantly forced to this conclusion, because I have claimed and felt all along that any Indian could be "worked" by other means; but absolute force is the only thing for him. There is no trouble with Little Big Man, Jumping Shield and Big Road, [who] are the strongest men in this band, though Iron Hawk and Little Hawk each have a good deal of influence. He Dog, also a strong man, has joined Red Cloud.

I regret very much that the delegation is so small–there should be thirty at least. The Indians are particularly anxious to have more go, and I heartily wish it might be increased. The Arapahoes feel that at least Black Coal, Sharp Nose and Friday ought to go. Spotted Tail wants Joe Merivale, and the Indians here, Hunter; and Grouard feels as though he had been e'enmost promised: this would leave but just about one man to each band. The additional cost of transportation would not be great as a car would be chartered. The Indians would be pleased to have Dr. Irwin also go along. (I promised them I would ask for the increase.)

Crazy Horse sent a delegation to Spotted Tail [Agency] secretly the other night, to try and induce the northern Indians there to come up and join him, but he got no comfort from them.

I think everything will go along all right, at least till the Delegation returns, but [I] am keeping a sharp watch, through some of the scouts I can fully trust, on both Agencies, and they keep me pretty well posted.

Spotted Tail said to me a few days since, (he came up to have a talk himself.) that nothing could be done with this band until their arms and ponies were taken away, and he would like to do it; but he is a Brule.

Very Respectfully & Sincerely Yours,
(sd.) W.P. Clark,
1Lt. 2d. Cavalry.

Telegram.   Omaha, Aug. 31, 1877.

Gen. Crook.
Comdg. Department,
On West-bound train, Fremont, Neb.

The following dispatch from Colonel Bradley just received. Crazy Horse and Touch the Clouds tell Lieut. Clark this morning that they are going out with their bands: this means all of the hostiles of last year. Probably more troops must be brought here, if this movement is to be stopped. I think General Crook's presence might have a good effect? Please acknowledge receipt and give me your instructions.

R. Williams.
Adjt. General

Red Cloud Agency, Neb.
Sept. 1, 1877.

To the Hon.
   Commissioner of Indian Affairs,
      Washington, D.C.
   Sir:
   I have the honor to report that at the time appointed last evening I met
Red Cloud, Little Wound, Young Man Afraid of His Horses, American
Horse and No Flesh, all chiefs of bands except No Flesh. Yellow Bear,
chief of the . . . [illegible] band of Sioux, sent word that he could not be
present, but that his mind was the same as of those that would come.
   I told them that I had not talked to them much about our civil matters,
but that I noticed some excitement among them and heard some bad talk.
I wanted to know what I could do as a civil agent to quiet the difficulties if
there were any. They nominated American Horse speaker, and he said in
substance—We moved our villages together ten or twelve days ago to
council upon the various subjects interesting to us. We have held councils
every day and done all we could to quiet Crazy Horse and bring him into
a better state of feeling; but we can do nothing with him—he has not
attended one [of these] councils. Today we held a final council to take the
sense of our people. There were eight hundred and sixty-four Ogalalla
men present: all the chiefs and head men, and the balance young men who
took an active part in the council; and we passed on many points with united feelings and a full and warm effusion of the young men. We want no
more fighting, and from this [day] out we will live in peace. We will be
responsible for our people a distance of twenty-two miles from our agency.
We will never go over twenty-two miles from our agency without permission. The military have been trying to do what is good for us in the end.
We want our agency at White Earth River—at any place the government
may select. We want to learn to take care of ourselves and not having the
Great Father always feeding us. We want the Great Father to give us wagons and farming tools and seed, stock . . . [illegible] cows for the land he
has taken from us.
   We would like to go to Washington and talk friendly and earnestly
with the Great Father about our present condition and our future
prospects. That we want Lieut. Clark and his interpreter and the agent
with his interpreter to go with us [so] that we may be impartially represented, and this latter we insist upon. We want you to send our words to
the Great Father tomorrow—they then said on their own authority that
they would see that Crazy Horse did nothing about the agency that would

hurt my feelings. Such was the result of our interview. Crazy Horse is very impudent and defiant, but has made no demonstration yet. General Crook is expected in the morning.

Very respectfully
Your obdt. servant
James Irwin
US. Ind. Agent

Telegram.

Grand Island, Neb.,
September 1, 1877.

General Bradley,
Camp Robinson, Neb.

Your dispatch received. I cannot come to Robinson. If Spotted Tail can, with his own people and the help of the troops now at Camp Sheridan, round up Touch the Clouds, you have sufficient force to do the same with Crazy Horse. If Spotted Tail has not sufficient force to do this, you might send some of your troops over to him and use those from Laramie for your command. The two movements should be made simultaneously as nearly as possible. I don't think that any disturbance will be made. If there is any danger of the Indians becoming alarmed by the arrival of troops from Laramie, you should so arrange matters that they shall arrive during the night and make the round up early the next morning. Use the greatest precaution in this matter. It would be better not to say anything to the Indians about it until the night previous when you can consult the head chiefs and let them select their own men for the work. Delay is very dangerous in this business.

George Crook,
Brigadier General.

Telegram.

Chicago, September 1, 1877.

General Crook,
on West-bound train,
Sidney, Neb.

I think your presence more necessary at Red Cloud Agency than at Camp Brown and wish you to get off at Sidney and go there. Colonel Bradley thinks Crazy Horse and others will make trouble if the Sioux scouts leave. I will ask Bradley to detain them until you reach Red Cloud. . . .

P. H. Sheridan,
Lieut. General.

Telegram.   Chicago, Illinois
                                             September, 1, 1877.

Gen. E. D. Townsend
Washington, D. C.

Crazy Horse and other head men at Red Cloud Agency made trouble yesterday & last night & prevented the scouts from going to join Major Hart's command. Col. Bradley telegraphed me that the departure of the scouts would probably bring on a collision. I therefore directed him to hold the scouts for the present, and ordered Genl. Crook, who was on his way to Camp Brown, to leave the train at Sidney & go to Red Cloud Agency, as his presence was needed there more than at Brown. He has done so. I very much fear that Crazy Horse has been treated too well & that he will give trouble. One hundred & fifty (150) of the scouts wanted to go, and [also] one hundred volunteer Indians. Crazy Horse & the malcontents pet their opposition on the ground that Major [V.K] Hart was going out to fight Sitting Bull.

P.H. Sheridan
Lieut. Genl.

Telegram.   Camp Robinson, Neb., Sept. 4, 1877.

General Crook,
Fort Laramie.

The Cavalry and Indians started out at 9:30 this morning. Crazy Horse's village broke up last night and when the Command got out to the ground, there were but few lodges to be seen and these making for the Bluffs; some of them came in and others were captured. We have about half the village—forty odd lodges—and the Agency Indians are after the balance and are sure to capture some of them. Crazy Horse left the village this morning with his sick squaw for Spotted Tail [Agency], and we have twenty picked Indians after him who promise to bring him in. All the friendly Indians behaved extremely well, Little Big Man among them. Will telegraph you to-morrow at Cheyenne.

Bradley,
Lieut-Colonel

Telegram.   Camp Robinson, Sept. 4, 1877.

General Crook,
Fort Laramie.

Quite a number of lodges of Crazy Horse's band left here last night; the rest commenced moving this morning before we started. As soon as we got within three or four miles, they promised to give up guns and move near the Agency, but most of them scattered like a frightened covey of quail, some going to camps here and quite a number to Spotted Tail. It is impossible to tell just now how many have left. Indians here acted well and were ready and would have fought, but they wanted the northern Indians to commence. Crazy Horse started down the river with only his one lodge. I at once sent a party to bring him back, and as soon as I learned further particulars, [I] sent No Water with ten men to arrest him and bring him to my house. I promised No Water two hundred dollars (200) if he accomplished his mission. I have great hopes that they will get him. Under all the circumstances, I believe it would be best to turn over the remnant of this band to the head men I spoke to you about and not try to take any ponies. We have been at work all day and can take no further action before morning. I have sent two couriers to Lee [at Spotted Tail Agency] to keep matters quiet there and intercept any who have gone there, if possible. I urged the arrest of Crazy Horse strongly to Lee.

Clark, 1 Lieut. 2d Cavalry

Telegram.   September 5, 1877

Asst. Adjt. Genl.
Mil. Div. Mo.
678 Michigan Ave, Chicago

The following telegram from Col. Bradley, dated Camp Robinson, Sept. fifth, just received and respectfully transmitted for information of the Lieut. Genl. Commanding [P. H. Sheridan].

The Companies of the Third Cavalry & about three hundred and fifty friendly Indians were sent out yesterday morning to disarm Crazy Horse's band. The village broke up very early in the morning and was stampeding when our force reached the ground. About seven miles out, about forty lodges were captured, and more were brought in last night. Friendly Indians are after the balance and will capture them, I think, as they went towards Spotted Tail. Crazy Horse escaped alone and went to Spotted Tail [Agency], was arrested there last night & is now a prisoner. Seventy-five people of Lame Deer's band surrendered at Camp Sheridan yesterday, and state that the rest of the band, numbering five hundred under Fast Bull, will be in in four or five days.

In absence of Genl. Crook,
R. Williams, Asst. Adjt. Genl.

————————————

Telegram.   Camp Robinson, Neb., Sept. 5, 1877.

Major Gillies,
Cheyenne Depot.

General Crook will reach Cheyenne on Laramie-stage to-day: please hand this to General Crook.

Crazy Horse was captured last night at Spotted Tail [Agency]. Seven more lodges were brought in last night, and the Indians are after the balance who went towards Spotted Tail. I think we shall get them all. Seventy-five of

Lame Deer's band surrendered yesterday. They state that five hundred more under Fast Bull will be in in four or five days.

Bradley,
Lieutenant-Colonel

Telegram.   Camp Robinson, Neb., Sept. 5, 1877.

General Crook,
Cheyenne.

Fifty lodges—seventy-three men—have been gathered up of Crazy Horse's band, and some others are being brought in. The new organization for this band will, I think, be perfected satisfactorily in a day or two. I believe not more than twenty lodges got away and went to Spotted Tail [Agency].

Clark,
1Lt. 2d. Cavalry.

Telegram.   Camp Robinson, Neb., Sept. 5, 1877.

General Crook,
Cheyenne.

Major Burke sends word that he, with Touch the Clouds, Swift Bear, High Bear and Crazy Horse are coming in ambulance to-day. He [Crazy Horse] will be put in guardhouse on arrival. I think he should be started for Fort Laramie to-night and kept going as far as Omaha, two or three Sioux going with him so that they can assure people on return that he has not been killed. I hope you will telegraph Gen. Bradley. Everything quiet and working first-rate.

Clark,
1Lt. 2d. Cavalry.

Telegram.   Cheyenne, Wyo., Sept. 5, 1877.

Colonel Bradley
Comdg. Camp Robinson.

Accept my thanks for the successful termination of your enterprise and convey the same to Lieut. Clark and others concerned. Send Crazy Horse with a couple of his own people with him, under a strong escort, via Laramie to Omaha. Make sure that he does not escape. Keep up your efforts until you get every Indian in, even if you have to follow them up to Powder River.

George Crook,
Brig. General.

Cheyenne, W. T.
September 5 [, 1877]

General P. H. Sheridan.

Your despatch of today received. Crazy Horse was at the bottom of whole trouble at both agencies & yesterday his band was dismembered by the soldiers & our Indians, mostly by the latter. The members of his band are being distributed among other bands. Crazy Horse is now a prisoner & I have ordered Bradley to send him here [Omaha]. I wish you would send him off where he will be out of harm's way. You can rest assured that everything at the agencies is perfectly quiet & will remain so. The advance of Lame Deer's party has already come in & the balance will be in in four or five days with the exception of five lodges, which went to hunt up Sitting Bull & I have given necessary orders about disarming them as they come in. This is the end of all trouble as far as all Sioux are concerned, outside of Sitting Bull.

(Signed:) Crook.

Telegram.   Chicago, Illinois
Sept. 5, 1877.

Captain Gillies, U.S.A.,
Cheyenne, Wyo.

Sending the following to General Crook.

Your dispatch of this date received. I will send to you at Green River Station, the latest news of the Nez-Perces. I wish you to send Crazy Horse under proper guard to these Hd. Qrs.

P. H. Sheridan,
Lieut.-General.

Telegram.

Camp Robinson, Neb.
Sept. 5, 1877.

General Crook,
Green River, Wyo.

Crazy Horse reached here at 6 o'clock: his pistol and knife had not been taken from him and in getting these, he made a break, stabbing Little Big Man in arm and trying to do other damage, but we have him all right and I think there will be no further trouble. I had selected several Indians here and cannot speak too highly of their conduct, particularly of Little Big Man. Crazy Horse's father and Touch the Clouds are now with him; the latter in the melee was cut in abdomen, but not seriously. The Indians I selected simply did better than I can express and deserve great credit, and I hope may get it.

Clark,
1Lt. 2d. Cavalry

Telegram.

Camp Robinson, Neb.
Sept. 5, 1877.

General Crook,
Green River, Wyo.

In the melee, Crazy Horse got a prod in the abdomen, possibly from a bayonet, but probably from a knife when he attempted to stab Little Big Man: the latter I am trying to persuade all Indians. The Doctor reports that he [Crazy Horse] has no pulse in either arm, and it will be impossible to move him to-night. His father will be allowed to move his lodge near the guardhouse and take charge of him should he be alive in the morning.

Clark,
1Lieut. Commanding.

Telegram.   Camp Robinson, Neb.
                                                   Sept. 5, 1877.

General Crook,
Green River, Wyo.

If you approve [I] will complete arrangements for payment of scouts, dis-
charging Crazy Horse to date August 31, and let the chiefs who are to take
charge of this band designate men to replace those whose arms have been
taken away. These chiefs are doing even better than I anticipated.

                                          Clark,
                                          1Lt. 2d. Cavalry.

Telegram.   Omaha, Nebraska
                                                   September, 6, 1877

Asst. Adjt. Genl.
Mil. Div. Missouri
Chicago, Ill

The following dispatch from Colonel Bradley, dated Camp Robinson,
September sixth, respectfully forwarded for the information of the Lieutenant General.

Crazy Horse was brought from Spotted Tail yesterday [as] a prisoner, and
was mortally wounded in trying to Escape last Evening. He died about
midnight.

                              In absence of General Crook
                              R. Williams, Asst. Adjt. General

---

Telegram.   Omaha, Neb
                                                   Sept 6

Genl. Sheridan
Commanding Mil. Div. Mo.
Chicago, Ill

Bradley reports that he does not anticipate any serious trouble in consequence of Crazy Horse's death. He says there is a good deal of excitement

among the Northern Indians, but the Agency Indians are quiet & the chiefs are acting with him in the effort to control the others.

> In the absence of General Crook,
> R. Williams, Asst. Adjt. Genl.

Telegram.

Red Cloud Agency, Neb
Sept. 6, 1877

Commr. Indian Affairs
Washington

Crazy Horse resisted last evening when about to be imprisoned. Had concealed weapon. Fought furiously and was killed. Considerable excitement prevailed through the night, and most of his band got away, but probably went to Spotted Tail to join other Northern Indians. I think everything is quieting down this morning. Little Big Man was wounded by Crazy Horse.

> Irwin, Agent.

Telegram.

Camp Robinson, Neb.
Sept. 6, 1877.

General George Crook,
En route to Camp Stambaugh, Wyo.

Crazy Horse died at 11:40 P.M., last night. Some lodges have left and gone to Spotted Tail, the exitement last night being intense; but the Indians here claim that they will get them and will be responsible that none go north. Everything seems to be working well, though we have not heard from Spotted Tail. The death of this man [Crazy Horse] will save trouble.

> Clark,
> 1Lt. 2d. Cavalry

Copy.

Headquarters Dist. Black Hills
Camp Robinson, Sept. 7th, 1877

Adjutant General
Department Platte, Omaha.

Sir:

When Gen. Crook arrived here on the 2nd inst. he ordered me to surround and disarm Crazy Horse's band the next morning, but I received information on the evening of the 2nd that Lame Deer's band was on the way in, and quite near. So Gen. Crook directed the movement to be suspended, fearing that, if the attack on Crazy Horse was made at that time, the northern Indians coming in might be alarmed, and driven back.

Gen. Crook left here on the morning of the 4th, and under his instructions I sent out a strong force about 9 o'clock of that date to surround Crazy Horse's village, situated about six miles below the Post (Camp Robinson). The column consisted of 8 companies of the 3rd Cavalry, and about four hundred friendly Indians; the Indians Scouts were under Lieut. Clark, the other Indians under Chiefs Red Cloud, Little Wound, American Horse, Young [Man] Afraid of his Horses, Yellow Bear, Black Coal, Big Road, Jumping Shield, and Sharp Nose. The Cavalry were under command of Col. [Julius W.] Mason, 3rd Cavalry.

When the command reached the site of the village they found it had broken up in the night, and most of it had disappeared—a part of the lodges returned to the Agency on their own accord, and joined the friendly bands; a large number were overtaken by the friendly Indians and brought back; and a few went to Spotted Tail Agency. Crazy Horse escaped alone, and went direct to Spotted Tail, where he was arrested the same day by friendly Indians, and was brought here under a guard of Indians on the 5th inst. My orders from Gen. Crook were to capture this Chief, confine him, and send him under guard to Omaha. When he was put in the Guard-House he suddenly drew a knife, struck at the Guard, and jumped for the door. Little Big Man, one of his own Chiefs, grappled with him, and was cut in the arm by Crazy Horse during the struggle. The two Chiefs were surrounded by the Guard, and about this time Crazy Horse received a severe wound in the lower part of the abdomen, either from a knife or bayonet, the Surgeons are in doubt which; he was immediately removed, and placed in charge of the Surgeons, and died about midnight. His Father, and Touch the Cloud–Chief of the Sans Arcs–remained with him till he died; and when his breath ceased, the Chief laid his hand on Crazy Horses' breast and said, "It is good; he has looked for death, and it has come." The body was delivered to his friends the morning after this death.

Crazy Horse and his friends were assured that no harm was intended him; and the chiefs who were with him are satisfied that none was intended; his death resulted from his own violence. There was a good deal of exitement among his people following his death, but it is quieting down. The leading men of his band—Big Road, Jumping Shield, and Little Big Man—are satisfied that his death is the result of his own folly, and they are on friendly terms with us. Crazy Horse's band is being reorganised under Big Road, a moderate, prudent man, and I think most, if not all, [of] the band can be kept quiet.

Very respectfully, your obed't. serv't.
(Sgd:) L. P. Bradley, Lieut. Col. 9th Inf.
Headquarters Dept. of the Platte
Asst. Adjt. General's Office
Omaha, Neb. September 10th, 1877

Official copy respectfully forwarded to the Asst. Adjt. General, U.S.A., Hdqrs. Mil. Div. of the Mo. for the information of the Lieut. General Commanding.

In absence of Brig. General Crook:
R. Williams
Asst. Adjt. General

Telegram.   Headquarters Department of Dakota
St. Paul, Minn., September 7, 1877

Colonel N. A. Miles
Tongue River

Care: Lieutenant Chubb, Bismarck, Dakota

.   .   .

Crazy Horse and band escaped from Red Cloud Agency a few days ago, and fled towards Spotted Tail's. His people were turned back by the troops, and he was arrested. He attempted to escape from [the] guard, received a bayonet wound, and died therefrom Wednesday night, September fifth.

.   .   .

By command of General Terry,
(Signed:) Ruggles,
Assistant Adjutant General
Telegram.   Camp Robinson, Neb.
Sept. 9, 1877.

Lieut. J. G. Bourke, A.D.C.
Camp Stambough.

Courier from Spotted Tail [Agency] with letter: no stampede of Lame
Deer's party. They will all be in there in a day or two, and everything [is]
going on well. Crazy Horse's remains were taken over there for burial.
The exitement caused by his death is subsiding. Indians have been making presents to his kin. Some few still making threats, but the majority
consider his death a blessing to his people. Scouts in from north say all
who did not come in to Camp Sheridan went north to join Sitting Bull.

Clark,
1 Lieut. 2d. Cavalry.

Camp Robinson, Neb.
September 10th, 1877.

Commissioner of Indian Affairs,
    Washington, D.C.

Sir:
    I have the honor to submit the following report of the operations con-
nected with the breaking up of Crazy Horse's band of Indians at this
agency, and the killing of that chief, who for some months had been
growing sullen and restless here, and was trying to gather up a sufficient
number of lodges to leave for the north.
    He told me that he did not like the country about here, that he never
promised to stay here, and that he was going north with his band; that he
had made up his mind and was certainly going.
    This man possessed wonderful influence over young braves as well as
chiefs. Remarkably brave, generous and reticent, he was a pillar of
strength for good or evil. Knowing this, every possible effort was made
through kindness, reasoning and just treatment to secure his influence for
good; but the most patient and persistent efforts failed, as he attributed
every concession and kind act to fear, and would listen to no reasoning
which did not have for a basis the placing of himself and people in the
northern country, roaming at large. The chiefs who came in with him
were more earnest and honest in making peace and anxious to secure a

better life for their people. They worked persistently to try and get him to change his mind; but as he would not listen to them, they all left him and joined other bands here.

So vicious had this man become that on General Crook's arrival here recently, he told his men to go to the council prepared for a fight as he was going to kill him. This calamity was in all probability avoided by the loyalty and prompt action of one of my scouts, called Old Woman's Dress, in informing me a few minutes before the council was to meet.

On Sept. 5th [4th], having armed a large number of friendly Indians in addition to the Indian scouts, this band [Crazy Horse's] was surrounded and dismembered by these friendly Indians and a force of some four hundred white soldiers, who were in the immediate vicinity to give moral force and, if necessary, assistance. The lodges [were] joining other bands; some few, however, making their escape to Spotted Tail Agency, Crazy Horse among the rest. The friendly Indians here were ready and would have fought had it been necessary to keep this band from going north, which means war with them; but they [the friendlies] did not wish to commence the fight.

Crazy Horse was promptly pursued and so earnestly that No Water, who had charge of one party, killed two ponies in his efforts to overtake and capture him. He [Crazy Horse] reached the camp of the Northern Indians at Spotted Tail, and shortly afterwards Big Crow, a Brule Indian, told him that he understood that he, Crazy Horse, never listened, but now he had got to listen and had got to come with him to the commanding officer; and this Indian with White Thunder took him to Major [Daniel W.] Burke who arranged to send him to this post under Lieut. [Jesse M.] Lee. Starting from [Camp] Sheridan with only some Northern Indians, and gradually being joined by scouts who could be trusted, Crazy Horse still had his pistol and knives and did not realize that he was virtually a prisoner until some distance from Sheridan.

On reaching here he was told he must give up his pistol and knives, that he was not to be hurt; but in attempting to disarm him he, though surrounded by white and Indian soldiers, made a violent effort to cut his way out, stabbing Little Big Man (who had hold of him) in the arm and, in the scuffle that ensued, [he] himself getting stabbed in the abdomen.

He seemed to think it was done by one of the soldiers' bayonets, but [this] is impossible to ascertain about the matter as the doctors, from the appearance of the wound, thought it must have been done with his own knife. He died at 11:40 P.M. that night. Of course, the exitement among all the Indians was intense, but matters are now nearly as quiet as ever.

The majority of the Indians consider his death as a real benefit to their people and justify the killing as he first drew his knife. Of course, there are some who do not consider the matter in this light and who swear vengeance; but the band is now broken up and the lodges going to other bands and the people will be subjected to better influence, and it is presumable that there will be no further trouble. It is claimed by the Indians that this dead chief had with his own hand killed thirty-four white men and four white women, not counting those killed in battle.

Black Coal and Sharp Nose of the Arapahoes, [and] Red Cloud, Young Man Afraid of His Horse, American Horse, Yellow Bear, Little Wound, Little Big Man, Big Road, No Water, Three Bears, No Flesh and many other chiefs of the Sioux as well as many young men have all acted in the most praiseworthy manner during these troubles, and are all anxious to have their people live at peace with the whites. [They] are earnest and honest in their efforts to have their people make some advance, and can, I think, be trusted to work well when they feel convinced that the good of their people will be promoted by their work.

They say they can and will control and govern their people; that by doing as they have in the past few days they have probably prevented another war, and they hope they will get some credit for it; that if the government will deal with them justly and honestly and help them to become more civilized, they will in a few years be numbered among its most loyal subjects.

I am Sir
Very Respectfully
  Your Obt. Servt.
W.P. Clark
  1st Lieut. 2nd Cavalry
  Comdg. Scouts

REPORT OF THE BRIG. GEN. GEO. CROOK

Headquarters Department of the Platte
Omaha Barracks, Nebr., September 23, 1878.

Sir: I have the honor to submit the following report of operations in this department during the year just ended.

After Crazy Horse and his people surrendered (in May, 1877) they were placed on the reservation near Camp Robinson, Nebr., where they remained for some time, apparently peaceable and well disposed; but after the lapse of a few months the restraints of their new position became irksome to Crazy Horse, who daily grew more and more restless, and fomented plans for involving his people in trouble with us and recommencing a general war. To prevent any serious difficulty it was found necessary to arrest Crazy Horse and confine him as a prisoner. While on his way to the guardhouse he broke loose from those about him, and attempted to make his escape by hewing his way with a knife through the circle of sentinels and other bystanders. In the melee which resulted he was fatally wounded, and died the same night (September 5, 1877). After his death general harmony reigned, and the main body of the Indians acted as if anxious to establish and maintain the most friendly relations with our people.

•　　•　　•

The Newspaper Accounts

Chicago Tribune, May 3, 1877

GEN. CROOK
News from the Front.

Gen. George Crook and First Lieutenant W[alter] S. Schuyler, Aide-de-Camp—the former commanding the Department of the Platte—arrived in this city Tuesday evening, and are stopping at the Grand Pacific Hotel, occupying Parlors 9 and 7. Gen. Crook is here to confer with Lieut. Gen. P[hilip] H. Sheridan in regard to business connected with the department, and when that is concluded, [he] will at once return to his post of duty.

Last evening a Tribune reporter sent up his card, and in good time was invited to the room of Lieut. Schuyler, a pleasant and genial gentleman. Gen. Crook referred the news-gatherer to his subordinate, as he did not desire to speak regarding matters in which he was personally concerned.

•   •   •

"When did you leave Red Cloud Agency?" [asked the reporter.] "We left Red Cloud on the 29th of April. When we left, Gen. Crook had received a message from Red Cloud, who had been sent to find Crazy Horse, and had then heard that Crazy Horse and his band were on their way to the agency to surrender. They had previously heard the same thing through the Cheyennes who had surrendered on the 21st of April last, and some Sioux who came straggling into the agency said that Crazy Horse was coming in to surrender. Crazy Horse had been moving very slow[ly], and as Gen. Crook had not heard direct from him, he wanted the matter of his surrender settled in order that he might know what to do, and whether he would have to detail a force to go and meet him. In order to decide these points he sent Red Cloud as an envoy to meet Crazy Horse, with instructions to ascertain with certainty whether he wanted to come in and surrender under terms with which he had been made acquainted, or whether he wanted to stay and fight it out on the plains. Gen. Crook sent word to the Indians that he didn't care much, but [that] he simply wanted to know what Crazy Horse intended to do. That worthy was found coming in, but very slowly, because his ponies were extremely weak and poor."

"How many lodges has Crazy Horse with him?" [asked the reporter.] "He has 248 lodges that has been counted. Red Cloud reported that the proportion of warriors was very large—much larger than ordinarily. This is accounted for by the fact that Crazy Horse's following consists of a great many young bloods from the agencies who went out with him before the Custer fight. They are the worst element that we had to contend with, because, as young men, they had not yet become known, and they had to make their reputation."

•   •   •

"Who has the chief fighting men?" [asked the reporter.] "The chief fighting man is Crazy Horse, as a chief, and he had the best fighting element with him. He is no doubt the bravest man. Sitting Bull is looked upon more as a council chief. When he [Crazy Horse] makes a charge, there is this peculiarity about him. Indians usually fight in an acute angle when making a charge; but when he makes a charge, he always leads, and never allows his men to close up on him. He is always thirty or forty yards ahead of them. He is only 29 years of age."

•   •   •

RED CLOUD AGENCY.

Special Correspondence of The Tribune.

Red Cloud Agency, April 26 . . . .

I have spent considerable time to good advantage in examining the array of firearms thus far surrendered, and which are now stored in the ordnance room at Camp Robinson. Almost every pattern of rifle and carbine extant is represtend, while Colt's improved army revolver is about the only small-arm turned in. The young and prominent warriors usually produced the best Sharp's sporting rifle or carbine; and the chiefs were, in numerous cases, armed with fine Winchester repeating rifles. Then the old men and the boys turned in muzzle-loaders of every pattern, from the small-bore Kentucky squirrel-rifle to a terrible weapon approaching the blunderbuss style. Although not compelled to surrender their bows and arrows, many braves gave those up voluntarily. The fine workmanship displayed in repairing and ornamenting rifles leads to the conclusion that an average Indian possesses mechanical ability of no low grade. Few of the sights attached to rifles by manufacturers suit the savage, and he will manage to resight his piece and make it shoot closer, no matter in what isolated wilderness he may be located. I found guns restocked with native wood; resighted with bits of bone or steel; original fastenings replaced with rawhide, sinew, or wire; and all accomplished in a manner as effective as it was original. It is plain that an Indian's very existence depends upon his possessing a weapon of some kind, for the Cheyennes who have just surrendered here had hardly turned in their arms than they commenced manufacturing their oldtime companion, the war club. But this only illustrates one of their strongest traits. The ruins of all their years' accumelations have scarcely fallen before they commence gathering together and building anew.

The Cheyennes are not feeling at all kindly toward their confederates, the Sioux, and, should any of the latter now persist in making war, the former would enlist with the government in a body, and assist in closing the war with all the ardor and ferocity of their natures. The Cheyennes are recognized as being possessed of more bravery, better judgment and more determination, than the Sioux. They rallied promptly to the assistance of the Sioux when the war broke out, and have done the bulk of fighting, considering their numbers. They have also been the heaviest loosers—in fact, are so miserably poor today that they can scarcely boast of a decent wigwam. When Gen. [Ranald S.] MacKenzie destroyed their village in the battle of last December, the survivors, with what few ponies they had left, made their way to the Sioux camp, expecting food and shelter. But, wounded, and frozen, and half-starved as they were, their reception was emphatically chilly; and this accounts for the sour milk in the cocoanut. If ever opportunity offers, they will remind their red allies of that frigid reception in the northwestern wilds in no uncertain way. Lieut. [William P.] Clark's detachment of Cheynne scouts will do service of incalculable value here at the agency, as much on account of the stimulus mentioned above as from any other cause. They make an excellent patrol or police force, and some have already exhibited the striking traits of detectives. Let an unruly young Sioux commence to stir up trouble, and the quick and anxious ear of the Cheyenne takes it in as a funnel takes water. No time elapses before the bad talk reaches Gen. MacKenzie or Lieut. Clark; the Sioux of bad blood is "spotted," and his fetters, though unseen, are drawn as securely as Cheyenne "shadows" can make them. If there is pilfering going on, if arms are concealed, or if hostiles attempt to come into the agency undiscovered, their same unerring savage instinct is ready to frustrate or to punish. Sioux scouts are also enlisted, and their vigilance over the Cheyennes is equally close. Jealousy, and pride, and revenge, make it a case of "dog eat dog." The Sioux scouts even bring in prisoners of their own tribes in order to prove their fealty to Gen. Crook. It is also stated upon good authority that such a remarkable control has the General gained over these people that many of them would not hesitate to shoot recreant members of their own bands, if such were caught in the act of sowing dissension. Crazy Horse recently sent in the message that he had managed to fight the white soldiers, but, now that his own people were turning against him, there was no hope, and he was ready to bury the hatchet. Perhaps the most remakable feature in the use of these allies yet developed, is that of their service as spies. Scarcely a move has been commenced by any of the hostile bands during the winter that was not heralded to members of Gen. Crook's staff by this flesh-and-blood telegraph almost before it could be execcuted. One or two of these scouts will mount their fleetest ponies at any moment, penetrate the heart of the hostile country 200 or 300 miles distant, enter a village, and , after a grand two or three days' powwow, silently steal back with information as minute as a white spy could hope to gather in civilized warfare. Not only has the General, with his characteristic keenness, worked these matters down to a very fine point, but the experienced [military] aids who surround him—Maj . [George M.] Randall and Lieuts. Clark, [John G.] Bourke, and [Walter S.] Schuyler—are ever at the outposts, carrying forward a work which requires no less skill than patience.

•   •   •

[signed:] Alter Ego

Greencastle [Indiana] *Banner,* April 26, 1877

SURRENDER OF HOSTILE INDIANS.

On Saturday, April 14, the village of Sioux coming in with Spotted Tail, surrendered to Gen. Crook at the Spotted Tail Agency. The village numbered about 1,000 persons, mainly Sanzaries [Sans Arcs] and Minneconjous, under Roman Nose and other chiefs. The Indians asked permission to approach the agency in the style commonly used by them upon entering a friendly village, which was granted them. About 10 o'clock the warriors to the number of perhaps 300 made a regular charge on the agency from several directions, yelling and firing pieces in the air. At 11 o'clock the main village filed past the post and went into camp on a spot designated by the agent. As the village approached, about thirty principal chiefs and headmen rode in line into the fort, advancing slowly up the parade to the commanding officer's quarters, where they were presented by Spotted Tail. The son of Lone Horn [named Touch the Clouds] first rode forward, and laying his gun on the ground, said: "I lay down this gun as a token of submission to Gen. Crook, to whom I wish to surrender." The chiefs all shook hands with Gen. Crook, and rode away to put their people in camp. On the next day a council was held, in which the Indians were told what would be required of them by the government. They said that their professions of peace were sincere, and this is fully credited by all who saw them. They turned over to the agents upwards of 1,430 ponies and horses, [and] also their arms. The exact number could not be ascertained, but the collection embraced many carbines taken in the Custer massacre. They are believed to have brought in many relics of that affair, and General Crook has given orders to spare no pains in the recovery of such things. In the afternoon the peaceable Indians gave the newcomers a feast, and together they danced the famous Omaha dance. Five hundred Cheyennes are at Hot [Hat] Creek. They notified General Crook, some days ago, of their intention to surrender.

The story of Spotted Tails' experiences in hunting and bringing in the hostiles is very interesting. He met two camps of Indians near the mouth of the Big Horn, and told them to remain there until he could go into the village at the mouth of the Little Powder River. He found a village of one hundred lodges of Minneconjous, Cheyennes, Ogallallas, Uncpapas and Sansaries. They had a council and all agreed to come in but fourteen lodges. These with one hundred and seventy lodges of the first camp mentioned, all of them straggling Indians, make one thousand Indians. Among the chiefs are Scabby Bull, Antelope, Broken Horn, and several chiefs of not very great prominence. Crazy Horse himself was not seen. He was out hunting with one lodge one hundred miles from camp. Only the unconditional surrender of ponies, arms, and ammunition will be received. At Crazy Horse's village are all the northern Cheyennes, numbering one hundred and twenty lodges. An Indian was sent with tobacco to this village, and a reply [was] received by Spotted Tail that they would leave for the agency in seven moons, but would have to move slowly. Red Cloud starts for a final interview with Crazy Horse, and word is sent by Gen. Crook that he must unconditionally surrender at once or he would commence fighting immediately. . . .

New York Herald, May 11, 1877

•   •   •

THE SURRENDERED HOSTILES.

•   •   •

Red Cloud Agency, Neb., May 2, 1877.

The first visit made was to the camp of the Cheyennes, who surrendered here under their old chief, Dull Knife, about three weeks since. They number nearly six hundred, and are a fine looking race, the men being tall and soldierly and the children very bright in appearance. The women, who do all the drudgery about the lodges, are generally haggard and careworn. These people are entirely destitute, and haven't even the commonest necessaries of life. Their village was destroyed by General Crook's cavalry in November last, under command of General [Ranald S.] MacKenzie . . . . Accordingly a large body, numbering some hundreds, under one of their principal chiefs, Little Wolf, came into Red Cloud Agency early in March, and made an unconditional surrender, only asking permission to send runners out to the rest of their band and tell them they too would be allowed to surrender. The Cheyennes complained with much bitterness of the unkindness of the Northern Sioux, who had not treated them with any generosity in the hour of their suffering. They wished to retaliate upon the Sioux by enlisting as soldiers in the ranks of the white men and going out to destroy Crazy Horse's village.

It was to frustrate this movement that Spotted Tail, head chief of the Sioux, determined to go out in person to meet Crazy Horse and induce him to surrender before the white men and his fierce Cheyenne allies could swoop down upon him. A word about the Indian soldiers may not be out of place. They number only 200, but are picked out from among all the Indians at the Red Cloud and Spotted Tail agencies, and may be taken as representative men of the Sioux, Cheyenne and Arapahoe nations. They are mustered in and paid exactly the same as white soldiers, but are not drilled . . . . They are divided into four companies, each of which is kept under charge of a commissioned officer, while the warrant or non-commissioned officers are full blooded Indians. The government supplies them with arms and ammunition, but the Indians provide their own ponies. As an internal police they are most effective, as your correspondent can assert from his own knowledge. Their invaluable qualities as scouts and guides is testified to by all the officers and soldiers who have campaigned in their company; wonderful stories are related of their keenness of vision, their powers of endurance, and their skill as riders and marksmen. Since your correspondent has been here, not a day has elapsed without their bringing up to the military headquarters one, two, three or half a dozen young warriors who belonged to the Northern bands and who had come into the agency. These have always been disarmed and their ponies taken from them, while their names and numbers have been duly registered.

The Indian soldiers claim that they wish to have peace, but that the Northern Sioux have always kept at war, and that the ony way to bring the hostiles to their senses is for the agency Indians to join the white soldiers.

This plan of making Indians fight Indians is the keystone of the wonderful success General Crook has met with in his management of the wild tribes. From all accounts he does not place much dependence in the abililty of United States troops to cope alone with the aborigines of the plains. . . . Indeed, one of the surrendered Minneconjou warriors said yesterday:

We want to shake hands now. We don't want any more fighting. We are not afraid of the white soldiers. We can always sleep well when they come after us. But now that this chief (meaning General Crook) has brought our own people out against us we can't fight. We are so afraid we can't sleep, and our squaws and children can't sleep because they are afraid all the time. They are afraid that our villages may be attacked at break of day and destroyed like the Cheyenne village was last winter (by General MacKenzie). When a strange Sioux comes into our village we are all afraid he is one of General Crook's spies, and we set young men to watch him while with us, and to follow him back to see where he goes.

The general management of the Indian companies is under the care of Lieutenant [William P.] Clark, of the Second Cavalry, and Colonel [George M.] Randall, of the Twenty-Fifth Infantry, both members of General Crook's staff, who have had great experience upon the frontiers and evince excellent qualifictions for the positions they hold. The muster roll of these Indian soldiers reads like a page from one of Cooper's novels. We find First Sergeants Spotted Tail, Sharp Nose, White Thunder and Red Cloud; Sergeants Keeps the Battle, Pretty-Voiced Bull, Yellow Shirt, Little Wolf, Fire Crow, Young Man Afraid of His Horses and Eagle Tail; Corporals Dull Knife, Standing Elk, Yellow Bear, Roman Nose, Makes Them Stand Up, Climbs the Hill, Broken Jaw, Black Foot,

Pawnee Killer, and so on to the end. The 200 privates bear equally high sounding names as the above, but as they are not so prominent in their tribes the list may be omitted.

•   •   •

Chicago Times, May 7, 1877

CRAZY HORSE WITH US

The Venerable Gentleman the
Guest of Lieut. Clark at
Camp Robinson.

[Special Telegram.]
A Grand Scene.

Camp Robinson, Neb., May 6.–While people in the East were attending divine service this morning, listening to gospel eloquence, and sleeping under the droppings of the sanctuary, a splendid scene was being enacted near this post, in the western wilds of Wyoming [*sic*!]. This morning Lieut. [William P.] Clark left Robinson with twenty of his Indian soldiers, accompanied by your correspondent, to meet Crazy Horse. About five miles from Red Cloud Agency they met Lieut. [J. Wesley] Rosenquest, of the 4th Cavalry, who had been out with a detachment of soldiers to carry rations to Crazy Horse, Red Cloud, and sixty more of Clark's [Indian] men, who went out some days ago to bring in Crazy Horse. These were about a mile in advance of the great warrior [Crazy Horse], who could be seen slowly approaching from the opposite direction. Clark waited until Crazy Horse got within half a mile, and advanced with his [Indian] soldiers to meet him.

Crazy Horse was in advance of his warrriors, riding a white horse. He dismounted and sat on the ground, unattended by any one. Clark also advanced alone and sat on the ground for a few minutes, a few yards in front of Crazy Horse. They remained in this position for five minutes, when Clark arose and, advancing to Crazy Horse, shook hands with him. He was followed by Rosenquest, your correspondent, and some of the principal [enlisted] Indians. About a hundred yards back of Crazy Horse were sitting three hundred of his principal warriors, divided into five different bands, each with its principal chief. The party advanced and shook hands with all these warriors; most of them gave a good hearty grip, and seemed to mean it. Three gave the left hand; a few just touched their fingers very politely, not even saying "How koola?" But nearly all gave good hearty evidence of submission. During this hand-shaking, Crazy Horse remained seated where Clark first shook hands with him. The party now turned to Crazy Horse and seated themselves immediately in front of him. His two chiefs, Little Hawk and He Dog, were with him. The scene of this little council was in a valley between two long sloping bluffs. The Indian soldiers were drawn up behind Clark, while behind Crazy Horse were three hundred picked warriors. The long bluff was literally covered and jammed with the squaws and children, old bucks and young warriors, lodges and lodge poles of Crazy Horse.

He Dog opened the council with a short speech. He said: "I have come to make peace to those only [that] I like and have confidence in. I give these." He removed his heavily beaded and elegantly embroidered war shirt and flung it over Clark's shoulders. He then put his war bonnet on Clark, who was now evidently ready for business, and seated himself by the side of Crazy Horse. It was now his turn to make a speech, and he did it well, saying: "We have come to make a lasting peace, never to be broken. We had a rain last night that has washed out all bad feelings that have ever been between us. The sun is now shining brightly. All shows the Great Spirit is pleased with our actions. To insure this lasting peace it is necessary to give up arms and ponies. This afternoon, when we reach camp, I will take the names of all Indians who turn in ponies and arms, and will send them to the great father at Washington. Gen. Crook is now in Washington, looking out for your interests. We want to count the Indians so as to provide them with rations, and keep them supplied." The only answer made by the royal personage, Crazy Horse, was: "I have given all I have to Red Cloud," meaning his personal effects. Red Cloud said: "Crazy Horse is a sensible man. He knows it is useless to fight [any] longer against the whites, and is now willing to give himself up."

Through Red Cloud they have asked permission to surrender their arms at the agency voluntarily, and not have them forcibly taken away from them, each Indian advancing and depositing his gun on the ground, giving his name at the time. The council is now ended. This is evidently a bitter pill to Crazy Horse. He has been north for the last twelve years, a good part of that time on the warpath. This is the first time he was ever here. Fort Laramie was the last place he was in in this section before going north. Great credit is due Red Cloud for the consummation of this movement. He has done well and acted in good faith, and with the sixty Indian soldiers has brought in Crazy Horse.

A word about Lieut. Clark is not amiss here. There is a personal magnetism about the man that attaches a person to him as soon as one meets him. This is used to great advantage with Indians. His Indian soldiers perfectly worship him. His word is law to them. His perfect control of them shows that Indians can easily be go[tten] along with if dealt with honestly, treated kindly, and with a firm hand. Clark may well be proud of the splendid reputation he is getting in the Indian war. At noon the council was over, and all resumed the march for the agency—Lieuts. Clark and Rosenquest at the head, then the Indian soldiers, while about a quarter of a mile back was Crazy Horse and the principal warriors, marching with the regular order of troops, stretched out over the bluffs, dressed in all sorts of gaudy colors, all kinds and shades of war bonnets, blankets, leggings, and trimmings; ornaments of silver, brass, tin, and glass; their ponies painted in bright colors. The sun shining on them made such a dazzling show as almost to blind the eyes. Behind the warriors [came] the two thousand ponies, then the tepees and lodge poles. It was a grand and imposing sight, presenting a great contrast to the Northern Cheyennes, who came in last week.

In this manner they marched five miles to the camping ground selected for them near the agency, which they reached at 2 P.M. On a large plain, bordered by bluffs, their tents are now pitched on the banks of White Earth River, three-fourths of a mile from the agency and two and three-fourths miles from Robinson. The first thing done was turning in the ponies, and an actual count of seventeen hundred was made by Mr. [Thomas] Moore, chief packer. A good number of ponies were seen going into the herd after he had given up counting. At the conclusion of turning in ponies, attention was given to the arms. The hostiles requested that all whites withdraw, apparently meaning to convey the idea that their pride was crushed that they did not want the further humiliation of having spectators at this scene. They were humored in this, all white people and Indian soldiers making themselves scarce and leaving a large open place in which they could deposit their arms, Clark and Rosenquest, with Lieut. [Charles A.] Johnson, acting Indian agent, and Interpreters [William] Hunter and [Leon] Pallardy alone remaining, and here a little scene ensued that looked bad, and as if the Indians were not quite up to the mark. After turning in forty-six guns and seventy-six pistols, they claimed that this was all they had. Clark refused to receive them; told Crazy Horse he knew about the number of guns they had; that it was part of the treaty, as essential as any other part; that every arm should be surrendered at once. Crazy Horse preserved his stoical silence, and said nothing. The hostiles took up their arms from the ground and went to their tepees with them. Clark imediately ordered up a government six-mule wagon, and with Rosenquest, the two interpreters above mentioned, and some Indian soldiers, searched every tepee for arms, taking everything of the kind he could find.

At 6 P.M. nearly half the tepees had been searched, and fifty guns and thiry-one pistols found. At this rate there will be about one hundred and twenty guns and seventy-five pistols. I just saw two fine Winchester rifles taken from Crazy Horse's tent. No objections were made, no assistance given. Nearly half the guns are Winchesters; a good many are Sharp's carbines.

8 P.M.–Clark is just in from his search for arms. One hundred and thirteen guns were found and taken up to this time. No rations will be issued until satisfied that all arms are turned in.

New York Herald, May 28, 1877

CRAZY HORSE'S BAND

• • •

Justice for the Red Man.
Red Cloud Agency, Nebraska, May 7, 1877.

There can be no more appropriate place for commencing a description of the American Bedouins than the arrival of Crazy Horse and his large band of Northern Sioux, who have long been looked for at this agency and finally made their appearance yesterday. A full outline of this was telegraphed to the *Herald* yesterday, but a few words may not be out of place at this point.

The evening previous Red Cloud and Crazy Horse camped on a branch of War Bonnet Creek, seven or eight miles from the agency. Early yesterday morning they were met while on the march in by Lieutenant [William P.] Clark, of General [George] Crook's staff, who is to have charge of them while on the reservation, and who came to show them the place where they should camp. When he approached, Crazy Horse dismounted and, seating himself on the ground, said he wished to shake hands while thus seated because that was the sign that the peace made was to last through life and forever. After shaking hands the subordinate chiefs, five or six in number, approached and shook hands likewise. One of them, He Dog, presented the Lieutenant with a very handsome war bonnet and a "medicine shirt" made of buckskin and trimmed with scalp locks. The buffalo robe upon which he had been seated during the "talk" was also handed to him and a pony given—all intended as an expression of good feeling and regard.

Soon [there] after the strange procession resumed its way to the agency; where, as may be imagined, it produced something of a sensation; and truly it was an odd, barbaric sight that long black procession of human figures, with the great herds of ponies moving down the distant hillside like a swarm of black ants. The sun was in the zenith of a sky almost cloudless, each ray was reflected back from the bright surfaces of the tinsel, bead and metal trappings, in which the savage so loves to attire himself. First came a column of stolid-faced friendly Indian soldiers—regularly enlisted in the United States army—under charge of [First] Sergeant Red Cloud. They looked neither to the right nor to the left, and sat their ponies as if both horse and rider had been carved out of the same block of wood. Next came Crazy Horse and his warriors in compact columns, many of them singing a rude and slow-measured chant called the Peace Song. Finally the squaws, old men and the children with the village itself.

Every one who could ride rode; walking is as much an indignity in the eyes of an Indian as it is in those of a Spanish hidalgo. Scores of little ponies trotted by, carrying upon their backs quaint paniers of painted buffalo hides (called parflèche in the language of the Plains), and dragging after them the lodge poles, to which were attached all the property of the little community. Very many had netting of thong lashed to the poles behind them, and in these were slung the little children too young or too tired to ride. How young a Dakota child is when too young to ride is a question difficult to answer. Those in the cavalcade of yesterday ranged from twelve years down to three. All managed their little ponies with equal grace.

Herds of loose animals, many brood mares with little colts trotting alongside, strung out over the country; and last of all the pickets and flankers who are on all occasions posted on the flanks and at rear of a moving column of Indians, rode by and entered the agency. Every little while some of the squaws would start a song, and the refrain, soon caught up by her companions, was hummed and droned along the column; little boys dashed at mad gallop hither and thither, and the whole scene could without alteration have been transplanted to the depths of the Sahara and pass for a village of Arabs.

The squaws delayed not a moment in erecting their tents or lodges, which, braced by twenty-two long poles of fir wood resist every vain attempt of the wind to overthrow them. The interior of these lodges is black and grimy from the sooty accumilations deposited by the smoke ascending from the little fire constantly kept burning in the center of the floor. A few old pans and a battered coffee-pot constituted the average wealth of kitchen goods, for be it remembered these people have been chased and hunted so much during the year past that they found it expedient to abandon all surplus baggage and lost much in their various encounters with the troops. The children run in and out, through and around the tepis, none of them arrayed extravagantly, but all sharing an equality of filth. They looked very keen and animated, and in the possession of robust health. Their ringing laughter gave an animation to the scene scarcely to be looked for in this dreary country. One or two of the squaws who were visible—most of them remained in the lodges, busy in cooking the evening meal–were dressed very prettily in their peculiar gowns of antelope skins, crusted over with fanciful bead work. They did not address the strangers, except to answer the questions put to them by the officials who were taking the census of the village; counting men, women and children to determine the amount of rations to be drawn.

When visitors approached from the other villages, if food was ready everybody was offered something; generally coffee and bread, the latter an indigestible compound of flour and water. Both men and women indulge in earrings, necklaces and bracelets, all made of pieces of brass and nacreous shells found in the Yellowstone. These earrings are stupendous affairs, some of them reach almost to the waist.

While the work of gathering in the arms and "rounding up" the herds of ponies was going on the Indian soldiers were stationed on the crest of the hills overlooking the village, not certain whether their services should be needed or not. Some of these are noble specimens of masculine strength and agility. Standing Elk, one of the lately surrendered Cheyennes and now a sergeant [corporal], is extremely handsome for an Indian and has a fine reputation among his own people for courage and dash. Six Feathers, an Arapahoe sergeant, never appears except in full uniform and feels the dignity of his position very much. By "full uniform" is meant that he always wears his sergeant's jacket closely buttoned up to the neck, and his black hat, issued by the military authorities. He has a lofty contempt for other portions of dress considered of importance by white men. The rest of his uniform consists of moccasins and blankets. He wears a fine pair of shell earrings, and parts his hair in the middle, letting it fall in long tresses over his shoulders, and keeping the median line and a small circle on his scalp painted a bright red.

The surrender of Crazy Horse's band ends the Sioux war, so far as it relates to the country between the Union Pacific Railroad and the Yellowstone. How long this condition of peace shall continue is a problem which depends greatly upon the fidelity with which the government of the United States shall adhere to its obligations. What the nature of these obligations is may as well be explained now. The Indians do not come in to the agencies simply to be fed—at least the Sioux do not—because there is yet a sufficiency of game of all kinds to be found in the country between the north branch of the Platte and the British Possessions. But they do come, because they can see that in all their conflicts with the whites, however successful they may be at times, the burden of the struggle rests most heavily upon themselves. They know it will not be long before wild game shall cease to roam over the Plains, and that to save themselves from extinction they must adopt the arts and mode of life of the white man. Here is where the Indian policy of the American government has displayed its inherent defects. The aborigines with whom treaties have been made have been gathered like so many swine upon reservations and fed, with greater or less honesty, during a period of years. They have been fed and sometimes blanketed. Neither blankets nor rations have been remarkable for their excellence. The shortcomings of the Indian Bureau and the speculations alleged against its agents have been the theme of much angry and perhaps some unjust criticism. The Indian Bureau has many faults to answer for, but the whole system of dealing with the savages is so faulty that unless the system be changed the channel of its operations will continue to be subject to harsh comment. No effort has ever been made to teach the Sioux Indians anything. They dress in the same style, have the same ideas and customs as they had twelve years ago. The children are allowed to grow up in idleness, which is the hotbed of vice among Indians as among whites. Having no standard of glory, except prowess in war, the idle young warriors chafed under the restraints of peace and sought the excitement of a mimic fray of a raid upon the flocks of the settlers, to be found within a few days' ride of the agencies. They were emboldened to this course by the impunity enjoyed, no instance ever having occurred of any of their people being detected or punished for complicity in such depredations.

It remains to be seen whether the new management of Indian affairs at the Red Cloud and Spotted Tail agencies shall be better or worse. It has much to be urged in its favor. It deals with the red man on the basis of justice, giving proper encouragement to the well disposed, and assuring the evil minded they cannot escape punishment if they persist in wrong doing. With its well organized establishment of Indian soldiers, under the guidance of officers of the regular army, the ingress of egress of truant Indians is next to impossible; the savages being divided among themselves they can offer but a weak and short-lived resistance, hence submit readily to the rules of discipline. It is the old adage of "Divide and conquer" over again. . . .

New York Tribune, May 7, 1877

SURRENDER OF CRAZY HORSE.

•   •   •

(By Telegraph to The Tribune.)

Red Cloud Agency, Neb., May 6.—The entire Crazy Horse bands [sic] consisting of about 900 Indians, surrendered here to-day. Gen. [Ranald S.] M[a]cKenzie trusted the management of the details of surrender to Lieut. Clark, 2nd Cavalry. Riding out five miles from the Agency, the lieutenant met the savages and had a short preliminary talk. Crazy Horse was riding a few steps in advance of his leading chiefs, while some 300 warriors, marshalled in six companies and advancing regularly in single line, followed. Though attired in purely Indian costume, there was a total lack of the usual pomp and parade manifested by the vanquished. The survey of the leader was evident upon every hand, and the perfect discipline of the warriors in their new sad role, with the quiet reigning throughout the vast cavalcade, was deeply imposing.

After ordering his followers to halt, Crazy Horse and his principal men dismounted, advanced to meet Lieut. Clark, and shook hands cordially. Mr. Clark briefly told the savages of the general desire for peace, and added that all bad feeling of the past must be buried. Crazy Horse told his spokesman to convey his sentiments, as he would say nothing. The answer was in effect that the chieftain would make peace for all time, and that as he smoked the peace pipe he would invoke the Great Spirit to make it eternal. All of his things, he said, he had given to his brother-in-law, Red Cloud. Another chief, He Dog, advanced and placed his war bonnet and war shirt upon Lieut. Clark as a sign of his submission and good will. The ceremony completed, Crazy Horse ordered an advance, and the vicinity of the agency was reached at 2 p.m.

As they entered the broad valley of White River, near the point selected for the camp, the warriors formed in five bands, 40 in each band, and filed across the stream, chanting songs suited to the occasion. Here the great train of camp equipage, with the ponies and the savages, formed a compact line two miles in length. The solemn peace chant echoed from front to rear and everything betokened utter submission of the once dreaded band. While the tepees were being pitched, the ponies, numbering over 2,000, were turned over to the Red Cloud band, to whom they are given as a reward for their cooperation in subduing the hostile bands. Many excellent American horses and mules were noticed in the herd.

At 4 p.m. the warriors gathered in the center of the crescent-shaped camp to surrender their arms. Crazy Horse, Little Big Man, He Dog, Little Hawk, and other chiefs laid their guns upon the green sward, and were closely followed by some fifty braves. Lieut. Clark then quietly informed them that every arm must be turned in; that now they could show their desire for peace in a conclusive manner. As they hesitated, he told them they could take their arms back to their tepees and he would search every one singly until all weapons were found. The warriors quickly picked up their rifles and retired, when the lieutenant ordered up a thorough search of the village. Thus far he has secured a hundred and seventeen stands of arms. Crazy Horse surrendered three fine Winchester rifles. The Indians exhibited no objections to having the tepees searched, and the work has been accomplished with no trouble.

Crazy Horse is an Ogallalla Sioux, tall, slender, and about 35 years old. He has been at war for 12 years, having left Fort Laramie in 1865 upon the occasion of the murder of his brother. He exhibits two bullet wounds, one through the face, leaving an ugly scar. In his tribe he rules as a despot, and his people dread him while yet most worshiping him for his wonderful bravery. He has not uttered five words to his conquerors; in fact, he talks to no one. A coincidence worthy of notice is that Crazy Horse tonight took supper with the scout Frank Truand [Grouard], who two years ago was his prisoner, and who has since led Gen. Crook's forces unerringly to the great chieftain's haunts.

• • •

New York Sun, May 23, 1877

THE END OF THE SIOUX WAR

Ceremonies Attending the Surrender of Crazy Horse.

• • •

FORT LARAMIE, W.T., May 12.–Gen. Crook was not present at the surrender of Crazy Horse, which occurred at Red Cloud Agency on the 5th inst. He was represented by Lieut. W. P. Clark of the Second Cavalry, who has had charge of the Indians there and at Spotted Tail Agency during the past five months. He has managed the Sioux with the most consummate ability. Major Randall and Lieut. Bourke were also present to represent the Commanding General of the Department. The official ceremony of the surrender comprised a meeting between Lieut. Clark and the redoubtable chief himself. Crazy Horse was escorted by three hundred picked warriors whose gaudy trappings and soldierly appearances recalled the splendid retinue of the old Barons of feudal times. Fully two hundred additional braves remained mounted and observant upon the neighboring bluffs. Immediately accompanying Crazy Horse were the chiefs Little Wolf, He Bear, and Little Big Man—his staff, so to speak. Indeed, no others among his adherents are permitted to familiarly address him or approach his person, and in this respect he is different from any Indian chief I have ever seen. He holds himself aloof from the common herd, and though greatly feared, is correspondingly respected. He is probably the ablest of their chiefs, not excepting Spotted Tail. Tall and about thirty-eight years of age, he is not unlike other fine-looking and intelligent Sioux, though bearing himself with greater dignity than any of them. His eyes are exceedingly restless and impress the beholder fully as much as does his general demeanor. A bullet wound through his left cheek, obtained, it is said, in a personal feud which first gave him notoriety, disfigures his face and gives to the mouth a drawn and somewhat fierce or brutal expression.

Crazy Horse advanced entirely alone to meet Lieut. Clark, and, after proceeding several rods, sat down upon the ground and awaited the coming of that young officer, who immediately followed this example. Crazy Horse then arose, and moving slowly over the distance which separated them, shook hands but said nothing, Subsequently a council was held, in which Red Cloud was chief spokesman for Crazy Horse, who continued to maintain his singular silence. The former stated for him that neither Crazy Horse nor his warriors were defeated or cowed into submission, but that he deemed it best as a matter of policy to surrender, and that they acquiesced in this as they would have in any decision he made.

From 1,000 to 1,500 bucks, squaws, and papooses surrendered, 500 of which were warriors. Twenty-two hundred ponies, in fine order, were turned in, but only 147 arms were received, most of which were, however, first-rate sporting rifles or else Springfield carbines, calibre 45, the same as now issued to United States troops. Beyond doubt the remainder of their arms were cached in some secure retreat, where they can be readily obtained in an emergency

Crazy Horse had not been to an agency on foot for twelve years, his last visit to any settlement having been made to this post. His proud and almost contemptuous behavior chafes the impatient Col. MacKenzie, who ill brooks the peaceable surrender of Custer's brutal butchers. He thinks that Crazy Horse would be benefited by a dose of the Camp Robinson guard house, and the excercise afforded by attending upon the post water wagon—and so expresses himself. The Indian villages, and particularly those of the Arapahoes and Cheyennes, that were in the vicinity of Crazy Horse's camp, have marched further away through positive fear of that wily and moody chief. The Cheyennes, indeed, have borne the brunt of the war, and were in a perfectly destitute condition when they arrived at the agency. They say they have had enough of fighting for the rest of their lives.

The utmost good feeling prevails between the troops and the Indians, the latter having abandoned the insolent and defiant attitude they had always before assumed when in force at the agency. Sitting Bull is reported north of the Yellowstone, and attempting the crossing of the Missouri river, now at its spring flood. The Seventh Cavalry is endeavoring to intercept him. Otherwise, but forty lodges of hostiles remain unaccounted for, and troops will probably scour the country in their pursuit as soon as the grass will sustain their horses. The Fourth Cavalry expects to march to Leavenworth in about two weeks, and companies of the Third, in that event, will probably replace them. "The war is over," says everybody, and the late hostiles are going to commence farming operations in a few days. This fact is significant, as it does not indicate their removal to the Missouri river this spring, as was anticipated.

Strange to say, the ponies surrendered by the different bands that have submitted, are to be retained by them or given to the friendly Sioux who have remained at the agency. It makes little difference. Community of goods and equalization of property are strong points among Indians generally, and there is little doubt that most of these animals will again find their way into the hands of their original possessors. Except for hunting and the war path, ponies are of little use to the Sioux. Few of them are taken to work in harness, and they are too small for this purpose. Neither are they suitable for farming. They should be converted into mules, or else sold at auction, and the proceeds utilized for the benefit of the Indians. Properly speaking, they should accrue to the Goverment to reimburse it for war expenditures, or else be used to satisfy properly authenticated claims of frontiersmen who have lost stock by Indian depredations. The Sioux possess a great many ponies, and they would sell readily to ranchmen. Their appropriation might be reduced no inconsiderable amount thereby, or the regular annuities (blankets, wagons, harness, agricultural implements, ect.) be increased. Anything would be better than the choice apparently made. It is recommended that one or two regiments of Indian scouts be mounted upon them and employed by the Government. The plan is a perfectly feasible and a good one; but even then there would remain a large surplus of horse flesh. Cen. Crook is expected at the agencies to attend a grand council and peace dance that is to occur shortly, and his presence may materially alter the disposition proposed to be made of these ponies. Dismounted, the Sioux can never again be formidable foes to the Government; but if permitted to retain their wiry and courageous little beasts, there is not the slightest doubt in the general border mind that the army will be pursuing these same Sioux next year if not sooner.

Here is an incident peculiarly characteristic of the Indian. When it was ascertained that Crazy Horse was approaching the agency to surrender, Lieut. [J. Wesley] Rosenquest of the Fourth Cavalry was sent with an escort and train loaded with rations to meet him. He was warmly welcomed by the hungry Sioux, many of whose stomachs had long been unacquainted with Uncle Sam's sugar, tea and hard tack, and they immediately went into camp. They would proceed no further, and that night and the next day they ate ravenously and without intermission, until all the rations were consumed. During two more days and nights they refused to stir, notwithstanding the protestations of the young officer at their delay, and [they] sluggishly remained in camp, their overladen stomachs slowly digesting the unusual–[illegible]. At last they moved. Near the agency a fright ensued, consequent upon the discovery by a party of young bucks in advance, of a large herd of antelope. Naturally suspicious, the rapid firing in the distance aroused their utmost fears, and supposing that they were attacked by the troops, the main body, and particularly the women, children, dogs, and ponies regularly stampeded, and took shelter among the neighboring bluffs. It was some time before quiet was restored and the scattered village collected. There were many handsome squaws among them.

New York Herald, May 7, 1877

CRAZY HORSE'S SURRENDER

•   •   •

[By Telegraph to The Herald.]
Camp Robinson, Neb., May 6, 1877.

The long expected surrender of Crazy Horse's band took place this afternoon at two o'clock. Lieutenant [William P.] Clark, of General [George] Crook's staff, met the party about seven miles north of the agency and was presented to Crazy Horse by Red Cloud, After smoking a peace pipe, Crazy Horse seated himself on the ground and said:–"I want to shake hands while seated, because that means our peace shall last."

He then presented Lieutenant Clark to the principal chiefs and head men who came up to shake hands. A war bonnet, scalp shirt, pony and buffalo robe were then given [to] Lieutenant Clark as an earnest of goodwill, and the village resumed its march for the agency, arriving at the hour above mentioned.

General [Ranald S.] MacKenzie ordered the surrendered Indians to go into camp on a little space below the agency buildings. First came Red Cloud and the company of Indian soldiers in goverment service, next Crazy Horse and his warriors, and finally the herds and pack animals. The lodges were soon put up, and the work of counting the Indians and taking away their guns commenced.

It is now dusk, and the work is not yet finished, but enough is known to give close figures. There are more than twelve hundred Indians under six chiefs—namely Crazy Horse, Little Hawk, Little Big Man, Bull Hawk [Black Hawk?] and Bad Road [Big Road, and He Dog].

The animals surrendered number between 2,300 and 2,400 and are all in very good order. Among them are a considerable percentage of American horses and mules. The lodges are not in good condition; many are badly worn and some quite useless.

Crazy Horse is very taciturn, and has the reputation of never saying anything. His face is very dogged and resolute, bearing out the impression that he is a stranger to fear.

Little Hawk, the second in command, is a handsome chief. His father received from President Monroe in 1817 a silver medal which the son yet wears.

Little Big Man, the third chief, is the same who threatened the lives of the Black Hills Commissioners at this place in 1875.

Many of Crazy Horse's band have never been on an agency until the present movement.

The guns turned in include the latest patterns of breech-loading arms of precision, but the Winchester was apparently the favorite. Of these Crazy Horse himself turned in three and Little Hawk two.

A council will be held by General MacKenzie with these Indians on Monday or Tuesday.

The number surrendering to General Crook at Red Cloud and Spotted Tail agencies aggregate over thirty-five hundred since March.

New York Herald, May 8, 1877
COUNT OF THE CAPITULATION.
Chicago, May 7, 1877.

The official report of the surrender of Crazy Horse's band at Fort Robinson puts the whole number of surrendering Indians at 889 of whom 217 were men. Two thousand ponies and 117 stands of arms were also given up. Other firearms are known to be in their possession.

The Cheyenne Daily Leader
May 16, 1877.

CRAZY HORSE SICK

•   •   •

Special Telegram From Red Cloud.

———————

(From Our Own Correspondent.)
RED CLOUD, May 15.

To the *Cheyenne Leader:*

Crazy Horse has been very sick since his arrival here; for several days he was not expected to live; since Sunday, however, he has been improving. His illness was caused by over-eating and the sudden change from buffalo straight, and but little of that, to wheat bread, coffee, sugar and strawberries and cream, which are furnished at this place of plenty, and it nearly killed him. ('Tis a pity it didn't.–Ed.)

Lieut. Clark, of Gen. Crook's staff, has enlisted Crazy Horse and fifteen of his head men; this was done to better control the Indians at the Agency. A remarkable scene occurred when these red soldiers were sworn into Uncle Sam's service. They swore with uplifted hands to be true and faithful to the whiteman's goverment. The sullen, discontented look worn by the hostiles when they first came in, is fast disappearing now. Three of the leading chiefs have been advanced to the grade of Sergeants: Spotted Tail, Red Cloud and Crazy Horse. The latter said at the last council before his enlistment, that he wanted to "get along straight and well" at the Agency, and "that he would like a hundred of his best men enlisted"; that if any change was made in the location of the Agency, it ought to be removed north, where the land is better and where the children would be properly brought up.

A fearful hail storm prevailed here yesterday, stampeding all the cavalry horses, breaking windows and raising Cain generally. The rainy season has set in on the bad lands, making the Sidney route terribly rough and muddy, and almost impassable. . . .

"Rapherty."

———————

Denver Daily Tribune, May 18, 1877

INCIDENTS OF THE SURRENDER.

Savage Toilet-Making–The Disposition
of Crazy Horse–A Dog Feast.

When Crazy Horse, says the Cheyenne *Sun,* was reported within fifty miles of Red Cloud agency and his people in a starving condition, supplies were sent out under escort of Indian soldiers [on April 30, 1877]. These Sioux soldiers desired to make a great spread and ado over their mission, and among other things determined to create a stunning sensation in the Crazy Horse camp by exhibiting to the suffering hostiles a first class toilet. Accordingly they bought up all the white shirts at the trader's store, and carefully stowed them away in their gaudy saddle pouches. They rode out to within five miles of the Crazy Horse camp, halted by the side of a stream, bathed and donned their reception attire. Other garments were thrown aside and the clean, white linen put on with its full length exposed. Again resuming their march, these white-robed reds soon made a triumphant entry into the dilapidated Crazy Horse village. As they circled gaily around the tepees on their frightened ponies the thoroughly wild Indians, who had never seen such a fluttering of white flags, were greatly rejoiced that there were so many peace ensigns to welcome them in.

On the second day after the surrender [May 8, 1877], General [Ranald S.] McKenzie [sic] held a council with the prominent men of the bands. In the course of his talk he stated that he knew that the arms had not all been turned in by the prisoners, and that to save trouble they had better go out and find those guns at once. Crazy Horse was very sick and could not attend the council, but when his people told him of the General's little speech he grew very much worried. Others were also afraid that the military was about to pounce upon them and kill them all because a few of their evil spirits had hidden guns. That night there was no sleep for the inmates of the Crazy Horse camp. Children were crying, squaws singing the death chant and warriors trying to find guns that they might appease the soldiers. Sick as he was, Crazy Horse went from tepee to tepee, consuming nearly the entire night, coaxing and commanding by turns, that if any guns could be found they must be turned in before daylight. So frightened were some of the warriors that they took ponies which Red Cloud had given them, went from camp to camp of the agency Indians and bartered for guns. When daylight came they hurried up to the agency, gave up the few rifles that had been thus obtained and piteously declared that they could find no more.

On the 11th inst. the chief Little Wound, who is only second to Spotted Tail in influence, called a grand council of both agency and the recently surrendered chiefs. About one hundred prominent men assembled in the council tepees. Among them were Crazy Horse, Little Wound and He Dog. Little Wound had placed two immense tepees side by side and formed a large apartment in which the chieftains were seated in four circles. After the utterance of a prayer, the custom common at those assemblages, the talkers arose one after the other in rapid succession, and spoke freely of reforms they wished inaugurated at the agencies. Meanwhile the caterer to his majesty, Little Wound, busied himself in preparing refreshments. About half a dozen large dogs were strangled, their hair singed off and the bodies artistically carved. Shoulders, ribs, heads, feet and tails were thrown into large pots, and these placed upon the fire in the midst of the assemblage. About the time the talk was finished, a dog war dance and another prayer heralded the feast. All were served to large sections of canine, and seemed to enjoy the dish hugely.

Lieutenant Clark and Mr. [Robert E.] Strahorn were the only guests present and of course were forced to eat with the savages, as to refuse would be taken as an unpardonable insult. The latter gentleman says he narrowly escaped being handed a tail by turning his head at the right moment. Dog's ribs, however, he sampled thoroughly and pronounces them of the rather indefinite quality of not being quite as good as mule meat, but somewhat superior in flavor to that of wild cats.

Denver Daily Tribune, May 20, 1877

NORTHERN INDIANS.

Return of Mr. Strahorn to Denver—
What He Says About the Surrender.

White and Red Wives of the Sioux.

Mr. Robert E. Strahorn, the "Alter Ego" of the Chicago *Tribune*, who has, by his reliable and well written letters, won a reputation in connec-

(Denver) *Rocky Mountain News,* May 20, 1877

THE INDIANS

• • •

Life at the Sioux agencies is full of interest and romance these days. The glory of warfare departed, the ridiculous phases of savage tranquility manifest themselves on every hand. On the day of the surrender of Dull Knife's Cheyenne tribe [early April of 1877], the warriors were scarcely disarmed before they were found constructing war clubs with round rocks and rawhide after their peculiar manner. The day after the Crazy Horse surrender, cattle were issued to them in the usual proportion of an Indian's ration; they asked as a favor that the herd of wild Texans be turned over to them alive, so that they could enjoy a sensation like that of a buffalo hunt. The request was granted; about twenty steers were turned loose upon the plain, and the savages—armed with bows and arrows and mounted upon ponies obtained from Red Cloud's peace band—gave chase. All the thrilling whoops of battle were shouted and the terrific feats of horsemanship and the skill of the savage with his rudest weapon were exhibited. . . .

A grand peace council was one of the interesting sights afforded a couple of visitors at Red Cloud agency the other day. Little Wound, one of the most powerful of Sioux chieftains, summoned the other leaders of his nation to his grand "council tepees," there to talk over a lasting peace and agency reforms. Two immense tepees were placed side by side and made to furnish room for one hundred men. As the deliberators were gathering in this gorgeously-ornamented chamber, the master of ceremonies and an assistant were slaughtering dogs for the feast which always follows such a momentous carnival of oratory. . . .

• • •

A striking evidence of generosity was exhibited during the feast. An old Indian, ragged, wrinkled, and fairly tottering in his weakness, entered the circle, introduced by a fiery young warrior. The latter said that his aged companion should be fed and otherwise cared for, and that it was a shame that such feasting should be indulged in by the young and strong while the old were suffering. Little Wound pulled off his fine new blanket and presented it to the old man. Others divested themselves of their only mantles and did likewise, while the stolid and relentless Crazy Horse gave the venerable visitor a pony, blanket, and other garments.

The Cheyenne Daily Leader

May 26, 1877.

GRAND POW-WOW

•   •   •

(From Our Special Correspondent.)

Red Cloud Agency, May 23.

To the Editor of The Leader:

At noon to-day the enlisted warriors of this Agency, numbering 600, with about 200 others, with Lieut. Clark, of Crook's staff, commanding, passed in review before Gen. Crook. Lieut. Clark formed the line east of the Agency buildings. The Indians broke into eighteen platoons, and executed the march in fine style.

Afterwards the chiefs formed in line, and rode [to] within a few paces of Gen. Crook, and then dismounted and shook hands with him.

Crazy Horse, who met the General for the first time, knelt as he took the General's hand. His example was followed by most of the others. Little Big Man was conspicuous for his almost complete nudity.

•   •   •

Rapherty.

Black Hills Daily Times

May 28, 1877

NEBRASKA.

Camp Robinson, May 25.

At noon to-day, the principal warriors of this agency to the number of 600 were passed in review by General Crook. Lieut. Clark formed a line on the plain east of the agency buildings, Crook taking station in front of the center. The Indians were broken into a column of 18 platoons, and executed a march past in good style. Having been again wheeled into line, the chiefs formed the line and rode to within a few paces of Gen. Crook, when they dismounted and shook hands with him. Crazy Horse, who now saw the general for the first time, knelt on the ground as he took his hand, and his example was followed by most of the others. Little Big Man was conspicuous from his almost complete nudity. Gen. Crook now led the way to the agency, the companies breaking into columns by fours to the front. All of the principal men having assembled inside of the agency stockade, an interval of silence ensued, while the Indians arranged the order of precedence in speaking. The council was opened by Crazy Horse, who is notobly [sic] a man of few words. Seating himself on the ground in front of Gen. Crook, he spoke in a low voice as follows: "You sent tobacco to my camp to invite me to come in. When the tobacco reached me I started and kept on moving until I reached here. Ever since my arrival my face have [sic] been turned toward the fort, and my heart has been happy. In coming here I picked out a place where I wish to live hereafter, and I put a stake in the ground to mark the spot. There is plenty of game in the country. All these relations of mine that are here approve the choice of the place, and I would like them all to go back with me and stay here together." Crazy Horse was followed by Young Man Afraid of His Horses, Red Cloud, No Water, Iron Hawk and others, who spoke at greater or less length to the same effect, all expressing a desire to abide by the decision of the authorities in all matters, and to behave themselves in [the] future.

Chicago Times, May 26, 1877

DOVES AND DEVILS.

•   •   •

BEFORE THE BIG TALK
[Special Telegram.]

Camp Robinson, Neb., May 24. . . .

A council will be held by Gen. [George] Crook to-morrow, the 25th, when there will be an advance and parade of [William P.] Clark's Indian soldiers. The Cheyennes, numbering twelve hundred souls, through their principal chiefs, Standing Elk, Big Wolf, Little Wolf, and Two Wolf, have made propositions which have been accepted, to go to Indian territory. Two Knife, and others of their prominent chiefs, objected. But

their objections were overruled by the nearly unanimous vote of their
tribe. These Indians will leave here on Monday in charge of Lieut. [H.
W.] Lawton, quartermaster of the 4th Cavalry, and an escort of twenty
men of the same regiment, and will include the wretchedly impoverished
Northern Cheyennes who recently arrived here.

Your correspondent has obtained some very valuable information in
regard to the Custer massacre from Crazy Horse through Horned Horse
as his spokesman, which is authentic and confirmed by other principal
chiefs. I interviewed these chiefs this afternoon, Lieut. Clark arranging
for the meeting and Wm. Hunter acting as interpreter, a man perfectly
reliable and thoroughly conversant with the Indian language. This is the
Indian version, and the first published. The attack was made on the village by a strong force at 11 o'clock in the morning at the upper end of the
village. This was the force commanded by Maj. [Marcus A .] Reno, and
very shortly afterward the lower end of the village was attacked by another strong force, that commanded by [Lt. Col. Ceorge A.] Custer.

The village was divided into seven different bands of Indians, each
commandcd by a separate chief, and extended in nearly a straight line.
The bands were in the order mentioned below, commencing from the
lower end, where Custer made his attack: First, the Uncapapas, under Sitting Bull; second, the Ogallalas, under Crazy Horse; third, the Minneconjous, under Fast Bull; fourth, the Sansarcs, under Red Bear; fifth,
the Cheyennes, under Ice Bear, their two principal chiefs being absent;
sixth, the Santees and Yanktonais, under Red Point, of the Santees; seventh, the Blackfeet, under Scabby Head. The village consisted of eighteen hundred lodges, and at least four hundred wickayups, a lodge made
of small poles and willows for temporary shelter. Each of the wickayups
contained four young bucks, and the estimate made by Crazy Horse is
that each lodge had from three to four warriors. Estimating at three made
a fighting force of over seven thousand Indians. This is the lowest estimate that can be made, for there were a good many Indians without shelter, hangers-on, who fought when called upon, and the usual number was
much above seven thousand. The attack was a surprise and totally
unlooked for. When Custer made his charge the women, papooses, children, and in fact all that were not fighters made a stampede in a northerly
direction. Custer, seeing so numerous a body, mistook them for the main
body of Indians retreating and abandoning their village, and [he] immediately gave pursuit. The warriors in the village, seeing this, divided their
forces into two parts, one intercepting Custer between their non-com-

battants and him, and the other getting in his rear. Outnumbering him as they did, they had him at their mercy, and the dreadful massacre ensued.

Horned Horse says the smoke and dust was so great that foe could not be distinguished from friend. The horses were wild with fright and [were] uncontrollable. The Indians were knocking each other from their steeds, and it is an absolute fact that the young bucks in their excitement and fury killed each other, several dead Indians being found killed by arrows. Horned Horse represented this hell of fire and smoke and death by intertwining his fingers and saying: "Just like this, Indians and white men." Three chiefs say they suffered a loss of fifty-eight killed, and over sixty wounded. From their way of expressing it, I should judge that about 60 per cent of their wounded died.

While this butchery was going on, Reno was fighting in the upper part of the village, but did not get in so as to get surrounded, and managed to escape. They say had he got in as far, he would have suffered the same fate as Custer; but he retreated to the bluffs, and was held there until the Indians fighting Custer, comprising over half the village, could join the northern portion in besieging him. These Indians claim that but for the timely arrival of Gen. [Alfred H.] Terry, they would have certainly got Reno. They would have surrounded and stormed him out, or would have besieged and eventually captured him. From what I know of Crazy Horse, I should say that he no doubt is capable of conducting a siege. In both the Rosebud fight and the Custer massacre the Indians claim he rode unarmed in the thickness of the fight, invoking the blessing of the great spirit on him—that if he was right he might be victorious, and if wrong that he might be killed.

Some details were also learned in regard to the Rosebud fight [of June 17, 1876]. The Indians say in the latter fight thirty-six Indians were killed and sixty-three wounded. Crazy Horse says from the time Gen. Crook left Goose Creek, forty miles distant from the Rosebud battlefield, he was continually watched by spies. The first attack on the troops was made by Cheyennes, Ogallalas, Minneconjous, and Sansarcs, whose combined force was about fifteen hundred. Above the point where the attack was made, about eight miles, Crazy Horse and Sitting Bull with about five thousand Indians were camped. The attack was made with the idea that when the Indians retreated the troops would then fall into their stronghold. It shows as much generalship to avoid a defeat and massacre as to win a battle, and in this case just such generalship was shown by Gen. Crook. In an interview this afternoon, these chiefs also said that they knew [of] the time that Lieut. [Frederick W.] Sibley left the main column, with Frank Gruard [Grouard] for a guide, on the famous scout where Sibley saved the detachment by leaving his horses [behind] and returning on foot [early July, 1876]; and but for the jealousy among the Indians the party would surely have been captured. But the Cheyennes insisted on the lion's share of horses and plunder and delayed their attack until Sibley finally escaped with the loss of only his stock and supplies. The above undoubtedly is a truthful version of the engagement mentioned. No one was present at the interview with your correspondent but the chiefs and [the] interpreter. Hesitation was at first manifested, but after some questioning and talking on minor topics, Horned Horse told his story readily, which met with the approval of Crazy Horse and Red Dog, a friendly agency Indian, who were present.

THE GREAT COUNCIL
[Special Telegram.]

Camp Robinson, Neb., May 25—The arrangement last night was that the parade of Indian soldiers and, in fact, all the Indian bands should take place at 10 this morning. The Cheyennes, however, were so dilatory that it was 12:30 before the parade commenced. The Indians were drawn up in line a short distance from Red Cloud Agency, on a level plain, under command of Lieut. Clark. The line, a single one, was about a quarter of a mile in length, divided into eighteen companies of about thirty [Indians] each, making at least five hundred and forty Indians, though six hundred would probably be nearer the mark, some companies having over thirty.

While waiting for the Cheyennes, the little Indians and halfbreeds were whiling away the time by racing in every direction. Red Cloud appeared near Gen. Crook's party and excused his absence from the review by saying he was no longer able to ride back of Gen. Crook. A long, sloping bluff was covered with young bucks, squaws, and ponies. At 12:30, the long line of mounted Indians wheeled into a column of companies, each company under an allotted chief, and passed in review before Gen. Crook. With him were Gen. [Ranald S.] MacKenzie, Maj. [George M.] Randall, and Lieut. [Walter S.] Schuyler, one of Crook's aids-de-camp. They [the Indians] marched by in excellent style with almost as much precision in turning their columns as regular cavalry.

After marching in review, and returning to the ground originally occupied—perhaps a quarter of a mile in front of Gen. Crook—the command was given by Lieut. Clark, "Left into line wheel," which was readily and handsomely obeyed, and the Indian troops resumed their former position in single line, Crazy Horse on the right of the line, next [to] Lieut. Clark. The principal chiefs, to the number of about twenty—including Crazy Horse, Little Big Man, Little Wound, Young Man Afraid of His Horses, American Horse, Yellow Bear, Black Coal, Sharp Nose, Friday, Standing Elk, and other prominent warriors–advanced a few paces in front of the line as soon as this could be formed, with Lieut. Clark on the right and the interpreters on the left. They then advanced to where Gen. Crook and his party were standing, stopping a few yards in front of him. They dismounted and advanced to the general, he going forward a few steps to meet them, each in turn shaking hands with him. First came Crazy Horse, he dropping on one knee as he did so, followed by Little Hawk, Little Big Man, Black Hawk, Little Wound, Standing Elk, American Horse, Yellow Bear, Three Bears, No Flesh, Black Coal and Sharp Nose, who followed the example of Crazy Horse.

These chiefs represented all the different tribes. The Indians were all present to-day. After the meeting between the chiefs and Gen. Crook the long line advanced, making a very fine show as they approached. The general told the chiefs they could now adjourn to the stockade at the agency, where the council would be held in a short time. The stockade was about a quarter of a mile from where the meeting had taken place. To this ground they all now repaired, the Indians acting as escort. Arrived here, they were dismissed, each of the [Indian] companies going to their separate camps, and the parade was closed. It was cetainly a success, reflecting great credit on the Indians, some of whom had been enlisted but a few days; on Lieut. Clark, who has entire management of these Indian soldiers, and on all concerned, and shows that the Indians can be drilled and used as soldiers.

There had been a constant waiting in a hot sun since early in the day. It was now 2 o'clock, and it was decided to adjourn half an hour and get lunch. At 2:30 the council commenced. About two hundred of the principal Indians were in the stockade, thirty of them in a half circle fifty yards in front of Gen. Crook and Gen. MacKenzie, who were seated in front of one of the large buildings forming a portion of the boundary of the stockade. Maj. Randall, Lieuts. Clark and Schuyler, Lieut. [Charles A.] Johnson, acting Indian agent, J. W. Dear, Indian trader, and H. M. Goewey, manager of the telegraph office, and others were present. At the special request of the Indians, Leon F. Pallardy, one of the best interpreters in the West, was selected as interpreter, and he was ably assisted by

[William] Hunter. After these preparations had been made, the circle of thirty advanced close up to where Gen. Crook was seated, all the other Indians falling behind them, making a solid wall of Indians, three to six deep extending around three sides.

The council now opened at about 3 o'clock, Crazy Horse first advancing, shaking hands with Gens. Crook, MacKenzie, and others, and making the first speech. It was very short; but Crazy Horse is a fighter, not a talker. All the Indians, in speaking to-day, squatted on the ground in their peculiar Indian fashion. Crazy Horse said:

> General: You sent us tobacco and provisions when we were hungry, to our camp. From the time I received it, I kept coming in and toward the post. All the time since I came in, I have been happy. While coming this way [prior to May 6], I picked out a place and put a stick in the ground for a place to live hereafter, where there is plenty of game (He meant where he wants the agency). All of these relations of mine who are here, were with me when I picked out this place. I would like to have them go back with me and stay there with me. This is all I have to say.

Crazy Horse was followed by Young Man Afraid of His Horses, who advanced and said:

> Three Stars (meaning Gen. Crook), you are a good man, and to-day you shall hear my voice. Young men like myself are here with me to-day to have a talk with you– to let you know what our decisions are. Bear Butte is a country to look ahead to. Over there in that country there is plenty of game. We can raise our children there. If my great father wants me to raise stock or learn my children to read or write, there is where we want to go . We don't want you to make us one with the Snakes [Shoshones]. All of the Sioux on the Missouri river talk as we do, and we all want to be there [Bear Butte] together. That is our country. The great father asked us for the Black Hills. We told him we would give it to him one hundred years hence, but we decided to go over there (meaning north) and be friendly with all the Indians. This we will do and be at peace with all Indians. Here is all there is of us. We are behaving ourselves, and all we want is an agency over there, north. We want you to speak to the Great father and ask him to help us along. Now you are asked here to help us. That country is a good country. We can raise what we want in that country. We can raise our children there. I look ahead and see nothing to do wrong ahead. This is the reason I talk to you as I do. I am done!

The old chief, Red Cloud, now spoke:

Three Stars, listen! I am going to talk to you. The first thing made was the sun and the moon. We have a different great father now, and I want to make arrangements with my great father for myself and [my] children. I hope my people will live peaceably on my ground in this country; but whatever my great father deliberates to be I want to do, and not go contrary to what he says. I don't want to dispute my great father's word. The disposition of the people from the north is good, and when they go north tell the great father I want school-houses to teach my children to read and write in. If the great father decides to give us houses, I want him to send us good teachers, women teachers, that will teach us right what to do. Look at me! I have been a white man the last six months. Look at all the men standing around! They have all got children. These people are all obedient to our great father's word, and we want wagons and tools of all kinds. My friend, help me! I want your help!

No Water had his say. He is one of the agency Indians.

Three Stars, Gen. MacKenzie, Lieut. Clark, and Spotted Tail: To-day we have laid down everything. Peace is made. Our hearts are good. We feel glad for what we have done. I hope we can walk hereafter with our faces uncovered. I hope you will help us. I hope our people will get rich hereafter. Those people in the middle (referring to the middle of the circle of thirty), you told us to go after and bring in. We did so, and their principal chiefs are in the center of that ring. I hope they will get their agency where they want it, and that we will all live together there from this on and hereafter. There is no more laughing at our great father. We can't take our great father's word up in our hands and go off and laugh at it any more. We want our great father to help us live like the whites, and we can get along well from this. We want to decide with the whites, and from this [day] out we will decide with the whites. This is now the agency, and we meet here to talk, but we want to move north. We want a red school-house built so our children can go and learn to read and write. I am glad you have shaken hands with all my people. I have nothing more to say!

Red Cloud now made his second appearance on the stage, saying:

My friends, look at all these people! I have been raised in this country with this people; wherever we go, this people go with us. If we have all this people with us, our children can learn better (It is supposed he had reference to half-breeds, squaw men, ect.). Won't you let us know before we go what you will pay us?

Red Cloud retired for the second and last time, and Iron Hawk, alias Sweater, with a modern white shirt on, buttoned in front, the bossom on his back, took part in the council. He said:

> My friends, I want to talk to you a little. When you hear of one thing one day, and another thing another day, we want to talk it over. My great father is way down below where the sun rises, and his words come from there. What he says we listen to. I said yes, and it is all good. My great father wants to do what's right by us. We all say yes to what he says. My great father desires for me to do right where I was raised, and I was well raised—well brought up (meaning that the great spirit brought him up well). The great spirit told me back here where I came from that everything we wanted to raise could be raised in that country. There is plenty of game there, so we can make a living. From this, and what you tell me, I will obey. I will be quiet, listen and obey those gubs [?] that you have given the Indian soldiers. By this I suppose you mean [that] we must be quiet and behave ourselves. We want all these people together in peace. They are all our relations and friends. We want to zet [get?] all the interpreters of the country to go with us and stay with us wherever we may go. I hope we will get along well together and help one another. This is the reason I speak here to-day. I hope the great father will hear whatever we say here to-day, and we will do well by doing this. I hope all will be well.

Chairs were now brought into the council by Touch Cloud. Joe Merrival [Marevale], the old interpreter at Fort Fetterman, and Tom Duryea [Dorion] were seated in two of them. Touch Cloud, High Bear, and Red Bear advanced and shook hands with Gen. Crook, Gen. MacKenzie, and the entire party. High Bear now spoke to the Indians, telling them he used to be a Brule, but had now joined the Minneconjous. Then he turned to Gen. Crook, and said:

> In the first place, my friends and interpreters, I sent you to be good and true to us here so we can have courage and strength. These men that have been talking to you recollect being brought up on this ground, and talking to you on this subject. On this spot of ground five different generations have been raised. You can see as many here to-day as you see me here. I suppose you know I have been brought up with men of this country. I am talking for the No Bows and Minneconjous now, just as I did before (referring to a speech made some time ago). That man sitting there now, Spotted Tail, Tom Duryea, and Joe Merrival heard what I said. They told you to talk straight. They told you then to make your writings close down

to the paper, and press the pen down tight. My friends, this is the way I am talking–straight. You piced [?] my people and they came in. I want to be related to some white man; I want a place somewhere in my own country north where we can get some game, where we can run around and see my people hunt buffalo. We want a large agency so we can be free.

Little Wound now spoke and said:

Gen. Crook, Gen. MacKenzie, and Lieut. Clark, this is what I said to Lieut. Clark the other day. Gen. Crook and Gen. MacKenzie, you see these men back here. They are good men. They went to Gen. [Nelson A.] Miles' camp. One got killed, but we will cover that up. They must pay for the killing of that man. We are sitting here, and this is our land we are sitting on. We have a right to sit on this land. We used to be at the old agency [near Fort Laramie] and got moved here without being paid for it. I don't want to move, anyway. I almost cried when we moved before. All my relations talk to you. That is all right. I made my speech to Lieut. Clark the other day. I hope it has got to my great father. The great father told us first to pick out an agency on the creek, where we could get wood and grass, and we came here. The great father did it. What we want to do is to understand each other and know what we are going to do. You told me you was not going to take any more horses away from me. We did turn in some, though, and to-day I want to know whether we get pay for them or not.

Spotted Tail made the closing speech [while] seated in his chair:

Three Stars, I thought to-day I would have a big talk over matters and things. The goverment are here destroying our grass and things. We can stand it no longer. You tell us [to] decide what to do every day. No decision is made. The way the whites live they make fences and survey their ground. If you don't put a fence there, you make a mark in the ground. After you do this you get paid for the ground. Whatever passes over or through your country you get paid for–get recompense. This country is ours. We claim it as ours. We look upon it in that way. Here is our country covered with roads. My friend, you should put a paper on the roads and stop them. Last summer a lot of commissioners came here, baldheaded men, and said there should be no more roads. In the old treaty I was told we would get ammunition for fifty-eight years. We recollect what they told us then. It seems the whites don't remember it now. At Laramie, Gen. [William T.] Sherman told us we would get paid for the Platte country. We have not eaten up that treaty yet. Last summer, when the commissioners came here, they told us they would give us provisions, but we did not get provisions. All these things I remember; yet when I think of all these things, and the whites crowding all the time, I don't know what to think of it. We have got a new great father now, who wants to throw it all away. We want to shake all the whites out of the Black Hills and have a talk with the great father. All of this back stealing is done by agents, who ought to be put [to] one side and a different class sent here. I want to pick out some young men and go and see the great father myself. The reason I tell you this is it occurs so often. I don't always reach Washington. It occurs so often that the speeches and talks made here never reach the great father. Last winter you and Gen. MacKenzie said you would help me to go look for Crazy Horse and Sitting Bull, and if I did not succeed in getting them in, you would go after them. I did not want to see my own people killed, and I went after them and brought them in. With the white people everything that is done is paid for in their country. I succeeded in getting Crazy Horse in. I suppose the great father has heard of our making peace. I hope you will tell the great father of this, and see [that] we are paid. These white people with us and these half-breeds, I helped to raise myself. They are of our people, and wherever we go, we want them with us. They can help teach us to farm and work around the agency. Whenever your people own a piece of land they get paid for it. Three roads run through our land. Who owns the land between them? They are thieves, who come to take all the land between them. Whoever owns a piece of land gets it surveyed. I ask you to tell this to my great father. When you left, whatever displeased me I told you. I want my children brought-up like white men. I want them to learn to read and write. In the states wherever people live, a good many of them teach the children. You send me what can't learn and can't teach. Down there you have more doctors. Those you send us don't know anything about medicine. At our agencies we have stores. All we have to trade is hides, and all they give us is $1 apiece. The young men have a little money –$10–(meaning Indian soldiers). You can't get much with that $10. I ask you to tell our great father that we want to live with the whites, and live like white men, and buy what we get like a white man. No white man pays as much as we do for things. I ask you to ask the great father to send a Catholic priest to us—one that wears a black dress. What we get we get by hard scratching. We want Bouchey and Bissnett for traders. We were raised with these people, and when we get hungry they will give us something to eat.

This ended the Indian speakers. Gen. Crook made a short reply, say-ing:

I am very glad to meet you all here as friends. There is no sense in our being at war with each other. If any are killed on either side, neither side has done any good. I sent out for these people to come in because I did not want to kill any more of them. Last summer they were numerous; we were few; a good many of you fell, and you kept getting weaker constantly while we kept getting stronger. So many joined the whites with the Crows, Snakes, and Pawnees, that not many would have been left much longer. Your ammunition was growing very scarce while we had plenty, you soon would have been killed off. I sent for you because I was your friend. I am glad you have listened to reason and come in. I am very glad to see you here to-day. We have enlisted some Indians as soldiers, given them guns and ammunition as evidence that they have our confidence, and they are to-day the same as our people. We want to live from this out at peace—the same as brothers. You know what treatment you have received, and must judge by that what our feelings are toward you. It is an easy matter to talk. We only want to be judged by our actions. You asked for a reservation in the upper country. This is taken down and will be sent to Washington. I cannot decide these things myself. They must be decided in Washington. The com-missioner promised he would let some of you go and talk to him at Washington. If you get this permission, I would like to have repre-sentative men go and see how it is for themselves. I had rather you would hear for yourselves. What I tell you I know I can carry out. In regard to commissioners coming out, I knew nothing about them. I carry out what I say. If they did not keep their word I couldn't help it. When Spotted Tail goes to Washington he can tell them all this. I will try and be in Washington myself, so I can hear both sides. Lieut. Clark will tell Little Wound about the matters he asked about.

And so ended the big council. The 4th Cavalry leaves to-morrow; Gen. MacKenzie will leave for Leavenworth day after to-morrow.

The Cheyennes still adhere to the proposition to go to the Indian Ter-ritory, and will leave twelve hundred strong, day after tomorrow, in charge of Lieut. [H. W.] Lawton, as mentioned in a former dispatch.

New York Tribune, September 7, 1877

PICTURES OF THE SIOUX CHIEFS.

•   •   •

(From an Occasional Correspondent of *The Tribune*.)

Camp Sheridan, Neb., July 15.– . . . I have just visited the camps of Crazy Horse and Spotted Tail, and let it be my task to describe them in their every-day life, among their followers and friends.

•   •   •

One mile northerly [of Red Cloud Agency] is Camp Robinson, the military post which protects the Agency. It was built four years ago on a site selected by Gen. John E. Smith, 14th Infantry. Gen. L. P. Bradley, one of Sheridan's lieutenants in the late [civil] war, commands since Gen. McKenzie's [*sic*] departure. The garrison consists of four companies of cavalry and three of infantry. Besides this garrison, three of the five companies of [enlisted] Indians are here. They are all commanded by Lieut. Clarke [*sic*], 2nd Cavalry. The other two of their companies are at Camp Sheridan. The chiefs and head warriors are the sergeants and corporals. Retaining their own garb, they carry our weapons. They furnish their own horses and are paid forty cents a day for their use. The morning I was at the Agency there was a council at Lieut. Clarke's quarters concerning the horse thieves, who are carrying off the Indians' stock. Now that the Indians have become peaceable, the country is overrun with these scoundrels. The Agency is in the State of Nebraska, and the military must not interfere too much. Yet the country is too poorly organized as yet to deal with them by law. How shall they be suppressed? How shall they be prevented from exasperating the Indians into new hostilities? Lieut. Clarke, sitting on the rim of an office chair, with his feet on the seat, high enough to see and be seen, talking with the Indians in the sign language that is universal to all Indians. Sitting near him in a chair was Crazy Horse. Squatting on the floor and passing round the pipe were Black Coal, Yellow Bear, Swift Bear, Little Wound, American Horse, Young Man Afraid of His Horses, and perhaps twenty-five others of lesser note.

After a few days stay at Red Cloud [Agency], we started to go to Spotted Tail Agency, forty-two miles to the northeast. Camp Sheridan is to Spotted Tail Agency what Camp Robinson is to Red Cloud–a military post placed there to control the Indians at such times as frauds, bad faith, and short issues rouse them to anger and compel the presence of the military. Two companies of infantry, Burke's and Lee's, and one of cavalry, [Lieut. Frederick] Schwatka's, and two companies of Indians, compose the garrison. We were welcomed to the bachelor headquarters, and found there Dr. Koerker [Captain and Assistant Surgeon Egon A. Koerper], the Post Surgeon, Capts. Burke and [George M.] Randall, and Lieut. [Fred S.] Calhoun. The two latter are with a mixed command of red and white soldiers now pursuing the horse-thieves that are stealing the Indian's stock.

•   •   •

Black Hills Weekly Times

August 19, 1877

Sioux Coming Northward.

Mr. Ed Cook, Division Agent for the Cheyenne and Black Hills Stage Company, arrived in our city [Deadwood] last evening, and informed us that he passed Crazy Horse, accompanied by a large band of Sioux, on Thursday night at Battle Creek, twenty-four miles this side [north] of Buffalo Gap, on the Sidney Route. They were accompanied by a small detachment of soldiers, and were on their way to the north, ostensibly to hunt.

Chicago Times, September 5, 1877

CRAZY HORSE AND TOUCH THE CLOUD ORGANIZE A
REBELLION AT
RED CLOUD AGENCY.

•   •   •

[Special Telegram.]
An Indian Insurrection.

Red Cloud Agency, Neb., Sept. 4.–Considerable excitement has prevailed at this agency for the last few days, caused by the declared purpose of Crazy Horse and Touch the Cloud to leave the reservation. All the available cavalry in this vicinity was ordered to Camp Robinson, for the purpose of surrounding Crazy Horse's village and taking him with his band prisoners. This morning about five companies of cavalry and one piece of artillery, under command of Col. [Julius W.] Mason, proceeded to his village, accompanied by two hundred Arapahoe scouts and a number of friendly Sioux.

On nearing the village Crazy Horse sent word that he would fight them. His camp was situated on White River, below the mouth of the Little White Clay. Part of the command took a position at the mouth of the Little White Clay, while the remainder made a detour around the village and came up from the rear. At this movement the Indians began to break camp and scatter in different directions toward the bluffs, but were speedily overtaken by the Indians and soldiers, who brought them back [as] prisoners.

At the first advance of the troops, one Indian, braver than the rest, rode up to Crazy Horse's [should be Clark's] scouts and commenced abusing them, when he was struck over the head several times with guns, and finally shot and his horse killed. This is the only collision which occurred in capturing the band. It was then learned that Crazy Horse had fled, and is supposed to have gone to Spotted Tail Agency. Thirty [Indian] soldiers were immediately dispatched in pursuit, and shortly afterward Lieut. [William P.] Clark, commanding the scouts, sent eight or ten Indians after him [Crazy Horse], telling their leader he would pay $200 reward to the man who brought the renegade chief back dead or alive. Some of his band who got away into the bluffs early this morning have returned tonight to the agency.

●   ●   ●

[To the Western Associated Press.]
Recaptured Reds.

Camp Robinson, Neb., Sept. 4.–Crazy Horse and a number of his lodges left this agency last night, and the rest commenced leaving this morning. Six companies of cavalry and about two hundred and fifty friendly Indians left here at 9:30 this morning and succeeded in turning nearly all back. The military expects to have them all back by to-morrow. No fighting or casualties occurred.

Surrender of Hostiles.

Shedding Bear, with fifteen lodges of Lame Deer's band, numbering about eighty persons, surrendered this morning to Maj. [Daniel W.]

Burke, of the 14th Infantry, commanding this camp. Fast Bull, with the remainder of the band, numbering between four and five hundred, will arrive in two or three days. These are the Indians that have been committing depredations in the vicinity of the Black Hills, and their coming in leaves that country and the Big Horn country entirely free of Indians. The [Indian] delegation sent out by Maj. Burke succeeded in inducing these Indians to return.

Chicago Times, September 6, 1877

THE CAPTIVE CHIEF.

Sensational Scenes at Camp Robinson
on the Arrival of Crazy Horse.

The Reports at Headquarters.

• • •

[Special Telegram.]

Red Cloud Agency, Neb., Sept. 5.–The arrival of Crazy Horse as a prisoner from Spotted Tail Agency, this evening, was attended with a number of exciting events. About 6 o'clock an ambulance drove up to the guardhouse at Camp Robinson, bringing Lieut. [Jesse M.] Lee, Indian agent at Spotted Tail; Crazy Horse, the fallen chief; Spotted Tail himself, and several Indians as guards. The ambulance was escorted by about eighty Indian soldiers, partly from [this] agency and partly from Spotted Tail. On arriving at Camp Robinson Crazy Horse was led by Little Big Man and Touch the Cloud into the post adjutant's office, which place was at once surrounded by Indian scouts and United States soldiers. The interpreter was then instructed to tell all the Indians that Crazy Horse would not be harmed, but would be put in the guardhouse and be taken charge of by the soldiers.

When they started to move him to the guardhouse he held back, but was forced along by Capt. [James] Kennington, who was officer of the day, assisted by Little Big Man. It appears that Crazy Horse's revolver and knife had not been taken from him, and on being disarmed in the guardhouse he secured his knife and attempted to make his escape. Little

Big Man, however, hung on to him like a tiger and received a severe cut in the arm from Crazy Horse. On emerging from the guardhouse he was at once surrounded by soldiers, some of them with fixed bayonets. In the scuffle which ensued Crazy Horse received a wound in the abdomen which is serious, but may not prove [to be] fatal.

During the struggle to retain him a number of the Indians who escorted him from Spotted Tail, rushed up—guns and revolvers, cocked in hand—motioning for the crowd to open so they might get a shot at him; but on receiving this wound Crazy Horse sank to the ground, groaning piteously. The Indians then refused to have him taken into the guardhouse, and when Capt. Kennington ordered four men to carry him in, one Indian, evidently a friend of Crazy Horse, leveled a pistol at the captain's head, but his arm was pushed upward by an Indian standing by him.

After having his arm dressed Little Big Man returned to the scene of the disturbance, and gave some orders, whereupon Crazy Horse was placed upon blankets, and carried by the Indians into the adjutant's office, where he still remains. There have been Indian couriers galloping to every village around the agency all the evening, for what purpose it is not learned, but some fears are entertained that should Crazy Horse's wound prove fatal, a serious disturbance may occur. All the troops at Camp Robinson are under arms and prepared for any emergency. There is a small guard of Indian soldiers stationed here at the agency, but [considered] not [more than] a handful in case of trouble. Capt. Kennington deserves credit for his unflinching nerve during the whole trouble.

NEWS FROM THE AGENCIES
[Special Telegram.]

Fort Laramie, Wyoming, Sept. 5.–Gen. Crook, accompanied by Lieut. [John G.] Bourke, one of his aides, arrived last evening from Red Cloud Agency, but only stopped two hours. At 8 o'clock he left on the Cheyenne and Black Hills stage for Cheyenne, which city he will reach for an early dinner to-day, and take cars for Green River, and go thence by ambulance to Camp Brown, toward which point the 5th Cavalry are now hastening. He reports the Indians at Red Cloud and Spotted Tail agencies as being more contented, and thinks he will have no further trouble with them. This uneasiness was doubtless caused by wild rumors of Indian victories in the north by their old enemies.

There are now five companies of the 3d Cavalry at Camp Robinson, near Red Cloud, and three conmpanies of infantry, in all about five hundred men. Three companies of the 3d Cavalry were sent from Fort Laramie when the Indian excitement was at the highest, and a portion of the company at Hat Creek. These troops will be kept at the agencies for the present.

A rumor was in circulation that Lieut. Clark would be put in command of all those disaffected Indians who were spoiling for a fight, and march them against the Nez Perces, but there is no truth for the rumor. Lieut. Bourke said it would require a march of four hundred miles to take them [to] where they are needed, and other and more effective troops could be gotten to the points where their services would be required, much quicker and easier. The general appeared to be in excellent health and spirits.

[Special Telegram.]

Cheyenne, Wyoming, Sept. 5.–Gen. Crook arrived here this noon, directly from Red Cloud Agency, and immediately started for Camp Brown and Wind River valley. He says he is satisfied with the situation at the agencies. While here he received word that Crazy Horse, who was the cause of all the late trouble, had been recaptured and will be brought to Cheyenne and confined until the lieutenant-general shall dispose of his case. All of the Sioux and Arapahoe scouts are to be retained at the agencies, instead of going west after the Nez Perces.

FROM LOCAL HEADQUARTERS.

The officers at army headquarters in this city [Chicago] were indebted to the exclusive enterprise of *The Times*, on yesterday, for the first intelligence of the flurry among the redskins at Red Cloud Agency, which occurred on Tuesday. For some time past Gen. Sheridan has known that Crazy Horse was a malcontent. He had not believed, however, that the disquietude was snared to any great extent by the lately sunrendered savages, nor had he feared that the discontent of the few would be expressed in overt acts. The other day the Sioux and Arapahoe scouts at Red Cloud asked to be allowed to go out and harvest some Nez Perces scalps. They wanted to join [Major V. K.] Hart's command. This request seemed reasonable enough, and permission was granted; but Crazy Horse interposed an objection, saying there would be trouble if the scouts were allowed to depart. His pretext was that the scouts, instead of going after Joseph and

his band, were to be used in a campaign against Sitting Bull. He was the
friend of Sitting Bull, and he did not propose to see his own kind turned
loose against him, and he was satisfied that the scouts were to be need[ed]
for that purpose. On this flimsy pretext Crazy Horse made such a row that
the order permitting the departure of the scouts was suspended. This was
the only course to pursue under the circumstances. There were only a few
hundred troops at the agency, and three or four thousand Indians—enough
of the latter to eat up the soldiers. Gen. Sheridan telegraphed Gen.
Crook, who was aboard a train going west on the Union Pacific, to proceed direct to Red Cloud [Agency,] and try and quiet the malcontents.
Gen. Crook did as he was ordered, and on Tuesday telegraphed Gen.
Sheridan that the Indians were quiet, and that he was about leaving for
Cheyenne. The stampede occurred subsequently and the word confirm-
ing it was received from Crook until late last evening . . . .

New York Sun, September 14, 1877

THE DEATH OF CRAZY HORSE

•   •   •

Red Cloud Agency, Neb., Sept. 6.–Crazy Horse, the redoubtable
Sioux chief and warrior is dead, his spirit having entered the happy hunting grounds at 12½ o'clock this morning. You have been informed by
telegraph of the main facts in connection with the recent agency troubles.
When Crazy Horse and the other chiefs of the Sioux at this post were
informed that the Great Father desired them to send two hundred of
their young men to fight the Nez Perces under Joseph, he and Touch the
Cloud demurred, and it is asserted by Lieut. Clark, who has general
charge of the Indians, and by his interpreter, Frank Gouard [sic], that
both threatened to go north again and war against the whites. Crazy
Horse said he had appointed a day and arranged for his departure. His village was situated about five miles north of the agency, on White River,
and numbered over one hundred tipis. Many of his principal men, including Little Big Man, Big Road, Jumping Shield, Iron Hawk, and Yellow
Bear, had left him to join other bands, having been incited thereto by jealousy, the action of Gen. Crook and his representatives, and the protestations of Red Cloud, Little Wound, American Horse, and Young Man
Afraid of his Horses, all enlisted Indians and Ogallala or Kiocie [Kiyuksa]
chiefs. His influence was rapidly waning, and at this juncture, especially,

much dissatisfaction prevailed because of his persistent refusal to go to Washington.

Little Big Man will be remembered as the instigator of almost a massacre of Senator [William B.] Allison and his Commission when treating [on September 23, 1875] for the possession of the Black Hills. Touch the Cloud is reported to have expressed himself with similar import and emphasis. He is a Minneconjou, of magnificent physique, standing six feet five inches in his moccasins, and without an ounce of surplus flesh, weighing 280 pounds. Notwithstanding his stature and avoirdupois, he is nothing if not poetical. "The Great Father," said Touch the Cloud, "washed the blood from our faces, and now would besmear them again! If he bid us [to] put it on, it must stay there." The interpreter construed this into highly insolent and mutinous language, and both Crazy Horse and Touch the Cloud were reported by telegraph to Gen. Crook, who, although rapidly traveling to Camp Brown, found time to visit this agency en route. While here he endeavored to see Crazy Horse; but the latter not only refused to come to Camp Robinson when summoned, but threatened to scalp the Gray Fox (Crook) if he ventured inside of his village. Touch the Cloud had returned to Spotted Tail Agency, where his people are encamped. Of course this ended amicable negotiations. Spies were at once set [sent?] to watch the supposed hostiles, numbering several hundred.

There are about 6,600 Indians at this agency, and at Spotted Tail not less than 7,000. Of the former, perhaps 2,000 are bucks. Here there were only four companies of the Third Cavalry and three of the Fourteenth Infantry–of whom it is said, however, "Russia has her Cossacks; Turkey, the Bashi-Bazouks; and the United States the 'bloody Fourteeners!'" At Spotted Tail, one company of the Third Cavalry and one of the Fourteenth Infantry occupied the neighboring post of Camp Sheridan. It was desirable to have more troops, and E and G companies of the Third Cavalry were ordered from Fort Laramie, and a part of F and all of D company (en route to the Black Hills) of the same regiment, from camp at Hat Creek. The troops thus consolidated entered Camp Robinson at midnight, and on the morning of the 4th inst., at about 9 o'clock, they proceeded to surround Crazy Horse and village. There were seven companies of cavalry, partly incomplete, numbering about 300 men, and commanded by Major J. W. Mason, Third Cavalry.

The reenforcements were accompanied by nearly 300 enlisted Sioux under Red Cloud, Little Wound, Young Man Afraid of his Horses, Little Big Man, and Jumping Shield, and about 100 Arapahoes of Friday's band led by Black Coal and Sharp Nose. A twelve-pounder brass Napoleon with the limber chestfuls of grapeshot and canister, and which evidently inspired both allies and hostiles with a wholesome fear, completed this martial array.

Arriving where but a single crest concealed the village, it was cautiously approached, when there was discovered an empty and uninhabited valley! Crazy Horse and village had vanished. A few scattered lodge poles and bundles showed that his departure had been somewhat hurried. His trail led north principally, in the direction of Spotted Tail [Agency], and thither American Horse, with one party, and No Water with another, were instantly despatched, with instructions to bring him in dead or alive. Two hundred dollars was offered for his apprehension. Meanwhile, several incidents occurred, peculiarly illustrative of the Indian character. At a time the troops anticipated coming upon Crazy Horse and his fleeing village at any moment, a coyote was discovered running along the bank of the river, and a dozen or fifteen shots were instantly fired at him. They were heard at the agency, and it was supposed the ball had opened in earnest. Later, the Arapahoes started a gray fox from the brush, and the entire one hundred [warriors] followed, chasing him into and through an adjoining village. These childish impulses are irresistible to the otherwise grave and dignified warriors of the plains. The latter tribe converse almost exclusively by signs, and no white man ever acquired their deep guttural tongue. It is said that not even two Arapahoes can make themselves understand in the dark, where their gestures are not discernable.

At about 2 a.m. yesterday, a courier was received from Lieut. Lee, Acting Indian Agent at Spotted Tail, reporting that Crazy Horse and many of his people had arrived at his agency, and that he would bring the former down on that day.

Gen. Crook had left Camp Robinson very early on the 4th inst., before the attempted "surround," in order to connect with the stage line at Fort Laramie, and [to] continue his journey to the front of the nose-pierced Joseph. Before he left, however, it is understood that he gave directions that Crazy Horse, if captured, should be confined in the guardhouse at Camp Robinson, until he could be secretly conveyed to Cheyenne, and thence to the Dry Tortugas; and although an arbitrary punishment, it was no means an excessive one, if the conduct of Crazy Horse, as an enlisted man in the United States Army, is considered.

Of course, everybody was eager to see the doomed chief, and about 7 o'clock p. m. he arrived, accompanied by some of his own people, Lieutenant Lee, and thirty of his agency Sioux. Touch the Cloud towered above all, and in his haughty bearing recalled the pictures of Warwick, the great king maker, which relation, indeed, he is destined to sustain to the future choice of the Minneconjous. The next in importance to, and possessing greater influence than even Crazy Horse, it is not unlikely that he will be his immediate successor.

Arriving [yesterday] at Spotted Tail, he [Crazy Horse] had reported that he desired to change his agency, as he was misinterpreted here [at Red Cloud], and Red Cloud and others were jealous of him. He was closely followed [yesterday] by the Indians sent after him by Lieut. Clark, and No Water openly declared his intention to shoot him. In this emergency, Crazy Horse was protected by his Northern friends, while Black Crow, old Swift Bear (a very eloquent Indian, who was chiefly instrumental in having Spotted Tail declared chief),Whirlwind, Spider, and Three Bears, chiefly Brules, forced him to accompany them to the [Red Cloud] agency. To allay his fears, Lieut. Lee started with only half a dozen Indians, three of whom were adherents of Crazy Horse; but on the road the number of friendly Sioux was purposely augmented, although his conductor was entirely unconscious of what awaited him here [at Camp Robinson].

At Camp Robinson, Col. Bradley, commanding the District of the Black Hills, ordered the prisoner confined in the post guardhouse, and Capt. Kennington, the officer of the day, was charged with its execution. The interpreters seemed to anticipate trouble, and noticeably absented themselves. Taking Crazy Horse by the hand, Capt. Kennington led him unresistingly from the adjutant's office into the guardhouse, followed by Little Big Man, [who] now became his chief's worst enemy. The door of the prison room was reached in safety, when, discovering his fate in the barred grating of the high windows, the liberty-loving savage suddenly planted his hands against the upright casing, and with great force thrust himself back among the guards, whose gleaming bayonets instantly turned against him. With great dexterity he drew a concealed knife from the folds of his blanket, and snatched another from the belt of Little Big Man, turning with them upon Capt. Kennington, who drew his sword and would have run him through but for another Indian who interposed. Many of them [Indians] were dismounted and were crowding around the guardhouse door, some protesting vehemenently against his confinement, while others coolly insisted upon non-interference.

Crazy Horse had advanced recklessly through the presented steel, the soldiers fearing to fire, and gaining the entrance he made a leap to gain the open air. But he was grappled by Little Big Man. This Indian, as his name implies, is remarkable both for his small stature and great strength; his double joints would secure him distinction, as well as competence, in the arena. Crazy Horse, though powerful, was held in a vise, until freeing his right hand, he was observed to thrust a long, keen blade into the muscular arm of his antagonist, who, avoiding the full force of the blow by a backward movement, reversed the hands which contained the dangerous weapon, and once more grasping Crazy Horse as he made a second leap for his freedom, the point accidently pierced the quivering groin of the chief, who sank in a doubled-up posture upon the ground outside the door.

Instantly every Indian present—and about fifty had gathered near—was observed to load and cock his carbine; and the silence that ensued was broken only by the dark figure writhing in agony on the gravelled earth, until an old Indian, Crazy Horse's father, suddenly leaped from his pony, and with bow and arrow in one hand, and a cocked revolver in the other, advanced upon Capt. Kennington. He [the father] was instantly hurled upon his back and disarmed by the friendly Sioux. Reassured by this, the officers and guard approached Crazy Horse to convey him to the guard room, this time for medical attendance; but again their movement was arrested by the click of cocking carbines. What could they do? No interpreter was present, and they did not know friend from foe. In this emergency the Indians themselves motioned to the open adjutant's office they had just quit as a compromise between their contending parties, and into this room they were permitted to carry the prostrate chief. Some of them subsequently desired to convey him to an adjoining village, but this request Col. Bradley refused to grant; and with the exception of a guard of enlisted Indians, Touch the Cloud and Crazy Horse, Sr., the crowd dispersed.

Until now it had been feared that the wily chief was only "possuming," but when his wound had been examined and dressed, Dr. Macgillycuddy [sic], the assistant post surgeon, pronounced it fatal. Touch the Cloud, [and] the old father of the dying chief, and several officers remained until the end, which approached slowly and painlessly under hypodermic injections of opium or morphine. He never rallied, and only once spoke indistinctly about bayonets, which, unfortunately, created the impression in the minds of the two Indians present that he had been stabbed with a bayonet. Dr. Macgillycuddy showed them the cross section of a bayonet by thrusting it through a sheet of paper, and also that of the knife, endeavoring to explain the different wounds the two would cause, but, I fear, with little success. The latter had originally been a butcher's knife, and had been ground or whetted down to a very slender and pointed blade, that appeared to correspond exactly with the wound. This was so small as to be scarcely noticeable. He bled internally.

As death approached, the old man related his son's deeds of prowess and of war. He was his last and only living child. He had another boy, equally brave and renowned, but he was killed by the Snakes or Shoshones. Neither had any children, although Crazy Horse had long possessed two squaws, and recently persuaded a beautiful half-breed, living at the agency, to elope with him. His family and name would become extinct with his own death, and he was sixty-six years of age. His son [Crazy Horse] would have been thirty-seven, having been born on the South Cheyenne River in the fall of 1840. His boy, he affectionately said, would never have fought the whites, but they [the military] hunted him and his village in their own country, and they had to defend themselves, all would have perished. He had enough buffalo in that country to last several years, and [he] wanted to stay. He fought only the Crows and Snakes and stole their ponies. But he was not left alone. Every courier that came North to him said, "Come in! Come in! Or the Gray Fox [Crook] will drive you after Sitting Bull!" At last he came. Spotted Tail and Red Cloud, the greatest chiefs of the Brules and the Ogalallas, had to stand aside and give him the principal place in council, and on this account they and their young men became jealous. They were the cause of his poor boy lying there. He was killed by too much talk. He had said.

The old man appeared [to be] so much exhausted by this discourse and his grief that the Doctor kindly gave him a drink of whiskey, which he seemed to relish amazingly. He rose and shook hands all around, exclaiming, "How could [cola]!" a significant expression of friendship. After a silence of several minutes, he resumed: "You gave me a drink, and made my heart glad; but thinking of my dead son, my heart grows sad again. Give me another whiskey straight?"

At about 3 in the morning, Crazy Horse's mother, a withered old hag, who was not yet aware of his death, was challenged by the outposts and admitted to the room. Her outbursts of grief, in which she was joined by her husband, seemed uncontrollable. They tore their gray hair, and shrieked so as to alarm the garrison. Finally they became quieter, and settled in a crooning matter on their knees, bending over and caressing the prostrate and lifeless form, both chanting in a indescribably weird manner the now famous Sioux death song. The deep guttural of the one blended wildly with the shrill treble of the other, and both were cracked by age. No one who witnessed or heard the old couple can forget the sad scene, or their strangely impressive, and mournful dirge. Touch the Cloud several times grunted "Washté! Good!" And once, pointing to the corpse, he said, "That is only the tipi (lodge): the rest has gone to the Great Spirit in the happy hunting grounds!"

At about 7 the body was conveyed by them in the post ambulance to the nearest village, and I learn that great excitement prevailed, especially among the young bucks. They propose to bury the dead chief with much ceremony at Spotted Tail, and many of his people are leaving for that agency. All day the squaws have been mourning for miles around, and tonight a number of dances are in progress.

It is impossible to predict what effect the death of this distinguished chief and renowned warrior may produce upon the nation. Last night there were several false alarms at Camp Robinson, and the troops are kept constantly under arms and on the alert.

New York Sun, September 23, 1877

•   •   •

The Last Honors to Crazy Horse. . . .

Spotted Tail Agency, Neb., Sept. 13.–I [correspondent] arrived too late to attend the funeral of Crazy Horse, and perhaps it would not have been advisable, up here, to participate in his obsequies. They were very solemn and imposing to the Sioux, of whom a large number assembled to do honor to the dead chief. The commanding officer at Camp Sheridan furnished the best coffin the Quartermaster's department could turn out. This was elevated about three feet above the ground by means of a rude scaffold, an unusually low grave for an Indian, many of whom sleep their last sleep in the top of trees. Here, upon an exposed mound or bluff, not far from the Agency, repose the remains of the famous Minneconjoux [Oglala], who is said to have taken the scalps of thirty whites with his own hands. To secure him immunity from fatigue and cactus, and enable him to outstrip his enemies in journeying through the happy hunting grounds, his favorite war pony was led to his grave and there slaughtered. In his coffin were placed costly robes and blankets to protect him from the colds, a pipe and some tobacco, a bow and quiver of arrows, a carbine and pistol, with an ample supply of ammunition, sugar, coffee, and hard bread, and an assortment of beads and trinkets with which to captivate the nut-brown maids of paradise. . . .

The grave was left in charge of the chief mourners, the remainder dispersing. In the several villages they have been dancing night and day, this being an exhibition of grief as well of gladness. Indeed, a Sioux dances upon any occasion, and the act in no manner betrays the character of his emotion. Meanwhile, without food or drink, naked, and hideously blackened, eight figures lie around the corpse and howl. Night and day they do nothing but howl, and every Sioux, be it a buck or a squaw, who passes near, howls, too. The women delight in it. I suspect these fellows who mourn so assiduously about the dead chief are the principal subscribers to his equipment fund, and stay there to look after the property. . . .

With a view of closer inspection I requested the agent to accompany me to the grave. He asked me if I was bald. It would appear that a man carries his scalp in his hand in this country, and I confess I prefer to live where it is worn on the top of the head. It was then suggested that we visit Spotted Tail instead, to which I immediately acquiesced. . . .

*   *   *

Chicago Times, September 7, 1877.

"THE MAN WITHOUT EARS"

Crazy Horse, the Unsubdued Savage,
Dies from the Effect of a
Bayonet-Thrust.

His Remains Taken to Red Cloud
Agency for Interment in
"Holy Ground."

*   *   *

Death of Crazy Horse.

[Special Telegram.]

Red Cloud Agency, Neb., Sept. 6.–Crazy Horse died last night from the effects of the wound received while attempting to make his escape. This morning the body was taken to his village, where the mourning friends paid their humble tribute to his memory, after which the village moved toward Spotted Tail Agency to lay the remains away. They say Red Cloud Agency is not on hallowed ground.

The feeling among the Indians is generally good. They say that Crazy

Horse was "The man without ears, who would not listen to counsel." His father remarked this morning that the whites had killed his son; but he was a fool and would not listen; it was a good thing. Good Voice, one of the Brule chiefs, says the Indians do not blame the whites for killing Crazy Horse, and that he brought it all upon himself. These assertions go to show that most of the influential men among them are on the side of the whites.

<hr>

Points from Headquarters.

There were no outward or visible signs of mourning around army headquarters [in Chicago] on yesterday, and the inference is that the timely, instead of untimely, death of Crazy Horse, in consequence of a bayonet thrust in the abdomen, and as the penalty of "conduct unbecoming an Indian and a gentleman," was not, in the estimation of the lieutenant-general and his staff, an event calling for a piquant degree of sorrow. Indeed, the death of this renowned warrior and mischievous malcontent is evidently regarded by the military as an auspicious circumstance, and it is presumed that a majority of the redskins themselves view the event in about ths same light.

A dispatch received by Gen. Sheridan early in the day announced C. H.'s demise. Other dispatches described the condition of things at the Indian camp, and later in the day the general telegraphed the secretary of war that there was considerable excitement among the northern Indians at Red Cloud Agency, and that he had information from Col. [Luther P.] Bradley, commanding at Camp Robinson, that the principal chiefs, including Red Cloud, Young Man Afraid of His Horse, Little Wound, and Big Little Man [sic], were exerting their influence with the military authorities to suppress the tendency to disturbance. The general assured the secretary of war that there was a fair prospect that the excitement would soon subside.

Gen. Sheridan, immediately on learning of Crazy Horse's belligerent behavior, telegraphed orders for his removal from the agency. Gen. Crook was instructed to send the chief, in charge of an escort, to army headquarters in this city, and that there should be no delay about it. The old fellow was not to be detained here, but, with the consent of the Washington authorities, was to be hustled off to keep company with the other Indian exiles in Florida. The bayonet thrust put him more effectually out of the way than mere banishment could have done. It is probable that as soon as this trouble blows over a number of the big chiefs will be transferred from the agencies to St. Augustine [Florida].

"Crazy Horse was a mischievous and dangerous malcontent, and it is a good thing for his people and us that he is dead," remarked Gen. Sheridan to a reporter of *The Times.* "He was the most vigorous and aggressive of all the Sioux chiefs," he added, "and but for him the late Indian war would not have been so formidable." The general went on to say that Crazy Horse wielded a potent influence over all these thousands of Indians who favored hostilities. Not only was he the recognized leader of his immediate following, but his influence extended to most of the other bands, and as a leader he stood head and shoulders above Sitting Bull. The latter has grown famous on supposititious achievements, and has taken credit for Crazy Horse's generalship, and such victories as he has won. Gen. Sheridan says he never heard of Crazy Horse until in the winter of 1875-76. He took a prominent part in the grand council which was held during that winter in the Little Horn [River in southern Montana], and was instrumental in bringing about the general war that ensued. His prominence and influence have been spreading ever since. He was the rival of the old chief, Red Cloud, and had the satisfaction of seeing the latter "laid on the shelf," so far as possessing or exerting any influence was concerned.

Crazy Horse was about 30 years of age. He understood some English, but would never converse with the whites except through an interpreter. He was haughty and imperious, and has been known to punish refractory members of his band most cruelly, and still his personal popularity was great, except with other chiefs, who will probably rejoice in secret at his death. He leaves a herd of horses behind him—mostly Crazy Horses, including four squaws, who were wives to the fallen chief, their numeroud progeny, and a lot of rational equines, which were not immediate members of his tribe.

The burial of this big chief will be made the occasion of a ceremonial blow-out. His favorite ponies will be slain and their carcasses piled up around his grave, convenient for mounting when he gets ready to doff the habiliments of his tomb and go galloping over the plains of paradise. For the next six weeks his wives and children will howl their anguish at his grave at daylight every morning, and boiled beaver, fried buffalo tongue, and other delicacies known to the Indian cuisine, will be heaped on his tomb in prodigality, that he may not want for grub while on his route to the "happy hunting grounds."

Chicago Tribune, September 11, 1877

CRAZY-HORSE

The Death of the Indian Chieftain

Special Correspondence of *The Tribune*

RED-CLOUD AGENCY, Sept. 6.–Crazy-Horse, after his flight on the 4th inst., was pursued by Indian soldiers from here, and found at Spotted-Tail Agency that night. He said he had left here for the purpose of taking his sick wife to her relatives at Spotted-Tail, and that he would return next morning. The Red Cloud Indian soldiers, with some Brule soldiers, next morning started with him for this Agency, being accompanied by Lieut. [JesseM.] Lee, Ninth Infantry, the Agent, and Spotted-Tail. They were announced as being near here on the evening of the 5th, and the Indians here sent word to their villages to have it harangued for none of them to approach the party as they were passing the Agency, as it was feared that some young men might become excited, and probably make an attempt to resque Crazy-Horse.

They passed the Agency unmolested, and, upon their arrival at the post, found that a considerable number of Indians had collected there; and, while Crazy-Horse was being conducted into the guard-house, he suddenly made an attempt to stab Capt. [James M.] Kennington, officer of the day,–having, it appears, a revolver and two knives concealed about his person. Capt.K[ennington] drew his sword; and, at this juncture, Little-Big-Man (Crazy-Horse's former right bower) grasped Crazy-Horse by the arm and attempted to hold him; but he resisted, backed out of the guard-house,–being at the time surrounded by the guard,–and made a thrust at Little-Big-Man, cutting him on the arm above the wrist. At this, Crazy-Horse fell, having been mortally wounded in some manner, in the right side just above the hip. Capt. Kennington then ordered the guard to take him [Crazy Horse] back to the guard-house; whereupon the Indian soldiers cocked their guns,–whether intending to attack the guard, or prevent interference from the northern Indians, is not known. Crazy-Horse's father jumped off his pony and made two attempts to shoot, but was seized by the Indian soldiers.

The Indians then objected to them [the guard] taking Crazy-Horse back. At this, the interpreters (half-breeds) fled, leaving the Captain and Dr. [Valentine T.] McGillycuddy, Acting Assistant Surgeon, with the guard, to manage the difficulty,–none of them understanding a word of Sioux, and unable to explain themselves or to take any action, and not knowing friend from foe. A halfbreed, John Provost, then made his appearance, and told the Indians that the Doctor wished to take Crazy-Horse in and attend him; but they decidedly objected to it, and said they [the guard] could take him in the office; which was done. He was attended by Dr. McGillycuddy and Dr. [Charles E.] Munn, the Post Surgeon, and at 2 o'clock last night died.

It is not known how, or by whom, Crazy-Horse received his death-wound. Little-Big-Man says that, when Crazy-Horse made the thrust at him the knife, after wounding him, from the force of the blow glanced off and entered Crazy-Horse himself. Crazy-Horse, however, before his death, asserted that he had been struck with a bayonet, as he felt it penetrate his side. After his father had been quieted, he made a speech in behalf of his son,–giving his family history, ect.; said that he [Crazy Horse] did not want to come to the Agency, but that he wished to remain north and be let alone; that the troops hunted him down, and he had to come in; that he wished to be put on a scaffold in the customary Indian way, and not buried in a coffin. He said that his son had been his only protection, and that, as he was now gone, he was poor and friendless; that, while they were north, his son had taken good care of him, and they always had plenty of game to eat. But this morning the old man has been haranguing that his son was obstinate, would not listen to good advice, and that now he was no more and it was well.

Touches-the-Cloud, a northern chief, said, after Crazy-Horse was dead, that he [Crazy Horse] had courted death ever since his arrival here, and that at last he had met it, and that he had got what he deserved.

Capt. Kennington and Dr. McGillycuddy deserve great credit for the cool and collected manner in which they acted under such trying circumstances,–having, it appears, singularly been left alone with the Indians, and not knowing who were soldiers or who were not, and whom to trust.

During last night much excitement prevailed, Indians were rushing to and from the post, women and children were crying, and matters indeed looked dubious for a while. The post was well guarded, and a party of Brule Indian soldiers slept inside the Agency-stockade. Many northern Indians stampeded during the night,–it is supposed for Spotted-Tail Agency.

The principal chiefs of the bands here do not seem to be at all excited over the affair. They all say Crazy-Horse would not listen to them; that he was obstinate, dictatorial, stubborn, and objected to every measure which was taken for their and his good; and that he brought his fate upon himself.

Early this morning the body of Crazy-Horse was brought in the ambulance from the post by Indian soldiers, and delivered to his relatives in the village near the Agency. There was a terrible amount of crying done by the women and children; and, just before noon, the relatives of Crazy-Horse took the body to Spotted-Tail Agency.

Crazy-Horse was a brave man, reckless and foolhardy, of very little intelligence, and had gained his notoriety through his brute courage and stubborn will. He was a very young-appearing man, although 37 years of age. Every effort had been made by the Indians here, and his own particular leaders, to induce him to listen to the whites and obey the orders given him,–but to no avail. He persisted in his refusal to go to Washington, talked impudently and defiantly, and opposed every effort made by the Agent, Dr. Irvin [James Irwin], the military, and the Indians, to pacify him, and to persuade him to listen to advice. He would not listen, and at last got his own people disgusted with him, and a number of Indians were known to have remarked, on the day the northern Indians were surrounded, that they would like to kill him like a dog if he resisted. Now his career is over, and it is probable that no more trouble will arise here, as his death has been to the Indians a good and effective lesson.

[signed] Philander

———————

Greencastle Star [clipping]

CAMP SHERIDAN, Nebr.
Sept. 18, 1877.

My next letter to your newsy newspaper was to have been a description of the Indian mode of burial; but I will defer that, and give you an account of the week of exitement we have just passed through, and which I hope will be the last of the kind while I remain here.

On the morning of Sept. 2nd, we started for Red Cloud [Agency] to visit our good friends, Major B. and wife, and that my husband [Lieut. Jesse M. Lee] might attend to some necessary business, intending to return on the 4th. On arriving at the post–Camp Robinson–we found something unusual going on, but of what nature the mysterious manner of the knowing ones precluded all possibility of finding out. Several companies of cavalry from other posts had arrived, and more were expected. Gen. Crook had arrived, and had an immense amount of talking to do.

All the day of the 3rd, there was much running to and fro and talking, and still the reason for it all remained a mystery, though we knew it had something to do with the Indians. In the evening my husband came in with the announcement that he was to return home the next morning at 4 o'clock, and I would remain two or three days longer with our friends. He was ordered to return that early that he might keep the Indians quiet here, should they hear of what was going on at Red Cloud [Agency].

The morning of the 4th brought a solution of the mystery and plenty of exitement. The plan was to surround a certain band of Indians, of whom Crazy Horse was the chief, take all their ponies, disarm them and take the chief a prisoner. The troops, composed of 600 cavalry and 250 Indian soldiers—all mounted—moved in two columns to the village, some 6 miles from the post, expecting to make short work with it. The Indians, however, had surmised that something unusual was going to take place, and it had made them very uneasy, so they silently and quickly "folded their tents like the Arabs and hurriedly stole away," so that when the troops arrived at the place, there was nothing to be found,

In the meantime a group of us sat on Major B's porch, from whence we could see any courier who might arrive with news from the "seat of war."

The first report came that Crazy Horse had been killed, and this was considered good news. Presently a second report came that Crazy Horse had not been killed, but that the village was entirely surrounded and captured. This was not quite so good news as the first, still it was satisfactory. Then came word that Crazy Horse had gotten away, but was being followed by Indian soldiers, and would certainly be caught. Again came the word that the troops were bringing the entire village to the Agency buildings, and the commanding officer would be there to witness the disarming and taking of the ponies. These were some of the reports we heard during our day of suspense.

Now the facts are these: When the troops got to the village, they found that the Indians had become alarmed, and were on the move in all directions. Crazy Horse had been gone some time, having started (as he said afterward) with his sick wife, to take her to her uncle's, who lived at Spotted Tail [Agency], and then he intended to return. The troops followed the fleeing Indians, overtook them, and turned their faces Agency-ward. In the canyons or ravines through which they had to pass, the Indians, a few at a time, hid themselves behind the trees and rocks and thus escaped. On passing through quite a large ravine, so many of them took to the hills that nearly one-half escaped ere it attracted the attention of the troops.

As one of the officers expressed it, "They brought in only the tail-end of the village." Even those who were brought in succeeded in getting away that night, and they all went up to Spotted Tail.

While all this was happening at Red Cloud, Crazy Horse was wending his way to his friends at Spotted Tail. On his arrival in the Indian village, which was 4 miles below the post, an Indian came with the news to our commanding officer, Major Burke. Word was sent back for Crazy Horse to come and have a talk as to why he was up here. Major B[urke], one doctor and my husband–who had just gotten in from Red Cloud–got into an ambulance and went out to meet him. He [Crazy Horse] was escorted by some 400 of the Minneconjous and Sans Arcs, or Northerners, as we call them, because they are the ones who came in last spring from the north, of whom I gave you an account. Our friendly, or agency Indians–Brules and Loufers–had mixed themselves in among these northerners, knowing they were in a very dangerous mood, because of their intense excitement.

They came on into the post, and for some time, it did seem as if someone would be hurt. It reminded one of an infuriated mob, waiting for someone to fire the first shot or throw the first stone. One Indian jumped from his horse and took violent hold of Major Burke, and declared that he would die for Crazy Horse, for their chief did not want to die. Finally, after much talking, Crazy Horse and the other chiefs were induced to dismount and go into a house where they could talk in quiet. Poor Crazy Horse was an object of pity, bad though he doubtless was. He was suspicious and very much frightened, and had the look of a hunted wild animal. He said he "knew something was going on at Red Cloud, but he did not know what it was. He wanted to do right, and live in peace, but he had been so much talked to since he came in from the north that it had confused him. He wanted to be transferred to Spotted Tail [Agency], where it was more quiet."

He finally consented to return to Red Cloud [Agency], my husband going with him, and have the trouble down there talked over and settled, my husband promising to ask permission to have him transferred to this Agency.

Accordingly, on the morning of the 5th, they started, Crazy Horse asking permission to ride his horse, as ambulance riding made him sick. He seemed very suspicious about starting, fearing that something was going to happen to him.

When they left here there were seven northern and two Agency Indians along with Crazy Horse; but after going a few miles they were joined by little bands of five to ten of the Indian soldiers till the number had reached to near forty. Crazy Horse then began to realize that he was a prisoner, and it troubled him, but my husband assured him that no harm would happen to him if he would keep quiet and act all right. On arriving near Camp Robinson my husband sent in a courier, asking where he should take Crazy Horse, and the reply was "To the Adjutant's office, where the officer of the day would take charge of him"– which meant that he was to be put in the guardhouse.

Crazy Horse had asked permission to say a few words to the Big Chief at Robinson, so my husband went to the Commanding Officer with the request, urging strongly that it be acceded to. The Commanding Officer refused, saying he had peremptory orders to the contrary, and he had no voice in the matter but to see that the orders were executed.

My husband returned with feelings that cannot be described, and told the Indian chief that nothing could be said that evening, but for him to go with the officer who came up to take charge of him, and he would promise that no harm should come to him, and that in the morning he should have a chance to talk.

Supposing he was to be taken into some room for safekeeping, he [Crazy Horse] quietly followed the officer to the guardhouse and entered, but when he saw it was a prison room, it greatly frightened him, and made him desperate, for in his ignorant mind he believed he was to be cruelly put to death. He threw up his hands and gave a spring toward the door, and at the same time jerked from some hidden place about his body a knife, which he endeavored to use upon the officer, and he would have succeeded had not an Indian, Little Big Man, caught hold of the maddened chief and prevented him from so doing, thereby receiving a flesh wound in his own arm.

Crazy Horse still continued fighting his way out the door, and while so doing was bayonetted by a soldier of the guard. He fell to the ground, moaning piteously. This greatly excited the crowds of Indians who were standing around, and they began yelling and running in the greatest confusion. They believed it was a pre-arranged plan on the part of the military to kill their chief, and it fired them with anger, and some of them were for instantaneous revenge for his murder. At first his friends refused to let him be touched, but finally they consented that he should be carried into the adjutant's office and that a doctor should examine him. The Indian soldiers who had gone down from here with my husband, became alarmed, fearing they were to be surrounded. So they came riding up in front of Major Bradley's quarters, where a group of us were standing. My husband followed them, and while talking to them, endeavoring to allay their fears, one of the northerners, Crazy Horse's uncle, rode up, and pointed his revolver at our interpreter, intending to kill either him or my husband, because they had brought Crazy Horse down there to be killed.

Two friendly Indians quickly took hold of his horse and led it away where he could not carry out his murderous intentions. My husband succeeded in quieting his Indians and getting them off to camp, and then word came that Crazy Horse wanted to see him. He found the chief suffering intensely, and being taken care of by some of his friends, among whom was his old father. He wanted to say that he did not blame my husband for what had happened; that had he but listened to the good words he spoke to him, he would not now be dying.

My husband's feelings were beyond description or imagination. This frightened, suspicious, untutored savage, seeming like some hunted animal, had placed implicit trust in his assurances; had, as it were, thrown himself upon his protection and mercy, and there was the end of it. He feared the Indians might think his word was never to be trusted [anymore]. My husband told Crazy Horse that at Red Cloud he [Jesse Lee] was a very little chief, and his word was not much listened to, but he would have spoken some good words for him on the morrow.

At midnight all that was mortal of Crazy Horse, passed away. The old gray-headed father and mother began crying, and singing the death-song, which they kept up till early morn, when the body was taken to a tepee, prepared for burial, and brought to this place and buried on a hill just in front of the post.

Thus ended the career of Crazy Horse, one of the bravest of Indians. No doubt he was a very bad man, and had done some wicked things, but there is something to say in his defense: He felt that he and his people had been most cruelly dealt with by the whites, who were taking all their country from them without giving them any equivalent, and he was trying to help his people out of this bondage. Finally he, a "wild Indian of the north," was induced, by offers of complete pardon and safety for himself and his followers, to come in to an agency and live a life that was new and strange to him, and many promises of good treatment and privileges were made to him. After his many years of wild roaming life, it seemed almost as though he was deprived of his liberty. Then, instead of leaving him in peace and quiet, to get used to his new mode of live, he was talked to, morning, noon and night, until his mind was in a whirl of confusion, which prevented his sleeping, as he sent word to Spotted Tail "for twenty-seven nights he had neither rest nor sleep."

His every request and whim was granted, until he mistook the kindness permitted him as fear of him, and began to consider himself of much importance. He became angry when refused permission to go on a buffalo hunt–which, by the way, had been promised him at some future time. Then he was forced to go to Washington to see the "Great Father," but he did not want to go, for, as he said, "he had no business with the Great Father and he would stay with his people and take care of them." He seemed suspicious of everything that was done for him or said to him. Feeling sure that were he to go to Washington it would have a good effect toward civilizing him, he was so strongly urged to go that he began to think there was some plan to get him away and not let him return, so he determinedly refused to go.

Then came the Nez Perce war, and the Indians were asked to go with our troops as soldiers or scouts, and this stirred them up like a nest of disturbed hornets. Said Crazy Horse: "The big chief, Gen. Crook, sent out word to us that if we would come in to the Agency we would be well treated, and should live in peace and quiet. We believed him, and we came in with our hearts good to every one; and now we are asked to put blood upon our faces and go on the warpath, almost in the same breath with the request to go on a mission of peace to Washington."

He could not understand it; it angered him so that he did many rash things. All of a sudden, those who had the management of him "flopped" over, and from considering him all right, and he doing just what they wanted him to do, they decided there was nothing good in him, and that he was too dangerous to have any freedom whatever, and must be deprived of all liberty. Preparations were huriedly made to surround his band, and take him prisoner, and the result of it all I have just given you an imperfect description.

•   •   •

. . . The sick wife, whom Crazy Horse brought up here, has since died, and today was laid by his side; and I can now hear the dismal howling of the mourners. My husband went over to the grave of the dead chief to superintend the erection of a fence around his body. He found there the old father and mother, who had been keeping watch over their son's remains for three days and nights, that nothing should molest them. They said they had been looking for some of their relatives and friends to come to them, but the white friend was the first to come.

We returned from Red Cloud on the 7th. As we were unavoidably late in leaving there we did not reach home till quite dark, and as our friends here knew we were to come, our being so late arriving had alarmed them very much, fearing something had happened to us on the road. They were just on the point of sending some Indians out to find us. We had started with an escort of fifteen Indians, and when half-way home we met others who had gone out to meet us, and by the time we reached the post we had a body-guard of some thirty Indians, who were delighted to have their "Father" (as they called the Indian agent) home again.

We found that much of the excitement at Red Cloud had been trans-ferred to Spotted Tail. All of Crazy Horse's band had come up here, and for a time it was feared there would be a general stampeding of Indians toward the north, The northerners were intensely excited, and threat-ened to kill someone in retaliation for the murder of their chief. The friendly Indians took matters into their own hands, and there is no doubt that they saved the lives of everyone at this post, as we are but a handful.

They placed a guard of their soldiers here, who patroled the post for several nights. They all moved up near the post, and from my door I can count hundreds of their tepees. Now everrything is again as quiet as though nothing had ever occurred. . . .

(Signed) L[ucy]. (Mrs. J. M. Lee)

The Cheyenne Daily Leader
Sept. 18, 1877.

SCENES AT SPOTTED TAIL

Graphic Description of the Doings at
That Agency Before and After the
Death of Crazy Horse—
Maj. Burke's Close Call.

Camp Sheridan, Neb., Sept. 11, 1877.

Seldom have we been called upon to pass through scenes of greater excitement than those occurring here during the past week. A brief recital of those may not be devoid of interest to your readers. Those who are conversant with the Indian nature can readily realize how that, which to the general public would seem of only passing interest, would to them seem fraught with greatest moment, and rouse them to a state but little short of frenzy. To such a condition were they brought by the recent events, which comprised the escape, capture, and death of Crazy Horse, and it was only through consummate tact, a correct appreciation of the situation and the Indian character, cool judgement and prompt action, that serious consequences were averted. To correctly appreciate the situation here you must take into consideration that there are now over 8000 Indians at this Agency (Spotted Tail), nearly one third of whom were recently hostile and as yet not thoroughly "reconstructed," many of them at an Agency for the first time, bound by ties of relationship, and as they regard it of common interest, with Crazy Horse and his people. In the "round up" of Crazy Horse's village at Camp Robinson, large numbers escaped, fully 900 seeking refuge with their friends here, and adding fuel to the flame.

This man, Crazy Horse, possessing considerable influence with those Indians lately hostile, was generally distrusted and disliked by the Agency Indians who regarded him as a fire brand in their midst, and they are doubtless not overwhelmed with grief that he has been removed finally and forever. It is difficult to form a correct estimate of his true charater; a prominent characterestic was reticence allied with stubborness, in the exercise of which at times he seemed not inaptly named. His prominence with his people was undoubtedly due more to his undisputed personal bravery [rather] than to any traits fitting him to counsel or guide them. The first knowledge of his escape was received here from some 20 Indian soldiers who reported that they had followed him in hot pursuit from Camp Robinson, traversing the distance (about 43 miles) in a little over 4 hours, and that he had taken refuge in the camp of the Northern Indians, located about three miles from the Post, whither they had not followed him, lest their reception might prove more warm than hospitable.

A few moments later Touch the Clouds, chief of the Minneconjous, arrived, laboring apparently under great excitement, and reported that while he had not come directly from his village, he had been informed of the arrival of Crazy Horse there, and desired information as to the course intended by the authorities here. He was assured by the commanding officers that while no personal harm would be inflicted on Crazy Horse, he must be prevented from leaving his camp until such time as his presence would be required at the Post. To this arrangement Touch the Clouds promptly assented and took his departure, Major Burke, post commander, and Lieut. Lee, acting Indian agent, shortly following him to his village for the purpose of allaying any excitement or apprehension that might have been occasioned there by the unexpected arrival of Crazy Horse under such circumstances, and to secure, if possible, his appearance at the Post, where any further steps necessary might be taken. Just before their arrival at the village they were met by a large number of Indians, having in their midst Crazy Horse, whom they were bringing to the Post, [he] with every mark of reluctance upon his part, that a conference might be had and a course for future action determined upon.

The news of the arrival of Crazy Horse here, the cause of his flight ect., greatly exaggerated, had spread like wild-fire amongst Indians, and large numbers of them, greatly excited, had huried to the village, mounted and many of them armed, doubtless prepared to take such action as in their excited imaginations might seem proper. To calm these people, allay their fears, and yet secure the detention of Crazy Horse, and his ultimate return to Camp Robinson, without exciting a collision which, if it did not result [dis]sastrously to the small garrison here, would at least cause a stampede of the northern Indians and still further complicate the vexatious Indian problem, was a task requiring great discretion and tact. All this was however accomplished and their confidence restored by the well directed efforts of Maj. D. W. Burke, 14th Infantry, and Lieut. J. M. Lee, 9th Infantry, aided and abetted by Spotted Tail and other chiefs.

A council was held and Crazy Horse accepted Lieut. Lee's proposition to accompany him to Camp Robinson on the following morning. He manifested the most intense dislike to a return, declaring that he had no friends there, either Indian or white, and desiring that it might be only for the purpose of explaining himself and securing a transfer to Spotted Tail Agency, where, as he expressed it, "he could live in peace." His departure the following day was not–[illegible] without further management of delay, as he evidently feared personal punishment at the hands of the authorities at Camp Robinson.

Of his attempted escape while being conducted to the guardhouse at Camp Robinson, of his vicious onslaught on parties there, his reception of a wound in the melee which subsequently caused his death, you have been informed. The excitement among the Indians here, which had to a great extent disappeared with his departure, was revived and augmented by that event. Several attempts upon the lives of white men were made by his friends and relatives, the most prominent of which was made upon Maj. Burke. While engaged in conversation with Rev. Mr. Cleveland and Lieut. Goodwin, Post Adjutant, none of the party being armed at that time, an Indian, a brother-in-law of Crazy Horse, fully armed, entered the house and coolly avowed his purpose to take the Major's life, The Major displayed great coolness and fortunately so serious an event was averted.

At his own request, Crazy Horse was buried here, no particular excitement attending the ceremony. The body now lies on an elevation in plain view of the Post.

Too much praise cannot be awarded the Agency Indians for their noble conduct during the crisis. The northern chiefs behaved well as soon as they properly comprehended the situation, and realized that no harm would come to them or their people if they conducted themselves properly.

Percy.

Camp Robinson, Neb., Sept. 17.

Lieut. W. P. Clark, commanding the Indian scouts at Red Cloud Agency, left here this morning with a delegation of Indian chiefs to visit Washington. The following are the names of the Sioux: Spotted Tail, Hollow Horn Bear, Little Hawk, Ring Thunder, Spotted Tail, jr., White Tail, Swift Bear, Good Heart, Red Bear, Touch the Cloud, Red Cloud, Young Man Afraid of His Horses, Little Wound, Yellow Bear, American Horse, Big Road, Jumping Shield, He Dog, Big Little Man [sic] and Three Bears. The Arapahoes are represented by Black Coal, Sharp Nose and Friday. The delegation expects to reach Sidney on the 19th, where they will take the cars for the east.

Omaha Daily Bee, September 13, 1877

CRAZY HORSE'S TREACHERY.

How He Laid a Trap for General
Crook, Who had a Narrow
Escape.

The readers of the BEE are familiar with the facts of the killing of Crazy Horse at Camp Robinson, Red Cloud agency, a few days ago, but there is a chapter of history previously connected with the affair which has not yet become generally known, and which now for the first time appears in print. It relates to the narrow escape of Gen. Crook from being treacherously killed by Crazy Horse, and therefore of considerable interest to the public. The facts are obtained from a friend of Gen. Crook.

Crazy Horse, it will be remembered, had been working among the Indians to get them to go on the war path, but could not succeed. Among the northern Indians he had been pretty powerful, but when he came to the reservation he found so many chiefs who were regarded his superiors that he lost all his influence and became angry and ill-natured.

Gen. Crook sent word to him that he wanted to talk with him, and had started out with Mr. Clark, an Indian agent and interpreter, to see him. On the way down to his camp Gen. Crook was overtaken by a courier, who stated that Crazy Horse, in a conversation with his men, had stated that he intended to talk pretty saucy to the General, and in case the General should say anything about it, he would kill him. General Crook, who was unarmed, as were also his companions, thereupon abandoned the idea of having a talk with Crazy Horse, and returned to his quarters. There is no doubt that he escaped death, or at least severe injury by so doing.

The officers, then, upon consultation, determined to send the soldiers down next morning and arrest Crazy Horse, as the friendly Indians were afraid to do it, as they knew he was desperate and aching to kill some one. Next morning soldiers were accordingly sent for him, but he had gone to Red Cloud agency [Spotted Tail Agency], where he was arrested by Little Bad Man [Little Big Man], whom he cut, and while resisting arrest a soldier ran a bayonet through him, from which he soon afterwards died.

Gen. Crook regretted very much that Crazy Horse had been killed, as he thought it would be a good idea to hold him as a hostage to control his followers, numbering about fifty lodges. It was the intention of Gen. [Phillip H.] Sheridan to send him to the Dry Tortugas, and keep him there.

Crazy Horse no doubt thought that by killing General Crook, all the Indians would have been held responsible for the deed, or at least that they might have thought so, and then there would have been an uprising, a result that Crazy Horse desired.

It appears that all the other chiefs, except Crazy Horse, had held a meeting and adopted resolutions to the effect that whereas the Indians had been a powerful people, but were now reduced to their present small numbers by fighting the whites, upon whom they were now dependent, resolved they were now in favor of peace These resolutions were passed unanimously by the Indians, except Crazy Horse and his lodges.

The leading chiefs, Red Cloud, Spotted Tail, Little Bad Man, Afraid of His Horses, No Water, and others, will go to Washington the last of this month to have a "medicine talk" with the Great Father.

Gen. Crook left for the East this afternoon, and will be in Washington when these chiefs arrive there.

New York Times, September 28, 1877

HOW CRAZY HORSE WAS KILLED.

The Schoharie [New York] *Republican* prints a private letter, addressed to Francisco Wood, of that village, by his son, Edwin D., who is in the Army, and, as one of the guard, was present at the capture and killing of Crazy Horse. The writer says, under [the] date of Sept. 16: "We have had considerable excitement here within the last two weeks on account of Crazy Horse. We started out on the 4th of this month with eight companies of the Third Cavalry to bring him [Crazy Horse] and his band into the agency, but did not succeed in capturing him. The next day he was brought in by a lot of friendly Indians, who are enlisted and paid as soldiers. There were also a number of his own warriors with him. When the carriage drove to the guardhouse, Crazy Horse got out and walked a short distance; then [he] refused to go in. Then the struggle began. The guard surrounded him, and one of them stabbed him with a bayonet. He was then taken into the Adjutant's office where he died in about six hours. There are all sorts of rumors about the way he was killed. Some of the papers say he stabbed himself, others say he was killed by another Indian, called Little Big Man; but I was one of the guard myself, and was there when he was stabbed, and know the man who did it. I think this was the only thing that saved a row, because there were a great many Indians there at the time, and one shot would have been sufficient to start a fight. But I think there will be no more trouble after this, because he was undoubtedly the greatest warrior that ever lived. His father was with him in all his battles with the whites; he was also with him at the time of his death. Crazy Horse was 37 years of age. He was born on the north fork of the Cheyenne River. He fought closer to the whites than any other chief that ever lived. He has killed 37 white men beside what he has killed in battle. The other chiefs were all jealous of him. He could have been chief of all the Indians, but he would not; he only wanted to roam around the country with his band and fight the Snakes and Crows and steal horses. The next morning [September 6] he was taken to Spotted Tail Agency, where he is buried."

Crawford Tribune, June 26, 1903

HOW CRAZY HORSE DIED.

. . . The telegraph reports sent out from Fort Robinson at the time of his [Crazy Horse's] death were contradictory and nebulous. No one seemed to know how he died, while the man who killed him—William Gentles of the Fourteenth United States Infantry—died with the secret locked in his bosom. There were only two witnesses to the act, and only one of them is now living. His name is Sergeant William F. Kelly, formerly of the Fourteenth Infantry, now a resident of E street, in Washington. The story that he only the other day told to a *Washington Post* reporter of the killing of Crazy Horse has never before been published. Sergeant Kelly had kept the matter a secret for twenty-seven years.

•   •   •

"Crazy Horse was taken to the adjutant's office, where the officer of the day, Capt. Kennington, and his enemy, Little Bad Man [sic], were waiting for him. Crazy Horse thought he was going to attend some manner of conference, and when Kennington and Little Bad Man started with him to the guardhouse, about 250 feet distant, he bucked so hard that they had their hands full getting him over to the building. It was then sundown, and the space between the guardhouse and the office was filled with Indians, soldiers and the guard, who with fixed bayonets were stationed there to prevent anyone from getting in the way of the two men and their recalcitrant prisoner.

"Just as they entered the prison, Crazy Horse caught sight of the grated bars and iron doors of the cell he was to occupy, and with one supreme effort threw Kennington in one direction and Little Bad Man in another. As he did so he drew a long butcher knife from up his sleeve and attacked Little Bad Man, cutting him on the wrist. The latter was game, and, grasping Crazy Horse by the arms, the two struggled for the mastery, out through the door and into the alleyway between the prison and the office. The guard formed a circle around the two men as they struggled, while Kennington was trying every way he could to get some one to part the two men and secure Crazy Horse.

"It was an exciting moment, when a shot would have started a massacre, and no one knew just what to do. Suddenly, as the two men surged forward in the direction of where I was standing, I saw Wm. Gentles, an old soldier and a veteran of the Mormon campaign of 1857, give Crazy

Horse a thrust with his bayonet. The thrust was delivered with lightning-like rapidity, and in the next instant he had his gun at carry, as though nothing had happened. Crazy Horse gave a deep groan, staggered forward and dropped his knife and fell.

"Only two men, myself and another, saw and knew how this was done; and the strangest thing of all was that many of the members of the guard imagined that they were guilty of the killing.

"Crazy Horse died at midnight. He was conscious all the while and never uttered a word."

APPENDIX A

The Conroy Letter

HOT SPRINGS, S. D.
DEC. 18, 1934

Mr. McGregor, Supt.
Pine Ridge, South Dak.

Dear Sir:–

I am writing to you today about my relationship to Crazy Horse. There are no living blood relations nearer to him than my sister and I. There are many who claimed relationship, but they were related to him through marriage [only]. I feel that it is important to give the truth. My grandmother–my mother's mother–and Old Crazy Horse, whose common name was Waglula [Worm], were sister and brother. They had the same mother and father. There were three [children] in the family: two boys and one girl, the girl being mine and Mrs. Pete Dillon's grandmother. One of the boys was killed; only one boy lived which was [Old] Crazy Horse. My grandmother's name was Tunkanawin [Rattling Stone Woman]–marriage name was [Mrs.] One Horse.

When Crazy Horse was killed at Fort Robinson, he was laid [to rest] near Beaver Creek. From here the Department [of Interior] ordered the Indians to the Missouri River at the Ponca Agency in Nebraska. So they all moved. Old Crazy Horse had two wives (stepmother[s] to young Crazy Horse), and there were my grandmother and Crazy Horse's wife

---

The Conroy letter is contained in the Dr. Raymond A. Burnside Papers, Iowa State Historical Department and is reproduced by special permission.

[Black Shawl], who was Red Feather's sister. These five traveled together, carrying the body of Crazy Horse—traveling in the rear of the procession of travois. These secretly buried his body between the Porcupine and the Wounded Knee [creeks].

. . . [When] they returned from Ponca where they had camped through the winter, Old Crazy Horse and his two wives and Mrs. One Horse, my grandmother, went back without Mrs. Crazy Horse, Jr., (whom they were afraid would marry again and reveal the burial place). The four who went back buried him in another place, which place is a secret. So the son of Waglula or Old Crazy Horse, famous in battle, who died at Fort Robinson—at the military post—was my mother's first cousin. My sister Lena Standing Bear, now Mrs. Pete Dillon, [and I] are direct descendants and are second cousins to him.

Crazy Horse married Red Feather's sister. They never had any children, [although] they lived together many years. Crazy Horse took Miss Laravere [*sic*] for a concubine to his wife; but he was a childless man, so there was no offspring. He only had Miss Laravere a month or so when he was killed. After his death, she continued to present the ration ticket of Crazy Horse to draw rations with. When she remarried, the name was still carried on the rolls without any change. Her new man had a [different] name, but he was called Crazy Horse just the same. From this man, Miss Laravere had several children—enrolled as Crazy Horse's children—but they were not related to Chief Crazy Horse who was killed.

There are many who claim to know where Crazy Horse is buried; but I do not believe they know, because the last one who moved him died years ago. Crazy Horse, Jr. [Senior] had a younger brother who was killed in battle with many others. Now, [Old] Crazy Horse's wife thought a good deal of her young brother-in-law, and in her grief she took a rope and hung herself to a tree. So [Old] Crazy Horse was left alone without a living relation; when Old Crazy Horse or Waglula took two [new] wives, they were childless, neither wife ever had any children.

All this information was given to me by my mother and my grandmother. It was familiar history to me, as my folks and [Old] Crazy Horse were in the same band and always camped together after our return from Ponca, Nebraska, near the Missouri River. I was eleven years old at the time of Crazy Horse's death, and I can remember the trouble and the long journeys we made in travois, and the winter camp at Ponca, Nebraska.

Crazy Horse had no uncles, because his only uncle was killed in battle.

. . . My mother, grandmother and his father were the only blood relations he had at the time of his death.

I am sending the names of those who could verify my statement: Mrs. John Dillon, Julian Whistle, and Henry Standing Bear. I want to say here that Mrs. Lone Hill is a second cousin to my grandmother, but she is not a blood relation, as she is of a different family stock. I hope that this will help to clear [up the lineage] . . . of Crazy Horse, of which there is so much confusion.

Very Respectfully,
Mrs. Victoria Conroy

Written or dictated to
Mrs. J. F. Waggoner
Hot Springs, S.D.

The Campbell Letters

Oct. 13, 1932. University of Oklahoma
Norman, Okla.

My dear Miss Hinman:

I have just come across some of my notes gathered this summer, while questioning Chief White Bull of the Minniconjou. I asked him for the war record of Crazy Horse as he knew it. This is what he told me.

[1.] Crazy Horse was in the fight with the people of the grass houses, and struck third. In this fight Crazy Horse was shot in the calf of his left leg. Date and place not given.

[2.] Crazy Horse fought the Skili (pronounced "skeelee"), a people described as living down near Omaha. Skidi Pawnees? He struck a woman first.

[3.] Crazy Horse, in a fight with the Grass House People (who lived where the Shoshoni do now), had his horse shot under him. Crazy Horse started on foot, and [an] enemy tried to head him off, and Crazy Horse killed the man, took his horse, and came home.

4. Crazy Horse struck 2nd and third in a fight with the Crows.

5. Crazy Horse fought the Crows on the Powder, and his horse was shot under him.

6. On the Big Horn, Crazy Horse's mount was shot in two places.

7. On two occasions his horse was shot in fights [with soldiers] on the Yellowstone . . . [one of these at the mouth of Pryor Creek, August 14, 1872].

The Campbell letters are contained in the Walter S. Campbell Collection, University of Oklahoma and are reproduced by special permission.

The last time White Bull saw Crazy Horse was after the Custer fight and before the battle at Slim Buttes. White Bull's party ran upon Crazy Horse and learned that Crazy Horse was on his way home from a raid with ten men, Low Dog among them. They met on Moreau [River] near Captive Butte (west of Slim Buttes). The raid was somewhere in the Black Hills. All the men with Crazy Horse were Oglala. White Bull slept beside Crazy Horse that night. Before they slept they danced a victory dance with Crazy Horse, and later [they] sat and talked of the Custer fight. That evening Crazy Horse wore white cloth leggings, and a white muslin shirt for a robe. His face was not painted. White Bull describes Crazy Horse as being about his own height (5 ft 10 [inch] now—perhaps taller once), but slimmer, with a light complexion, [a] small, sharp aquiline nose, quiet in manner, and rated a good warrior. As to [the battle of] Slim Buttes [September 8, 1876], White Bull does not know where Crazy Horse was, as he [White Bull] was not present. But he says that he never saw Crazy Horse on a white horse, as described by [correspondent John F.] Finerty. . . .

I don't know that this will be of any use to you, but it may be. I am sorry I could not get more data. Much of this is secondhand, coming from Owns Horn, Crazy Horse's cousin.

Cordially,
(signed:) W. S. Campbell

The University of Oklahoma
Norman, Oklahoma

July 16, 1948

Dear Editor:

With regard to the hairdo of Chief Crazy Horse:

Chief White Bull (Pte San Hunka), the nephew of Sitting Bull, described the battle dress of Crazy Horse as follows: In a fight he generally wore a white buckskin suit, both shirt and leggins (as did at the Battle of the Little Bighorn), painted his face with small white spots put on at random by dipping his finger tips in white paint and then lighting [lightly?] touching his face here and there. His hair he wore loose and flying. This costume, paint, and hairdo were the *wo-ta-we* or battle-charm of Crazy Horse.

•   •   •

(Walter S. Campbell)

Genealogy of Crazy Horse

1. Crazy Horse, born 1840, killed Sept. 5, 1877
2. Black Buffalo Woman (first wife)
3. Black Shawl woman (second wife), born ca. 1843, died ca. 1927
4. Nellie Laravie (third wife)
5. They are Afraid of Her (daughter), born 1871, died 1873
6. Little Hawk (half brother), born ca. 1846, killed 1870
7. Unknown sister, born ca. 1838, died ca. 1900
8. Worm (father), born 1811, died 1881
9. Rattle Blanket Woman (mother), born ca. 1815, suicided 1844
10. Unknown stepmother, died 1877
11. Unknown stepmother, died 1884
12. Unknown uncle, born ca. 1813, killed 1844
13. Long Face (uncle)
14. Rattle Stone Woman (aunt), born 1815
15. One Horse (uncle)
16. Unknown cousin
17. Lena (cousin), born 1846
18. Makes the Song (grandfather)
19. Black Elk (granduncle)
20. Victoria (second cousin), born 1866

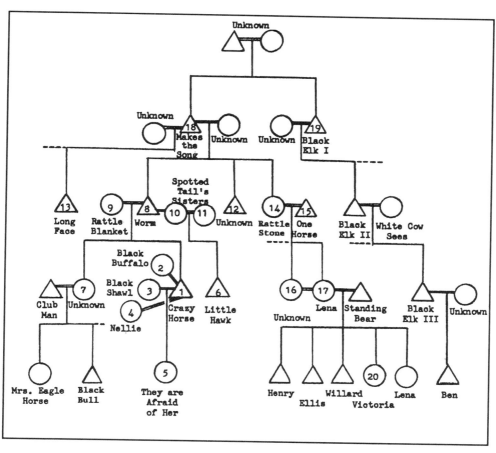

GENEALOGY OF CRAZY HORSE

Bibliography

ARCHIVAL SOURCES

Bloomington, Indiana. Univ. of Indiana Library. Manuscripts Div. Robert S. Ellison Collection: Walter M. Camp Manuscripts.

Columbia, Missouri. Univ. of Missouri Library and State Hist. Soc. Joint Collections: John G. Neihardt Collection.

Crawford, Nebraska. Fort Robinson Museum Files.

Crow Agency, Montana. Little Bighorn Battlefield National Monument. Walter M. Camp Collection.

Denver, Colorado. Denver Public Library. Western History Div. Robert S. Elllison Collection: Walter Mason Camp Papers.

Des Moines, Iowa. Iowa State Hist. Museum and Archives. Raymond A. Burnside Papers.

Laramie, Wyoming. Univ. of Wyoming Library. Special Collections: Agnes W. Spring Collection.

Lincoln, Nebraska. Nebraska State Hist. Soc. Frank F. Aplan Collection; Eleanor H. Hinman Collection; Eli S. Ricker Collection.

____ . Univ. of Nebraska Library. Special Collections: Susan Bordeaux Bettelyoun Collection; Richard G. Hardorff Collection; Mari Sandoz Collection.

Milwaukee, Wisconsin. Marquette Univ. Library. Records of the Bureau of Catholic Indian Missions: Holy Rosary Mission Records.

New Haven, Connecticut. Yale Univ. Library. William Robertson Coe Collection: Colonel Thomas M. Anderson Manuscript.

Norman, Oklahoma. Univ. of Oklahoma Library. Western History Collection: Walter S. Campbell Collection.

Pierre, South Dakota. State Hist. Soc. Doane Robinson Papers.

Provo, Utah. Brigham Young Univ. Library. Manuscripts Division: Walter Mason Camp Manuscripts.

Washington, D. C. National Archives. Record Group 75: Records of the Bureau of Indian Affairs; Record Group 94: Records of the Adjutant General's Office; Record Group 393: Records of United States Army Commands.

____. Smithsonian Inst. National Anthropological Archives: Hugh L. Scott Collection.

West Point. Military Academy Library. Special Collections: John G. Bourke Diaries.

PRINTED SOURCES—BOOKS

Blish, Helen. *A Pictographic History of the Oglala Sioux.* Lincoln: Univ. of Nebr. Press, 1967.

Bordeaux, William J. *Custer's Conqueror.* Sioux Falls: Smith and Co., Publ., n.d.

Bourke, John G. *On the Border with Crook.* Henrieta, NM: The Rio Grande Press, Inc., 1969.

Brininstool, E. A. *Crazy Horse: The Invincible Oglala Sioux Chief.* Los Angeles: Wetzel Publ. Co., 1949.

Brown, Dee. *Fort Phil Kearny: An American Saga.* Lincoln: Univ. of Nebr. Press, 1971.

Brown, Joseph Epes. *The Sacred Pipe: Black Elk's Account of the Seven Rites of the Oglala Sioux.* Norman: Univ. of Okla., 1963.

Burdick, Usher L. *David F. Barry's Indian Notes on the Custer Battle.* Baltimore: Wirth Brothers, 1949.

Cheney, Roberta Carkeek. *The Big Missouri Winter Count.* Happy Camp, CA: Naturegraph Publishers, Inc., 1979.

Clark, Robert A. *The Killing of Chief Crazy Horse.* Lincoln: Univ. of Nebr. Press, 1988.

Clark, W. P. *The Indian Sign Language.* Philadelphia: L. R. Hamersley, 1885.

Clowser, Don C. *Dakota Indian Treaties.* Deadwood, SD: privately printed, 1974.

Cook, James H. *Fifty Years on the Old Frontier.* New Haven: Yale Univ. Press, 1923.

Crawford, Lewis F. *Rekindling Camp Fires: The Exploits of Ben Arnold.* Bismarck, ND: Capitol Book Co., 1926.

DeBarthe, Joe. *Life and Adventures of Frank Grouard.* Norman: Univ. of Okla. Press, 1958.

DeMallie, Raymond J. *The Sixth Grandfather: Black Elk's Teachings Given to John G. Neihardt.* Lincoln: Univ. of Nebr. Press, 1984.

Eastman, Charles Alexander. *Indian Heroes and Great Chieftains.* Boston: Little, Brown, and Comp., 1918.

Flannery, L. G. *John Hunton's Diary.* 7 vols. Lingle, WY: Guide-Review, 1960.

Gilbert, Hila. *"Big Bat" Pourier: Guide and Interpreter, Fort Laramie, 1870–1880.* Sheridan, WY: The Mills Company, 1968.

Graham, W. A. *The Custer Myth: A Source Book of Custeriana.* Harrisburg: Stackpole, 1953.

Gray, John S. *Centennial Campaign: The Sioux War of 1876.* Ft. Collins, Colo.: Old Army Press, 1976.

Hammer, Kenneth. *Men with Custer.* Ft. Collins, CO: Old Army Press, 1972.

Hardorff, Richard G. *Markers, Artifacts, and Indian Testimony: Preliminary Findings on the Custer Battle.* Short Hills, NJ: Don Horn Publications, 1985.

____. *The Oglala Lakota Crazy Horse: A Preliminary Genealogical Study and an Annotated Listing of Primary Sources.* Mattituck, NY: J. M. Carroll & Company, 1985.

____. *Lakota Recollections of the Custer Fight: New Sources of Indian-Military History.* Spokane, WA: Arthur H. Clark Co., 1991.

____. *Hokahey! A good Day to Die! The Indian Casualties of the Custer Fight.* Spokane, WA: Arthur H. Clark Co., 1993.

Hassrick, Royal B. *The Sioux: Life and Customs of a Warrior Society.* Norman: Univ. of Okla. Press, 1964.

Heitman, Francis B. *Historical Register and Dictionary of the United States Army.* 2 vols. Washington, D.C.: Government Printing Office, 1903.

Hyde, George E. *Red Cloud's Folk: A History of the Oglala Sioux Indians.* Norman: Univ. of Okla. Press, 1937.

____. *A Sioux Chronicle*. Lincoln: Univ. of Nebr. Press, 1956.

____. *Spotted Tail's Folk: A History of the Brulé Sioux*. Norman: Univ. of Okla. Press, 1961.

Jaastad, Ben. *Man of the West: Reminiscences of George Washington Oaks, 1840–1917*. Tucson: Lawton Kennedy, 1956.

Kadlecek, Edward and Mable Kadlecek. *To Kill an Eagle: Indian Views on the Last Days of Crazy Horse*. Boulder: Johnson Books, 1981.

Liddic, Bruce R. and Paul Harbaugh. *Camp on Custer: Transcribing the Custer Myth*. Spokane, WA: Arthur H. Clark Co., 1995.

McCreight, M. I. *Firewater and Forked Tongues*. Pasadena, CA: Trail's End, 1947.

McGillycuddy, Julia B. *McGillicuddy, Agent: A Biography of Dr. Valentine T. McGillycuddy*. Stanford: Stanford Univ. Press, 1941.

Neihardt, John G. *Black Elk Speaks: Being the Life Story of a Holy Man of the Oglala Sioux*. Lincoln: Univ. of Nebr. Press, 1961.

Olson, James C. *Red Cloud and the Sioux Problem*. Lincoln: Univ. of Nebr. Press, 1965.

Parkman, Francis. *The Oregon Trail*. Boston: Little, Brown and Co., 1891.

Powers, William K. *Oglala Religion*. Lincoln: Univ. of Nebr. Press, 1977.

____. *Sacred Language: The Nature of Supernatural Discourse in Lakota*. Norman: Univ. of Nebr. Press, 1987.

Radin, Paul. *The Winnebago Tribe*. Lincoln: Univ. of Nebr. Press, 1990.

Report of the Secretary of War, 1878. Washington, DC: Government Printing Office, 1878.

Robinson, James M. *West from Fort Pierre: The Wild World of James (Scotty) Philip*. Los Angeles: Westernlore Press, 1974.

Sandoz, Mari. *Crazy Horse: The Strange Man of the Oglalas*. New York: Alfred A. Knopf, 1942.

Schmitt, Martin F. *General George Crook: His Autobiography*. Norman: Univ. of Okla. Press, 1946.

Speck, Gordon. *Breeds and Half-Breeds*. New York: Clarkson N. Potter, Inc., Publ., 1969.

Spring, Agnes W. *Caspar Collins: The Life and Exploits of an Indian Fighter of the Sixties*. Lincoln: Univ. of Nebr. Press, 1969.

Standing Bear, Luther. *My People the Sioux*. Lincoln: Univ. of Nebr. Press, 1975.

Steinmetz, Paul B. *Pipe, Bible, and Peyote among the Oglala Lakota.* Knoxville: Univ. of Tennessee Press, 1990.

Terrell, John Upton and George Walton. *Faint the Trumpet Sounded.* New York: David McKay, 1966.

Utley, Robert M. *The Last Days of the Sioux Nation.* New Haven: Yale Univ. Press, 1963.

Vestal, Stanley. *Sitting Bull, Champion of the Sioux.* Norman: Univ. of Okla. Press, 1957.

_____ . *New Sources of Indian History, 1850–1891: The Ghost Dance—The Prairie Sioux, A Miscellany.* Norman: Univ. of Okla. Press, 1934.

_____ . *Warpath: The True Story of the Fighting Sioux Told in a Biography of Chief White Bull.* Boston: Houghton Mifflin, 1934.

Walker, James R. *Lakota Belief and Ritual.* Lincoln: Univ. of Nebr. Press, 1980.

_____ . *Lakota Society.* Lincoln: Univ. of Nebr. Press, 1982.

PRINTED SOURCES—ARTICLES

Anderson, Harry H. "Indian Peace-Talkers and the Conclusion of the Sioux War of 1876." *Nebraska History* (December, 1963).

Brininstool, E. A. "Chief Crazy Horse: His Career and Death." *Nebraska History Magazine* (January-March, 1929).

DeLand, Charles E. "The Sioux Wars." Par II. *South Dakota Historical Collections* XV (1930).

Dickson, Ephriam D., III. "Crazy Horse: Who really wielded [the] bayonet that killed the Oglala leader?" *Greasy Grass* (May 1996).

Gilbert, James N. "The Death of Crazy Horse: A Contemporary Examination of the Homicidal Events of 5 September 1877." *Journal of the West* (January 1993).

Grange, Jr., Roger T. "Fort Robinson, Outpost on the Plains." *Nebraska History* (September, 1958).

Greene, Jerome A. "The Lame Deer Fight: Last Drama of the Sioux War of 1876–1877." *By Valor and Arms* (No. 3, 1978).

Hardorff, Richard G. "Stole-One-Hundred-Horses Winter: The Year the Oglala Crazy Horse was Born." *Research Review, the Journal of the Little Big Horn Associates* (June, 1987).

_____ . "The Frank Grouard Genealogy." *Custer and His Times: Book Two.* Fort Worth: Little Big Horn Associates, 1984.

Hinman, Eleanor H. "Oglala Sources on the Life of Crazy Horse." *Nebraska History* (Spring, 1976).

Howard, James H. "Dakota Winter Counts as a Source of Plains History." *Anthropological Papers.* Smithsonian Institution, Bureau of American Ethnology, Bulletin 173 (Washington, 1960).

Lee, Jesse M. "The Capture and Death of an Indian Chieftain." *Journal of the Military Service Institute of the United States* (May-June, 1914).

Lemley, H. R. "The Passing of Crazy Horse." *Journal of the Military Service Institute of the United States* (May-June, 1914).

Marshall, Robert A. "How Many Indians Were There?" *Research Review* (June, 1977).

Trenholm, Virginia Cole. "The Bordeaux Story," *Annals of Wyoming* (July, 1954).

NEWSPAPERS

Black Hills Daily Times, 1877
Black Hills Weekly Times, 1877
Cheyenne Daily Leader, 1877
Chicago Times, 1877
Chicago Tribune, 1877
Crawford (Nebraska) *Tribune,* 1903
Denver Daily Tribune, 1877
(Denver) *Rocky Mountain News,* 1877
Frank Leslie's Illustrated Newspaper, 1877
Green Castle (Indiana) *Banner,* 1877
New York Herald, 1877
New York Sun, 1877
New York Times, 1877
New York Tribune, 1877
Omaha Daily Bee, 1877
Sheridan County (Nebraska) *Star,* 1954

Index